Gay Macho

D1570959

Gay Macho

The Life and Death of the Homosexual Clone

Martin P. Levine

EDITED WITH AN INTRODUCTION BY

Michael S. Kimmel

New York University Press

NEW YORK AND LONDON

NEW YORK UNIVERSITY PRESS
New York and London

Library of Congress Cataloging-in-Publication Data
Levine, Martin P.
Gay macho : the life and death of the homosexual clone / Martin P.
Levine ; edited with an introduction by Michael S. Kimmel.
p. cm.
Includes bibliographical references and index.
ISBN 0-8147-4694-2 (cloth : alk. paper).—ISBN
0-8147-4695-0 (pbk. : alk. paper)
1. Gay men—United States—Psycholology. 2. Gay men—
United States—Attitudes. 3. Gay men—United States—
Sexual behavior. 4. Masculinity in popular culture—United
States. 5. Machismo—United States. 6. Stereotype
(Psychology)—United States. 7. AIDS
(Disease)—United States. I. Kimmel, Michael S. II. Title
HQ76.2.U5L49 1998
306.76'6—dc21   97-21215
                                        CIP

Grateful acknowledgment is given to the following for granting
permission to reprint from copyrighted material: chapter 7 is
reprinted with permission, from "Gay Men's Health Crisis, Inc.,
Newsletter," 1984; chapter 8 © 1989 by Michael Kimmel and
Martin Levine. All rights reserved. Reprinted with the permission
of the authors; chapter 9, "Myth of Sexual Compulsivity," is
reprinted with permission of the *Journal of Sex Research.* 25 (3)
1988; chapter 10 © 1989 by the Society for the Study of Social
Problems, Inc. Reprinted from *Social Problems,* Vol. 36, No. 4,
October, 1989, pp. 368–383, by permission; chapter 11 is reprinted
with the permission of the authors.

New York University Press books are printed on acid-free paper,
and their binding materials are chosen for strength and durability.

Manufactured in the United States of America

10 9 8 7 6 5 4 3 2 1

For everyone we've lost to AIDS

Contents

Editor's Preface

"So Many Men, So Little Time" was "the" big disco song in the summer of 1983, the year I moved to Manhattan and met Marty Levine. It was on a bright sunny Sunday afternoon in June, at the Gay Pride Parade, where I was marching with a group of my students from a course I was teaching at Rutgers on the Sociology of the Male Experience. By marching in the parade, the class had embarked on a sort of "gay support field trip" to participate in our own (and others') homophobia, experiencing what it felt like to have all the spectators believe, for at least those few minutes, that we were gay. (Some of us were, some were not.) Quite a consciousness-raiser, as they moved from the march to the assembled throngs watching from the streets, and back into the march snaking down Fifth Ave.

A mutual friend who was marching with Marty introduced us. We had heard of each other, and I had read the breakthrough book he had edited, *Gay Men,* in preparation for my teaching. I'd just been invited to be a Visiting Professor at NYU that fall, where I was scheduled to teach a course called "Society and Sexual Variations" — a course Marty had designed and taught as a graduate student several years before. We exchanged telephone numbers and agreed to have dinner later the next week.

Our first dinner was one of those rare experiences during which time seems somehow truncated, or lost entirely, as we were both so absorbed in the thrill of discovering someone who saw the world sociologically in the same way. We were both struggling to critique the very culture in which we also found ourselves. And we shared an outlook supportive of feminism and gay liberation, and especially their implications for a transformation of masculinity. Marty had earlier completed his dissertation—the work that is now the first part of this book—which developed a loving critique of his own community, an ambivalent work in which he critiques the self-absorption, misogyny, and hyper-masculinity of the gay clone, even as he reveled in his participation in that community. Meanwhile I had been working to develop a pro-feminist male sensibility, a critique of traditional definitions of masculinity that would not be so self-effacing as to renounce all aspects of my own gender. We had a lot in common.

There was one difference, which, at the time, seemed relatively minor to us, and even less significant as we worked together over the next several years. We developed a tag-team joint lecture about how both heterosexual and homosexual male identities and sexualities were best understood through the prism of gender, of masculinity. Our friendship, too, tended to downplay different sexual orientations and emphasize our common concerns with gender issues. And we wrote op-ed pieces, later expanded into the essay "Men and AIDS" (included in this volume) to try and apply this gender perspective to the health crisis that was beginning to ravage the gay community.

Of course, that relatively minor difference turned out to be not so insignificant after all. That's why I am left to edit Marty's work.

And, of course, I already knew what Marty would tell me when he called to have coffee at The Peacock Coffee Shop on Greenwich Street in the Village in October 1988. I knew he would tell me that he was HIV positive. How could it be otherwise? For years, we'd known he was in the highest risk group—urban gay men, 30–45, who had been sexually active since the early 1970s. And I knew because over the years, we'd met at the Peacock whenever we had something really important to discuss.

Though I knew, I was not ready. "This is not what I imagined," I said to him. "It's 50 years too soon. I want to sit with you on a deck chair by the pool in Miami Beach in our eighties, like two old Jewish *altekackers*, and talk about everyone else's death. 'Remember him? Cancer.' 'Remember him? Liver.' That's what I want."

"Get over it, honey," he said. "It's the 80s. My whole social world is crumbling. There's going to be no one left."

He was more right than I could ever have imagined. When Marty first became symptomatic with full-blown AIDS in late 1991, he had already lost his lover, his best friends from high school and college, his first roommate, and the friend he had originally come out with. Of the seven guys in his clique, the group that used to go dancing and partying together virtually every weekend, only one was still alive. Him.

The sinews of his community had been stretched and broken. There was virtually no one left who knew Marty before 1973, when he first came to New York. I kept imagining what my world would be like without those people who are both developmental signposts and living breathing parts of a coherent and stable life—or if Marty, for that matter (whom I had met in 1983, remember) had suddenly become one of *my* oldest friends.

When Marty got really sick, in late 1991, he said he'd been to fifty-four funerals in the preceding five years. I'd been to exactly two in the preceding twenty years—both for people in their seventies. What had been, to us, a relatively minor difference, had caused a most profound difference in our lives.

One of the cruelest ironies of the AIDS epidemic is that its primary target—younger, urban gay men in late twentieth-century America—is probably the most independent group of individuals in the history of the world. Here were men who lived alone, without families (many of which had distanced themselves or even repudiated them), with virtually only same-sex peer relationships to sustain them. And yet here is a disease that progressively erodes precisely that independence, which makes the sufferer ever more dependent on both technology and social support, where the body literally disintegrates, decomposes while you're still inside it, while you're still young enough and conscious enough to understand what's happening to you.

I knew that Marty had many friends who would provide support. And he was so pleased by the dedication and compassion shown by his twin sister, Hope, his brother, Steven, and other sister, Jackie, throughout the months of his illness. Even his parents, from whom he had been painfully and angrily estranged for many years, came to his bedside and had a tearful reconciliation.

But I was also determined to be as much a part of Marty's illness and death as he had been a part of my life. One summer, when I had broken up with my then-girlfriend, I was distraught and despairing. Marty talked with me every day, sometimes for hours, meeting me at the Peacock, even if only for a few minutes, just to make sure I knew I had his support. There was no way I would let him be alone now.

In the winter of 1992–93 I was teaching at Berkeley, and trying to make a transcontinental marriage work logistically, so I arranged my schedule to teach Tuesday through Thursdays, and come back to New York for long weekends. My then-wife and I spent New Year's Eve eating Chinese take-out at Marty's dining room table, while he slept fitfully through the night. Our first task on New Year's Day 1993 was to arrange for a regular nurse to administer his daily TPN nutrient intravenous feeding, when we couldn't do it anymore.

I was honored, and a bit frightened, when Marty asked me in late 1992 to become the executor of his estate and his literary executor. We wrote and revised several drafts of his will. He even planned his memorial service (he really wanted to be there!), down to the kind of cake we would serve, and his friend Meredith Gould-Ruch videotaped a final farewell to be played at the service. On several visits, we walked around his apartment and he attached little stickers to his possessions to remind me who was to get what. Impish with a "queeny" gallows humor to the end, Marty had placed stickers on everything that read "I'm dying for you to have this!"

With the publication of this book, I fulfill my final obligation as the executor of Marty's estate. But my debt to him, for his friendship and his love, can never be repaid.

"So Many Men, So Little Time." Who knew then how deadly accurate was that title, or how many layers of meaning could be laid upon a simple little disco number?

Acknowledgments

Many people helped to bring Marty Levine's work to publication. I would like to thank his friends and colleagues at New York University, including his other dissertation advisors, Ed Schur and David Greenberg (I served as his third reader during a year as a Visiting Professor). I am also grateful to Marty's many friends, colleagues, and students who were as generous with their time and energy and support as Marty had been with his. I hope they will forgive me for being unable to mention them all by name here.

During his illness, I was supported and sustained by his care team that included his twin sister, Hope, his brother, Steven, his sister, Jackie, and various friends, including Karen Butler, John Gagnon, Cathy Greenblat, Harold Kooden, Iona Mara-Drita, Meredith and Richard Ruch, Dan Schluter, and David Whittier. His physician, Dr. Lawrence Grossman, was deeply caring.

I am grateful to Carla Howery of the American Sociological Association for the concern she showed Marty during his illness, and the dedication with which she helped establish the Martin P. Levine Memorial Dissertation Fellowship at the ASA, to which all royalties from this book will be directed.

Tim Bartlett at NYU Press has been an exemplary editor. I know that Marty would have been thrilled to have his book published by the press at his home university.

Editing a friend's work was a new challenge for me, transporting me back to the era and the circumstances in which Marty first produced his work. It's been emotionally draining at times, exhilarating at others. Several friends, including Marty Duberman, John Gagnon, Michael Kaufman, Mary Morris, and Lillian Rubin have been especially supportive. And, as always, Amy Aronson has shared it all with me.

—M.S.K.

New York City

Part I

The Birth of the Gay Clone

Martin Levine's Ph.D. dissertation was written in the early 1980s and filed formally in 1984. Based on field work conducted in the late 1970s in New York's growing gay community in Greenwich Village, *Gay Macho* chronicled the rise of a specifically masculine gay subculture, an articulation of male homosexuality that stressed gender conformity to traditional masculinity. He described this gendered homosexual type, the clone, in a language both celebratory and critical. The specter of AIDS did not yet hang over the work, as it did not yet hang over his community.

In that sense, *Gay Macho* captures a moment in time, an exuberant period when gay men had thrown off the opprobrium of social stigma as failed men, and wildly, ecstatically, and somewhat recklessly articulated a new kind of gay masculinity. No more were gay men the "pitiful effeminates" that Magnus Hirschfeld had called them, the inverts, men trapped in women's bodies. Gay men were real men, and their sense of themselves as gay was shaped by the same forces by which they experienced themselves as men: traditional masculinity. The ideals of masculinity, the homophobia, the sexism that are attendant upon traditional masculinity were all, in different doses, ingested by gay men in their development and articulated by them as they elaborated their new sexual styles.

One of the more important implications of Levine's effort to explicate this new gay masculinity is that it revealed the variety of masculine styles within the gay male community. In a sense, then, one cannot speak of a singular definition of homosexuality any more than one can speak of a singular monolithic gender identity for all males or all females. There are many homosexuali*ties*, variations of homosexual identity and behavior that are dependent upon different race, ethnicity, age, and, of course, gender.

The gay clone is a specific articulation of gay masculinity that emerged in the major urban centers of gay life in the era between the Stonewall riots of 1969, which signaled the birth of the gay liberation movement, and the beginning of the AIDS epidemic, in the early 1980s. It is a specific construction of masculinity that used sexual activity as a major vehicle for gender confirmation.

I have edited the chapters of the dissertation for style and consistency, occasionally adding a few lines to bring forward the theoretical arguments in a more direct way. I've also changed the titles of the chapters to those of popular disco songs of the time. I'm sure Marty would have approved.

Introduction: "So Many Men, So Little Time"

Toward a Sociology of the Gay Male Clone

Men coming home from work thronged Christopher Street late one afternoon. The sultry weather caused many to undo their ties and carry their jackets. As I watched the parade of tired nine-to-fivers, I noticed another onlooker a few feet down the block, standing at a popular meeting spot. He was positioned opposite me, leaning against the side wall of the Village Cigar store.

By clone standards, he was very handsome, possessing a beautiful face, black hair, and a thick mustache. Tight jeans and a white tee shirt revealed his ample "basket" and pumped-up body.

As he stood there, he glanced every so often at his watch. Judging from his behavior, he was waiting for somebody. After awhile, he began to look at the passing crowd. Many men "cruised" him. A few bold ones even stopped and sat on parked cars. Though he responded with an occasional smile and wink, he was not interested.

About five minutes later, he perked up. Two new men had arrived, each sitting on a car at opposite ends of the row. Both were quite good looking and were unabashedly "cruising" him. He eyed them back, first staring at one, then at the other. After a couple of minutes, one of the newcomers broke into a smile, got up, and walked towards him. He smiled back and said, "Hello." The smiler returned his greeting. Looking crestfallen, the third man leaped up and headed down the street. As he went by, he "cruised" Tee Shirt one more time. Although Tee Shirt returned the "cruise" with a half-hearted grin, his gaze remained focused on Smiler, prompting the disappointed man to hurry away.

Tee Shirt and Smiler began to talk. After chatting for a bit, Tee Shirt looked at his watch, and whispered something I could not hear into Smiler's ear. Smiler grinned, reached into his gym bag, pulled out a pen and note pad, and wrote something down. He then tore that note off the pad, handed it to

Tee Shirt, who read it, smiled, folded it up and placed it in his back pocket. The other fellow then kissed him good-bye, picked up his bag, and left saying, "Call me."

A few seconds later, another good-looking man came down the street. As he walked past, he cruised Tee Shirt, who returned the stare. The new arrival looked back over his shoulder and cruised him again. Tee Shirt nodded, causing the other man to spin around and walk towards him.

Just then yet another man rounded the Seventh Avenue corner and waved to Tee Shirt, who grinned, waved back, and went over to him. They hugged, kissed, and started talking. Looking dumbfounded, the first man stopped dead in his tracks and stared inquisitively at Tee Shirt, who shrugged his shoulders, grinned sheepishly, and pointed to the message, "So many men, so little time," printed on his chest. The other man smiled, shook his head, turned around and walked away.

Just another warm spring evening in Greenwich Village. And, for me, just another field trip into the gay community—a world that was organized as socially and sexually separate from the mainstream of American society, with connecting, orbiting economic, political and social institutions that gave it an air of a totally enclosed social space. The year was 1975. I was 25, having recently returned to New York to pursue graduate study at New York University. This was the community I was going to study.

That this was also "my" community was already well-known to me; I'd known I was gay since I could remember. But my new interest in the emerging gay male world was more than social or sexual—although it was also that—it was intellectual. I was determined to map this emerging terrain, understand the origins of the gay male world, its institutional dynamics, and its sexual practices. And, most important, I wanted to demonstrate that this world was a gendered world, that, contrary to all psychoanalytic predictions, gay men were as much "real men"—and saw themselves as such—as were heterosexual men.

This book is about the emergence of that gay male world from the explosion of gay liberation in the early 1970s, through the beginning of the AIDS crisis of the mid-1980s. It is a book about the ways in which gay men confronted, challenged and transformed existing stereotypes about male homosexuality, and the ways in which gender—masculinity—became one of the chief currencies of that transformation. I argue that gay men enacted a hypermasculine sexuality as a way to challenge their stigmatization as failed men, as "sissies," and that many of the institutions that developed in the gay male world of the 1970s and early 1980s catered to and supported this hypermasculine sexual code—from clothing stores and sexual boutiques, to bars, bathhouses, and the ubiquitous gyms.

Of course, that world has been radically transformed in the 1990s. In part, the prolonged health crisis among gay men has necessitated a transformation of that community, as would any epidemic in any socially cohesive community. In part, though, the transformation wrought by AIDS has also been different from other epidemics, and transformed many of the most specifically gendered institutions and sexual practices among gay men in major metropolitan areas. Many of the older bars and bathhouses have closed, replaced by other gay-identified institutions.

Other trends besides the AIDS crisis have transformed the world of the circuit and the tribe, dancing away 'til dawn at discos and clubs in major cities. Gay men and lesbians have become integrated into mainstream American society in ways that were nearly unthinkable in the early 1970s. For one thing, many of these gay fads and fashions of the 1970s have become institutionalized in a more generalized, sexually fluid, youth culture. What gay men wore in the late 1970s is today's trendiest haute couture. Discos and dance clubs in the 1990s are populated by gay, straight and bisexual people, dancing and partying together in ways that were unheard of in the 1970s. Indeed, bisexuality has become almost trendy among rock stars, Hollywood celebrities, and its idolizing youth. Many, from basketball stars to rock singers, flirt with gender transgression and flout traditional strictures. Gay men and lesbians turn up on the covers of mainstream magazines, not as the stories of personal tragedies but as role models and triumphant successes. A recent article in *New York* magazine promised to investigate "the mainstreaming of a once-edgy subculture" (Mendelsohn 1996).

In our current political debates, we wonder whether gay men and lesbians can serve in the military or be legally married; only two decades ago, we debated whether gay men or lesbians should be barred from becoming teachers, parents, or could be legally protected from discrimination in housing or employment.

Of course, that is not to say that there are not still enormous areas of backlash, and that legislative efforts to sabotage gay marriage before it even is legalized, or statewide ordinances to reassert the right to discriminate against gays and lesbians have not blighted the political scene. But such ballot initiatives have been declared illegal, and gays and lesbians increasingly are finding protection from discrimination in the courts. It is probably only a matter of time before all legal restrictions are lifted against gay men and lesbians assuming their rightful place in the nation's armed forces, with equal access to housing, employment, and the rights and privileges of legally sanctified unions.

This book, then, takes us back in time, to the emergence of that gay male subculture—the world of the "clones"—from the first stirrings of gay liberation through the mid-1980s. Virginia Woolf once wrote that "on or about December, 1910, human character changed." And well it might have, especially for the company she kept in London before the War. For gay men, on or about 1984, the world changed— and the world they had struggled to build, a world in which they could demonstrate and prove that gay men were real men after all, came tumbling down around them. Since that time, they have struggled mightily, heroically, to rebuild their communities, to heal their cultural and social pain as well as tend to those who have been stricken with HIV. This study, then, is about the world that gay men built—a world which, in some ways at least, we have lost.

This book is an empirical investigation of a world that gay men inhabited in those years and its subsequent changes. The gay community has not been destroyed by AIDS, nor has it disintegrated. Though far more resilient in the face of the most terrible health crisis that one American subculture has ever faced, the gay community has certainly been transformed by AIDS. And yet one of the constants which I probe in this book is the constancy of gender affirmation by gay men. In the 1970s and early 1980s, it was through gender—the explicit conformity to specific normative codes about the enactment of masculinity—that some gay men in the major urban environments sought to resolve the crisis of identity brought about by both their similarities to heterosexuals and the stigma attached to their sexual orientation. And in the 1990s, it has been gender confirmation that continues to animate much of gay life.

To explore the intersection of gender and homosexuality, I undertook a broad investigation into New York's largest gay enclave, the West Village, from 1977 to 1984. This study involved both systematic and nonsystematic field work, and, for some time, complete immersion in the community, including participation in the daily round, affiliation with various friendship cliques, and attendance at local bars, discos, and bathhouses. Comprehensive field notes were recorded after each visit to the research setting.

This is a book about the gay "clone," a specific constellation of sociosexual, affective and behavioral patterns that emerged among some gay men in the urban centers of gay American life. The clone was the indigenous life form of the urban gay enclave (Levine 1979b; Holleran 1982). Although there were surely other social types—such as gay liberationists, "twinkies, "drag queens" and "leathermen"—prior to the AIDS epidemic, clones constituted the community's most defining social type. Clones filled gay neighborhoods across America, marking such areas with a certain sameness. As Altman (1982, 311) puts it, these neighborhoods "seem at first sight to be populated almost entirely by men under the age of forty-five, dressed in a uniform and carefully calculated style and dedicated to a hedonistic and high consumption life style."

Clones symbolize modern homosexuality. When the dust of gay liberation had settled, the doors to the closet were opened, and out popped the clone. Taking a cue from movement ideology, clones modeled themselves upon traditional masculinity and the self-fulfillment ethic (Yankelovitch 1981). Aping blue-collar workers, they butched it up and acted like macho men. Accepting me-generation values, they searched for self-fulfillment in anonymous sex, recreational drugs, and hard partying. Much to the activists' chagrin, liberation turned the "Boys in the Band" into doped-up, sexed-out, Marlboro men.

The clone was, in many ways, the manliest of men. He had a gym-defined body; after hours of rigorous body building, his physique rippled with bulging muscles, looking more like competitive body builders than hairdressers or florists. He wore blue-collar garb—flannel shirts over muscle-T-shirts, Levi 501s over work boots, bomber jackets over hooded sweatshirts. He kept his hair short and had a thick mustache or closely cropped beard. There was nothing New Age or hippie about this reformed gay liberationist. And the clone lived the fast life. He "partied hard," taking recreational drugs, dancing in discos till dawn, having hot sex with strangers.

Throughout the seventies and early eighties, clones set the tone in the homosexual community (Altman 1982, 103; Holleran 1982). Glorified in the gay media, promoted in gay advertising, clones defined gay chic, and the clone life style became culturally dominant. Until AIDS. As this new disease ravaged the gay male community in the early 1980s, scientists discovered that the clone life style was "toxic": specific sexual behaviors, even promiscuity, might be one of the ways that the HIV virus spread in the gay male population. Drugs, late nights, and poor nutrition weakened the immune system (Fettner and Check 1984). To survive, many gay men abandoned the clone life style.

Today, gay masculinity has been absorbed by the mainstream culture, even as that mainstream culture has found new avenues for discrimination, and continues to maintain similar patterns of stigmatization. Gay masculinity has also become more visibly diverse, as more and more gay men have adopted heterosexual patterns, developing lasting partnerships and longer-term "marriages," families with adoptive or biological children, and more mainstream professions. At the same time, the gay community has grown large enough and diverse enough that major gay centers continue to support gay institutions— from gay travel agencies to insurance salesmen, banks and financial services, to dry cleaners and restaurants—that allow gay men and lesbians to live their lives almost completely within their community.

In the chapters that follow, I will explore the making of gay masculinity through an ethnography of the gay clone from 1977 to 1984. Chapters 1 and 2 show how gay men experienced the same developmental processes as heterosexual men and how stigmatization prevented many gay men from articulating manly behavior. Gay liberation then removed those barriers to the expression of masculinity by gay men, and paved the way for the emergence of the clone. The ethnographic chapters document the linkages between the patterns of clone life, masculine dictates and the self-fulfillment ethic. I describe the social structure of the clone community (chapter 2), and its interactional styles (chapter 3). Chapter 4 details the gay male presentational styles, and chapter 5 portrays the specifically sexual patterns of clone life. The next two chapters describe its erotic practices and its sociosexual relationships. In a sense, then, this book has an elegiac quality, sounding, as it does, a requiem for the gay clone. That he has been both absorbed into the mainstream and abandoned as a cultural ideal does not diminish his importance, both to the gay community and to the culture he inhabited.

Chapter One

"It's Raining Men"
The Sociology of Gay Masculinity

The aims, then, of a sociological approach to homosexuality are to begin to define the factors—both individual and situational—that predispose a homosexual to follow one path as against others; to spell out the contingencies that will shape the career that has been embarked upon; and to trace out the patterns of living in both their pedestrian and their seemingly exotic aspects. Only then will we begin to understand the homosexual. This pursuit must inevitably bring us—though from a particular angle—to those complex matrices wherein most human behavior is fashioned.

— William Simon and John Gagnon (1967b)

The straight world has told us that if we are not masculine we are homosexual, that to be homosexual means not to be masculine. . . . One of the things we must do is redefine ourselves as homosexuals.

— Tony Diaman (1970)

Who was the clone? Where did he come from? What was his view of himself as a man? As a gay man? Emerging in the 1970s, the clone was a product of the confluence of several forces at once: the postwar "baby boom"—the clone was a younger to young middle-aged man, between early twenties and early forties in age—and its attendant social movements, from Civil Rights and antiwar movements, to feminism and gay liberation. He was most often white (in fact, black men had some visibility and currency in clone circles, but it was often because of the association with danger, and a rougher masculinity); he was a child of relative suburban affluence. But he was also the product of discrimination, both systemic and interpersonal; from the earliest time he could remember he had endured the threats and realities of violence against him because of who he was. When he moved to the main gay enclaves that sprang up in major metropolitan areas in the 1960s and 1970s, he found people like himself.

The clone embodied—literally and figuratively—two of these cultural processes at once: the socialization of boys to traditional American definitions of masculinity, and the self-fulfillment ethic of both the counterculture and the "sexed-up, doped-up, hedonistic" styles of what Tom Wolfe called the "me decade" of the 1970s (see Wolfe 1979, 103). In this chapter, I describe the developmental processes of enculturation. The clone was, first and foremost, a man, whose sexual experiences were shaped by masculine socialization and the stigmatization of homosexuality.

The Clone as a Man

Gender identity and sexual behavior are learned, socially constructed sets of attitudes, traits, and behaviors that socially demonstrate successful acquisition of an identity. Men become men through an elaborate process of socialization, negotiations between the individual and his environment. And we learn to be sexual not through any biological predisposition to engage in some practices and avoid others, but through the successful mastery of sexual scripts, that "give the self, other persons, and situation erotic abilities" (Simon and Gagnon 1967a, 10). Defined as a set of norms, values, and sanctions governing the erotic acts, statuses, and roles recognized among a social group (Long and Schwartz 1977, 1–2), the sexual script constitutes a cultural definition of sexuality, organizing and directing sexual expression, as well as describing the processes of pleasure so that they will be recognizable.

All men in our culture, regardless of future sexual orientation, learn the male gender role and sexual script, mainly because our culture lacks an anticipatory socialization process for adult homosexuality. Regarding same-sex love as a loathsome aberration, the agents of socialization prepare all youths for heterosexual masculinity (Dank

1971). Like every other male, prehomosexual boys undergo this training. Families, schools, and churches teach all boys, including those who later become gay, how to be manly.

As boys develop, they acquire different aspects of the male gender role and sexual script. From birth onward, socialization agents treat the sexes differently in regard to "expectations, behavioral responses, names, apparel, toys, furniture styles and games" (Richardson 1981, 49). This differential treatment teaches infants gender identity, the psychological sense of being male or female (Gagnon 1977, 422; Richardson 1981, 49–50). Psychoanalysts had earlier theorized that boys who grew up to be gay had failed to develop a masculine gender identity (Harry 1982). Empirical research, however, suggests otherwise, that gay men do indeed acquire this identity as men (Harry 1982; Bell, Weinberg, and Hammersmith 1981).

In childhood, boys begin to engage in the process of learning the masculine sexual script. Here, like all men, they run into the contradictory nature of the traditional sexual script. The script is multiple, and carries many messages. From a more traditionally conservative, procreational script, we learn that sex is dirty, sinful, and wrong, except when it occurs between husbands and wives who are trying to have babies. As a result, it bans nudity and all nonmarital and nonreproductive forms of erotic expression. It also defines open discussions of sexual matters as taboo. At the same time, there are sexual scripts that are relational or recreational in orientation (DeLamater 1981). Regarding sexual activity as "a means of expressing and reinforcing emotional and psychological intimacy" (DeLamater 1981, 266), the relational script prohibits sex outside a committed affiliation. But within the relationship, any act is appropriate, provided both partners agree. Viewing pleasure as the sole purpose of sexual activity, it approves of contacts between mutually interested partners and permits them to engage in any agreed upon act, provided it enhances erotic pleasure.

At the same time, boys also begin to learn what it means to be a man. This role also takes a variety of forms; there are multiple definitions of masculinity based on other social factors such as age, race, ethnicity, region of the country (Stearns 1979). The culturally dominant construction is the male gender role stereotype, which includes a wide variety of traits and behaviors. Sociologist Janet Saltzman Chafetz listed seven areas of characteristics of traditional masculinity: (1) Physical—virile, athletic, strong, brave. Sloppy, worry less about appearance and aging; (2) Functional—breadwinner, provider; (3) Sexual—sexually aggressive, experienced. Single status acceptable; male "caught" by spouse; (4) Emotional—unemotional, stoic, don't cry; (5) Intellectual—logical, intellectual, rational, objective, scientific; practical; mechanical; public awareness, activity, contributes to society; dogmatic; (6) Interpersonal—leader, dominating; disciplinarian; independent, free, individualistic; demanding; and (7) Other Personal Characteristics—aggressive, success-oriented, ambitious; proud, egotistical, ambitious; moral, trustworthy; decisive, competitive, uninhibited, adventurous (see Chafetz 1974, 35–36).

In a similarly analytic, but far more humorous mode, psychologist Robert Brannon provided the four basic rules of manhood: (1) "No Sissy Stuff": Never, ever do anything that is even remotely considered feminine; masculinity is the relentless repudiation of femininity; (2) "Be a Big Wheel": masculinity is measured by the size of one's paycheck. Wealth, power, status are all markers of masculinity. He who has the most toys when he dies, wins. (3) "Be a Sturdy Oak": Men are reliable in a crisis because they never show their feelings. Like a rock, impervious to emotional display. (4) "Give 'em Hell": Exude an aura of daring and aggression. Always go for it. Take risks.

Taken together, these descriptions capture the essence of the traditional masculine stereotype—a stereotype that defines what it means to be a man in contemporary America. The traditional male role, according to psychologist Joseph Pleck, emphasizes physical prowess, same-sex bonding, and a recreational erotic style:

> In the traditional male role, masculinity is validated ultimately by individual physical strength and aggression. Men are generally expected not to be emotionally sensitive to others or emotionally expressive or self-revealing, particularly of feelings of vulnerability or weakness. Paradoxically, anger and certain other impulsive emotional expressions, particularly toward other males, are expected or tolerated.
>
> The traditional male prefers the company of men to the company of women and experiences other men as the primary validator of his masculinity. Though bonds of friendship among men are not necessarily emotionally intimate, they are often strong. In the traditional male role in marital and other relationships, women are seen as necessary for sex and for bearing children, but these relationships are not expected to be emotionally intimate or romantic, and often seem only pragmatic

arrangements of convenience. The traditional male expects women to acknowledge and defer to his authority. There is also strong adherence to a sexual double standard that views sexual freedom as appropriate for men but not women. Further, men often view women in terms of the madonna-whore complex, in which some women are categorized as morally superior, and other women morally inferior to men. (Pleck 1981, 140–41)

By contrast, Pleck allows that a more "modern" male role has sprung up alongside the traditional one, never fully supplanting it, but also beginning to articulate a somewhat different sensibility, stressing occupational prowess, opposite-sex bonding, and relational erotic style:

In the modern male role, by contrast, masculinity is validated by economic achievement and organizational or bureaucratic power. Interpersonal skills and intelligence are esteemed insofar as they lead to these goals. Emotionally, the modern male role strongly values the capacity for emotional sensitivity and self expression in romantic relationships with women. It holds that these emotional bonds should occur only with women. Overall, maintenance of emotional control is a crucial role requirement. Anger and other traditional male impulsive behavior are thus discouraged.

The modern male prefers the company of women. Women, rather than men, are experienced as the primary validators of masculinity. Men's relationships with women are now expected to be intimate and romantic. . . . Men now see heterosexual relationships as the only legitimate source of emotional support they need. Women now soothe men's wounds and replenish rather than defer to their authority in the family. Though it still persists, the sexual double standard is less marked. Masculinity is now proved less by many sexual conquests than by truly satisfying one woman's sexual needs. Men's emotional relationships with other men have become weaker and less emotionally important though a high level of competence in conducting work relationships is expected. (Pleck 1981, 141)

Boys are taught both the dominant sexual script and male gender role as well as the alternative formulations appropriate to their social situation (Gagnon 1977). But they also leave some parts out. Owing to prevailing mores, they sidestep explicit instruction in sexual acts and feelings. Families, schools, and churches, for the most part, avoid teaching boys about the "facts of life." When pressed about these matters, they limit their comments to generalities about morality and reproductive biology. Socialization into these matters is relegated largely to the media and the peer group. This training gives boys an imprecise understanding of erotic practices. As Gagnon (1977, 45) notes, boys:

> have simply a bundle of disconnected knowledge, none of which has been assembled in a way that makes sense. A child may know that babies come out of a mother, but know nothing about intercourse. A child down the street may know nothing of where babies come from. Another child may have a large vocabulary of dirty words and yet know nothing of sexuality.

After all, as Gagnon (1977, 95) continues:

> At the beginning of puberty, what do most children actually know about sex? The answer must be "extremely little." While they may be able to tell you where babies come from, and that during intercourse the penis goes into the vagina, and mommies and daddies (or, from liberal parents, women and men) enjoy it, they know very little else of those matters that will turn out to be important to them. They do know that men do some things and women do other things, that the typical living arrangement in U.S. society is two adults, male and female, husband and wife, most often mother and father. They have a rough idea of what boys are supposed to do and feel, and what girls are supposed to do and feel, and they may have learned and forgotten the "facts of life."

In addition to this fragmented and often inaccurate sense of sexual conduct, they also learn that social standing depends upon peer evaluations of their masculinity. During childhood, boys socialize in a homosocial world, shunning cross-sex associations for those with all-male play groups (Gagnon 1977). Within each group, gender role performance determines social rank (David and Brannon 1976). Boys who perform well are considered manly; those who perform badly are called "faggots" and treated with contempt. From this, boys learn that masculinity is a means of achieving status in the eyes of other males.

The experience of gay men during childhood is relatively similar. Gay men undergo essentially the same enculturation as heterosexual males (Gagnon and Simon 1973). Agents of socialization teach all boys, including those who later become gay, portions of the erotic codes and the masculine roles (Harry 1982, 17). As a result, homosexuals learn the role and the script. The degree to which gay youths diverge from masculine prescriptions remains unclear. Although research indicates extensive conformity to these expectations, it also reports a rate of noncompliance that is significantly higher than that among heterosexuals. Harry (1982, 51–52), for example, found that 42 percent of his gay respondents were "sissies" during childhood. Only 11 percent of his heterosexual sample were gender role nonconformists. Bell, Weinberg, and Hammersmith (1981, 188) reported that half their male homosexual subjects practiced gender inappropriate behavior in childhood. Among their heterosexual males, the rate of noncompliance was 25 percent. And Saghir and Robins (1973, 18) found that one-third of their gay male respondents conformed to gender role dictates. Only 3 percent of their heterosexual men deviated from the role.

But this nonconformity does not signify nonenculturation but rather nonperformance. Like all boys, homosexual and heterosexual "sissies"learn the male gender role stereotype during childhood. But specific training doesn't always spell appropriate role performances. People are not "cultural dopes" blindly enacting role expectations (see, for example, Cicourel 1972; Garfinkel 1972). Individual men negotiate their way through a thicket of contradictory norms and expectations—one can't be a sturdy oak and "give 'em hell" at the same time—engaging in a process called role negotiation. "Sissies" tailor masculine prescriptions to fit their personalities and needs. This may involve partial rejection of manly expectations, particularly those governing games, pastimes, and friendships (Bell, Weinberg, and Hammersmith 1981, chap. 7; Harry 1982, 49; Saghir and Robins 1973, 18).

Gender role nonconformity elicits harsh sanctions. Because our culture stigmatizes male gender role nonconformity, peers and other socialization agents tease, mock, reject, and even physically attack "sissies" (Saghir and Robins 1973, 17–18; Bell, Weinberg, and Hammersmith 1981, 74–84), making them feel unworthy, inadequate, and miserable (Harry 1982, 20). These punishments have the added effect of reinforcing gender role training. To ward off sanctions, "sissies" actualize this training in late childhood or early adolescence. They "de-feminize," replacing feminine activities with manly behavior, becoming appropriately masculine (Harry 1982, 20; Saghir and Robins 1973, 18–19).

As boys enter adolescence they take with them their incomplete knowledge and begin to add the missing pieces of adult masculine heterosexuality. Early in adolescence, between 11 or 12 and 15 to 16, boys learn to make sense of the physical changes that are transforming their bodies. The information acquired here shapes the meanings boys place on pubescent erotic development, particularly the bodily changes and feelings accompanying their budding adult sexual responsiveness. At this time, "tentative sexual-like behaviors and the physical signs of adolescence are enriched by differential adult and peer amputations of motives, desires, and needs, which through their very imputation become the occasion for the child's learning them" (Gagnon and Simon 1973, 52–53). The key socialization agent for males during early adolescence is peers. For the most part, parents and other adults avoid teaching boys how to interpret and respond to their emerging erotic abilities, largely because of mores prohibiting candid discussions of sexual matters with young people (Gagnon 1977, 166; Sorenson 1973, 71–80).

Peers teach each other at first about the activities associated with their new sexual capacities (Gagnon 1977, 95). Up till now, boys have had a vague understanding of what people do sexually. They now acquire more specific information, learning about erotic acts, statuses, and roles. They learn that these activities can occur alone, as in the case of masturbation, or more preferably, with the opposite sex, in intercourse. They also learn that the audience for role performances is the peer group. And they learn that the bodily changes accompanying puberty signal the advent of physical manhood and the advent of erotic adulthood (Simon and Gagnon 1969, 12). Emerging sexuality and its physical signals are thus means of articulating their masculinity to peers.

The traditional procreative sexual script also leaves boys with mixed feelings about these activities. While most boys are delighted to finally be able to perform these behaviors, they also feel guilty and ashamed, chiefly because the script condemns sexual desire and masturbation as moral wrongs (Gagnon and Simon 1973, 34). Calling for modesty and discretion in erotic affairs, the script, moreover, causes youth to perform these acts in private, disclosed to no one save peers (Gagnon 1977, 154). So the boys strive to become proficient, so as to demonstrate their masculinity, but do so without explicit guidance on sexual pleasure. Thus, they fall back upon *gendered* proficiency, interpreting sexuality through gender role prescriptions. If men are aggressive and dominating, they will initiate sexual contact. If men are achievement oriented, they come to see sexual conquest and orgasm as measures of erotic success. If men are competitive, they will pit their performance of these acts against those of other males. If men are independent and individualistic, they will divorce these activities from emotionally binding relationships. Gay youths also undergo this training (Gagnon and Simon 1973; Harry 1984), although this can result in serious psychological distress. After all, having learned that men are supposed to be attracted to women, they find their lack of heterosexual interest and corresponding homosexual attractions profoundly disturbing. Masturbation is the first and primary site of adolescent gendered sexual training (Sorenson 1973, 132; Simon and Gagnon 1969, 13). Most adolescent males regularly and routinely masturbate, and prior socialization shapes the ways in which they do (Sorenson 1973, 130–32; Gagnon and Simon 1973, 65). In sexual fantasy, they enact a masculine pattern—active, in control. Sex becomes, for all boys, regardless of future sexual orientation, organized as detached from emotion, privatized, phallocentric, and objectified (Gagnon and Simon 1973). In fact, homosexual boys probably learn these teachings better than heterosexual youths, largely because they masturbate more frequently. Saghir and Robins (1973), for example, found that 92 percent of homosexual respondents performed this act more than once a week prior to turning 15, while only 62 percent of heterosexual males did.

In a sense, both heterosexual and homosexual males acquire an erotic code that combines the recreational sexual script with a clearer demonstration of masculinity. Sex is equated with physical pleasure, a testing ground for manly prowess. In later adolescence, from age 12 to age 15 or 16, these themes become elaborated in their initial sexual contacts with others. Here, however, differential gender training actually thwarts boys' efforts at sexual competence. Adolescent girls have been taught a very different, more emotionally laden relational and procreative sexual script—seductive, submissive, passive. They are taught to be adept at managing intimate emotional relationships and to believe in the ideology of romantic love. Adherents of the relational scripts are taught that sexual activity is permissible in a committed emotional relationship. For girls, gender nonconformity to the feminine sexual script, acceptance of a recreational sexual script, for example, brings peer sanctions and disapproval as well; girls are labeled as "slut" or "whore" and their identity is damaged by sexual agency and activity. Girls learn to be "good girls" and stay chaste, lest they be shunned in the marriage market.

Gendered sexual development thus impedes male erotic development in late adolescence (Gagnon and Simon 1973). Regarding sex as an activity isolated from emotional intimacy, boys search for females with whom they can engage in advanced erotic acts. Taught to respond only in the context of an affective connection, most girls refuse these overtures. Unless they occur within a romantic involvement or marriage, they are just not interested. Only "bad girls" are willing to have casual sex. For the most part, boys thus experience intercourse at first with "bad girls," typically in a one-shot, impersonal situation (Sorenson 1973, 198).

Adolescent culture, however, stigmatizes more permanent unions with "bad girls." According to these norms, "loose women" are fine for sex but wrong for relationships. But having a girlfriend, chosen from the ranks of good girls, is also necessary. Thus, adolescent boys undergo a new round of sexual socialization—this time by young girls. Girls teach boys the techniques required for sociosexual relationships. These techniques replace recreational norms with relational ones. Boys are urged to redefine sex as an activity expressing emotional intimacy.

All boys, however, do not receive this training, and those who do, do so incompletely and inadequately, if current statistics on date rape, gang rape, and sexual assault on college campuses are to be believed. Sexual "resocialization" by girls happens more to middle- and upperclass boys, and, naturally, only to heterosexual boys. In working-class communities, boys learn a more traditional male role (Pleck 1981, 140; Balswick 1972; Whyte 1943; LeMasters 1975; Rubin 1975; Komarovsky 1964) and a sexual script that combines procreation with recreation, but rarely includes relationships. Men have sex with women but they form their deepest emotional bonds with other men.

This is also true for homosexual youths. Aware of same-sex desires since early teens, many of these boys eschew heterosexual dating and intercourse (Saghir and Robins 1973; Bell, Weinberg, and Hammersmith 1981), and thus never acquire these new relational capabilities. Succumbing to peer and parental pressures (Harry and DeVall 1978), others attempt dating and intercourse, but regard these behaviors as unsatisfactory and discontinuous with their nature (Saghir and Robins 1973, 35–36, 101; Bell, Weinberg, and Hammersmith 1981, 107; Harry

1982, 113). Participation in these activities thus causes them to further split, rather than integrate, erotic and affective feelings. In this sense, gay men may remain more fully committed to the masculine sexual scripts of early adolescence, more fully wedded to nonrelational, non-procreative, and fully recreational notions of sexuality than are hetero-sexual boys. One might problematize this by arguing that gay men remain developmentally "stuck" in an earlier phase of sexual develop-ment—a tack taken by psychologists for decades who sought to make homosexuality a developmental disorder. But one might also say that homosexual adolescents are one of a group of males (including work-ing-class males) whose sexual scripts remain "undiluted" by feminine strictures, whose sexual scripts remain fully and traditionally mascu-line.

Yet another large force operates on the recognition and expression of homosexual sexual scripts. Homosexuality and heterosexuality are not enacted in a social and cultural vacuum, in which boys and girls come to their sexual socialization in a value-free world that values all manner of sexual expression equally. They come to their sexual awareness in a society that is organized around the systematic denial of homosexuality. If clones were men, subject to sexual and gender socialization as men, they were also gay men, shaped within a context of homophobia and heterosexism.

Stigma and Gay Masculinity

Throughout the formative period of clone life, from the end of the Second World War until the first eruption of the AIDS epidemic in the early 1980s, America stigmatized homosexuality as a kind of gender deviance that required strict social control. Gay men were regarded as "failed men," men who deviated from masculine norms because they were either mentally or morally disordered. Gay men had a limited range of stigmatized identities from which to choose, including "hope-less neurotics," "moral degenerates," and "nelly queens."

The stigmatization of homosexuality fostered harsh social sanctions designed to isolate, treat, correct, or punish gay men. Most states criminalized homosexual contact, which exposed gay men to police harassment, imprisonment, and blackmail. Moreover, psychiatry re-garded homosexuality as a treatable form of mental illness, which left

gay men open to mandatory psychotherapy or psychiatric hospitaliza-
tion. Finally, family and friends frequently taunted, ostracized, and
even violently attacked gay men.

The gay world of the sixties functioned as a deviant subculture.
This symbolic world constituted a relatively "impoverished cultural
unit"; that is, the threat of sanction effectively limited structural and
cultural elaboration within this world to covert sets of socially isolated, self-hating social networks and gathering places, which were
primarily designed to facilitate social and sexual contacts and the
management of stigma (Simon and Gagnon 1973, 183). Three techniques for neutralizing stigma largely shaped the patterns of life
within this world: passing, minstrelization, and capitulation. Passing
accounted for the secrecy that characterized this world and included a
set of behaviors that were designed to hide a gay identity under a
heterosexual facade.

Minstrelization explained the patterns of cross-gendering associated with "camp," a behavioral style entailing the adoption of feminine dress, speech, and demeanor. And capitulation accounted for the
feelings of guilt, shame, and self-hatred associated with the damaged
sense of self that resulted from believing that homosexuality was a
form of gender deviance.

Passing and capitulation prevented many gay men from engaging
in the recreational sex associated with the male sexual script. The
threat that recognition and police raids or entrapment posed to heterosexual passing forced some gay men to shun opportunities for recreational contacts present in the sexual marketplace of bars, bathhouses,
and public restrooms. In addition, the belief that same-sex desires
constituted gender deviance blocked others from engaging in recreational sexual contacts. Thus clandestine and covert sexual assigna-
tions were more a *consequence* of homophobia than they were the
cause of antigay sentiments and discrimination. Prior to gay liberation, observers frequently commented on the inconsistency of gay
men's behaviors. At times they seemed fully manly, while at other
times, among themselves, in the safety of the gay bar or party, they
could become outrageously effeminate (Karlen 1978; Cory and LeRoy
1963; Newton 1972). As one observer (Stearn 1962, 29) put it:

> They have a different face for different occasions. In conversations with
> each other, they often undergo a subtle change. I have seen men who

> appeared to be normal suddenly smile roguishly, soften their voices, and simper as they greeted homosexual friends. . . . Many times I saw these changes occur after I had gained a homosexual's confidence and he could safely risk my disapproval. Once as I watched a luncheon companion become an effeminate caricature of himself, he apologized, "it is hard to always remember that one is a man."

Acquiring society's formulation of same-sex love, gay men viewed themselves as "failed men." This was misunderstood by psychologists who believed that male homosexuals' apparent embrace of heterosexual views of them as failures or as deviant was the defining feature of their lives, a condition known as "internalized homophobia." While it is certainly true that gay men could not help but internalize the homophobia of the culture, they also creatively coped with that homophobia in ways that also indicated a certain resilience, creativity, and defiance.

"Camp," for example, expresses this apparent acceptance of a failed gender identity. Once a culturally dominant homosexual pattern (Altman 1982, 154–55), this practice involved feminine performances known as "swish" and "drag" (Newton 1972, 34–37; West 1977; Cory 1951). To "swish," gay men sashayed with limp wrists, shrieked in falsetto voices, and used feminine pronouns (e.g., her, she) and superlatives (Sonenschein 1969; Tripp 1975, 180–82):

> Extravagant language is common. Such expressions as "Oh my word!" "Good heavens!" and "Oh, my dear!" are readily associated with other aspects of a feminine man. In describing ordinary experiences the male variant is likely to use such words as "terrific," "amazing," "completely devoted," "horrible," "tremendous," "sublimely," "charming," "appalling," "vicious," "loathed," and "madly." Exaggerations are made more conspicuous by placing undue or erroneous emphasis on certain syllables and intonations which leave little doubt of the effeminacy of the speaker. (Henry 1955, 291).

"Drag" required womanly apparel, ranging from slight makeup and a few feminine garments, typically hats, gloves, or high heels, to a total getup, complete with wigs, gowns, jewelry, and full makeup (Newton 1972, 34–36; Read 1980).

Some pre-Stonewall homosexual pastimes also expressed this identity. Many gay men rejected manly activities for such womanly pursuits as fashion, gossip, and culture, especially opera and theater

(Karlen 1971; Hooker 1956; Altman 1982, 154). Other feminine practices entailed bitchy humor (Read 1980, 105–8), "drag" balls and shows (Newton 1972; Cory 1951: 129–34), old movies (Dyer 1977), and celebrity worship (Tipmore 1975). The sexual activities of gay men participating in "closet" culture were also inconsistent. As youths, homosexuals acquired scripts urging high-frequency recreational sex and discouraging emotional affiliations. They thus should have engaged in extensive casual sex and formed few relationships as adults. However, the actual patterns diverged from these expectations. To a large extent, stigma evasion accounted for these differences. Covering, capitulation, and passing hindered articulation of masculine erotic behavior. Surveys of homosexual erotic conduct (Spada 1979, 68–71; Bell and Weinberg 1978, 73–76; Jay and Young 1977, 226–253; Saghir and Robins 1973, 53–56) consistently reported transient contacts were widespread among gay men:

> The homosexual male does not "date" or "court" another male in the usual heterosexual sense. Soon after seeking and meeting a potential partner, he embarks on a sexual contact that usually ends the relationship immediately afterward. Frequently he does not know the name of his sexual partner and often does not care to know or to give him his own name. (Saghir and Robins 1973, 63)

Gay men may have had many partners, but they also had few intimate relationships (Bell and Weinberg 1978, 85–86; Saghir and Robins 1973, 59).

Nevertheless, these contacts did not always signify high levels of erotic activity. Though homosexuals had many partners, they appeared to have relatively infrequent sex (Harry 1984, 14). The Kinsey researchers (1948) were among the first to note this. Defining average sexual outlet as approximately once every other day or 3.5 times per week, Kinsey found that 94 percent of predominantly homosexual males had fewer than 3.5 contacts per week. Later research corroborated these findings. Westwood (1960, 65–67) reported that 89 percent of his sample had fewer than three same-sex contacts per week. The corresponding figure is 66 percent among Spada's (1979, 326) respondents, and 85 percent among Bell and Weinberg's (1978, 298) sample. (Only Saghir and Robins [1973, 59] reported high frequencies of sexual contact among gay men, finding 70 percent or more of the homosexual men were having four or more homosexual outlets per week. However, this finding was probably a sampling artifact; they recruited their respondents from homophile organizations located in major urban settings.)

It is possible that evasive forms of stigma management caused this discrepancy. Covering, for instance, impeded erotic expression, particularly among religious and middle- or upper-class men (Cotton 1972; Cory and LeRoy 1963; Helmer 1963; Way 1977).

To normalize same-sex love, coverers adopted culturally dominant erotic codes, recasting them to fit the homosexual experience (Humphreys 1972, 139). As a result, they favored relational over recreational sex (Humphreys 1972, 139). Regarding casual contacts as whorish (Cory 1951, 120), they avoided the sexual possibilities of the erotic marketplace, locales facilitating anonymous pickups such as bars, baths, or restrooms (Hooker 1965), which obviously reduced the frequency of sexual contact (Blumstein and Schwartz 1983, 296; Cotton 1972; Cory and LeRoy 1963). Coverers also restricted erotic practices, viewing analingus, sadomasochism, and group sex as equally "whorish,' they shunned these for more "conventional" acts, such as fellatio and anal intercourse (Cory and LeRoy 1963; Helmer 1963).

Capitulation and passing also constrained sexual activity. Acquiring cultural constructions of same-sex love (e.g., sin, illness), capitulators despised their sexuality, which caused them to remain inactive. "The sickness model had been drummed into me," writes Martin Duberman (1982, 43). "That's why I waited so long to have sex." Several surveys provided additional evidence of reduced sexual activity among capitulators. Bell and Weinberg (1978, 134) found that gay men who had the most regrets about their sexual orientation were also those who were most likely to be sexually inactive. Similarly, Harry (1984, 102) reported that unhappiness over homosexuality was most prevalent among his respondents who had never had a lover.

Passing was more complicated. To protect their fronts and avoid penalization, "closeted" gay men avoided activities risking exposure (Warren 1974, 93–99). "Cruising" the sexual marketplace might jeopardize one's cover owing to the threat of police raids, entrapment, or recognition (Schur 1965; D'Emilio 1983, chap. 4). Casual pickups carried similar risks because of the dangers of "queer bashing" and blackmail (Schur 1965; Vining 1983). Suspicions about the nature of close male friendships made coupling also dangerous (Hoffman 1968, 172–73). As a result, many closeted gay men shunned anonymous encounters and coupling, which lessened their sexual activity. What's more, they often obfuscated the mechanisms or locations for homosexual contact, a strategy which prevented other gay men from finding partners (Kinsey, Pomeroy, and Martin 1948, 632).

The coupling patterns of homosexuals also differed from masculine expectations. As surveys of same-sex behavior repeatedly indicated (Spada 1979, 176–85; Jay and Young 1977, 339–54; Harry and DeVall 1978, chap. 5), relationships were commonplace among gay men. Harry (1984, 102), for example, reported that 89 percent of his respondents had been coupled at least once. Among Saghir and Robins' (1973, 56) and Bell and Weinberg's (1978, 86) subjects, the figure was nearly 100 percent. When taken together, the studies show that at any given time somewhere between 25 to 50 percent of homosexuals are in relationships (data in Harry 1984, 90; Bell and Weinberg 1978, 132–33).

Covering partly explained this divergence. To normalize homosexuality, coverers accepted relational norms. As a result, they valued intimacy in erotic contacts (Harry 1984, chap. 4). They thus became "home builders," actively seeking and forming affiliations as lovers with other men (Silverstein 1981, chap. 4). However, gay relationships were far more likely to be nonexclusive than those of heterosexuals or lesbians. Most coupled gay men engaged in recreational sex with outside partners, even when agreeing to fidelity (see, for example, Bell and Weinberg 1978, 101–2, 132–33; Saghir and Robins 1973, 57; Harry and DeVall 1978, 8; Peplau and Cochran 1981; Kinsey, Pomeroy, and Martin 1948; Blumstein and Schwartz 1983, 257–302). According to Gagnon and Simon (1973, 180–82), this nonexclusivity reflected gender dictates. Taught recreational norms, homosexuals eschewed monogamous coupling for open relationships or covert nonexclusivity.

The Impact of Gay Liberation

The gay liberation movement of the 1960s fundamentally altered forms of gay life. Many early gay rights activists had participated in either countercultural, antiwar, or civil rights movements and were therefore prepared to advocate libertarian values and the destigmatization of homosexuality. For example, they championed an ethic sanctioning self-expression, especially in regard to experimentation with drugs and sex. They promoted a construction of same-sex love that stripped homosexuality of its discrediting association with gender deviance, holding instead that same-sex love was a moral, natural, and healthy form of erotic expression among men who typically conformed to cultural expectations for manly demeanor and appearance. Finally, they actively campaigned to reduce the level of criminal, psychiatric, and social sanction and succeeded in forcing some localities either to repeal sodomy statutes or to cease police harassment of gay men, in compelling the mental health professions to remove same-sex love from the official list of psychological disorders, and in provoking a growing acceptance of gay men in the family, media, and workplace.

Participation in these movements caused gay radicals to abandon evasive for more confrontational techniques of stigma management (Humphreys 1972). The philosophical doctrine of liberation led them to engage in conversion and militant chauvinism. They stripped homosexuality of its discrediting features and changed the meaning of being gay (Humphreys 1972, 142). As one activist put it:

> Homosexuality is not a lot of things. It is not a makeshift in the absence of the opposite sex; it is not hatred or rejection of the opposite sex; it is not genetic; it is not the result of broken homes inasmuch as we could see the sham of American marriage. Homosexuality is the capacity to love someone of the same sex. (Wittman 1972, 331)

Another argued that "[w]e need a thorough housecleaning. We've got to get rid of all the garbage straight society stuffed into our heads. That means questioning every one of the values they have given us, turning them upside down" (Alinder, in Teal 1971, 56).

The doctrine of social reform prompted gay activists to politicize stigma and fight the forces oppressing them (Schur 1979, 322; Bayer 1981; Marotta 1981). Activists held marches, demonstrations, and "zaps" (public confrontations) against police harassment, sodomy statutes, and the classification of homosexuality as a mental illness (Marotta 1981; Teal 1971). These protests led to the decertification of homosexuality as a mental illness, the repeal of many local sodomy laws, and the end of police persecution in many places (Marotta 1981; Altman 1982; Bayer 1981).

Gay liberation discredited camp and other evasive techniques. Homosexuality did not necessarily mean immorality, pathology, effeminacy. Camp was more about self-hatred than self-acceptance. One liberationist aptly made this point:

> Christ, that apartment. It looked like the Castro showroom on Times Square, only not as masculine. Everything . . . embellished. You know: not a straight line in the whole apartment. He had this old Ethel Merman record. And Judy Garland—everything of Judy Garland. . . . It really struck me as weird, that a guy who feared women could relate only to these female singers—Ethel Merman and so on. Some of his buddies came up, and they drank a lot and kept arguing about how Ann Sheridan laughed. I mean they cling to this trivia to avoid reality, which was, to them, the old guilt bit. . . . I think camp was a way for queens to distract themselves from guilt and today who needs it—there used to be this syndrome of drink, guilt, camp. (Burke 1969, 306)

To gay liberationists same-sex love was a natural, healthy, and worthwhile form of self-expression (Fischer 1972; Young 1972; Berlandt 1972). "Gay was good" and they refused to apologize for their sexuality, proclaiming, instead, how "we *like* making love with people of the same sex. We feel good and whole making love. We want to remain homosexual." As one writer put it:

> Homosexuality is the ability to relate sexually and spiritually to someone of the same sex. Human beings need to unite with other human beings and homosexuals unite with people who have the same genitals. That's a great thing, and we who are homosexual, and groove on each other, have nothing to hide or escape. (Nassberg n.d.)

"Coming out" became the term of the era of gay liberation, tearing off the veil of secrecy from the gay world.

To some, gay liberation meant no longer capitulating to heterosexual definitions. In a widely read essay, Wittman (1972, 333) wrote that gay men must "stop mimicking straights," no longer organizing same-sex relationships along heterosexual morals, roles, and marriages, and suggested that gay men engage in recreational sex and erotic experimentation. Politically, confrontation strategies erased the obstacles to masculine expression in the closet culture. Militant chauvinism reorganized the cultural meaning of homosexuality, which allowed gay men to express masculine demeanor and interests. Conversion lessened the sanctions surrounding same-sex desire, which enabled gay men to pursue manly erotic conduct. Gay men had become real men, and in their affect, attire, and attitudes celebrated their newfound masculinity—and nowhere more than in sexual self-celebration.

The Birth of Gay Macho

Gay activists formulated radically different images of the postcloset homosexual (Marotta 1981, chaps. 5–6). Some gay liberationists viewed this man as a politicized hippie who eschewed traditional manliness, conventional aspirations, and established institutions. He avoided the quick sex associated with the sexual marketplace and formed instead lasting relationships. And he wore "gender fuck" attire that mixed masculine and feminine (beards and dresses). Gay reformists, by contrast, viewed the postcloset homosexual as a "butch" rebel who had sex with "anyone, any way, any time" (Marotta 1981, 144). He actively participated in the sexual marketplace, "cruising" and "tricking" in gay bars, bathhouses, and pornographic bookstores. The liberationist image gathered few converts as most gay men found gender fuck too radical (Burke 1969; Humphreys 1971). They opted instead for the reformist image of the postcloset homosexual (Marotta 1981, chap. 5).

This image heralded the masculinization of gay culture. Gay men now regarded themselves as masculine. They adopted manly attire and demeanor as a means of expressing their new sense of self. They also adopted this look to enhance their physical attractiveness and express improved self-esteem. Since American culture devalued male effeminacy, they adopted manly demeanor and attire as a means of expressing a more valued identity.

At first, some gay men took on the look of hip masculinity favored in the counterculture (Humphreys 1971; Burke 1969). They wore long hair, beards, vests, and bell-bottomed jeans. Some even took drugs and had promiscuous sex. They became "an unfettered guiltless male child of the new morality in a Zapata moustache and outlaw hat, who couldn't care less for Establishment approval, would soon as sleep with boys as girls, and thinks that " 'Over the Rainbow' is a place to fly on 200 micrograms of lysergic acid diethylamide." In this sense, they were "virtually indistinguishable from heterosexual hippies" (Burke 1969, 178).

But by the early 1970s, gay men embraced other marginalized, but far more masculine definitions of masculinity. They expressed their new sense of self by wearing the attire of the working class (Altman 1982), which led to the emergence of the clone. Traditional masculine themes were heartily embraced—in part as a new kind of camp (as in the various over-the-top displays of gay disco groups like The Village People), and in part as a vigorous assertion of a newfound, and passionately embraced successful masculinity.

_____

Chapter Two

"Y.M.C.A."
The Social Organization of Gay Male Life

I live in an all-clone world. All my friends are clones.
I live in a clone building, in a clone neighborhood,
and work in a clone bar. My family stopped talking to
me and I stopped talking to my straight friends.
—New York clone, age 27

At seven o'clock in the morning, the party was finally winding down. Earlier, the club had been packed, jammed with hundreds of handsome men, all "ripped to the tits," dancing to the hottest music in town. Now the hard partying was over. The crowd had thinned, the music had slowed, and the men were coming down. By now, the dance floor was nearly empty. The remaining merrymakers gathered in the lounge, clustering in groups.

Some stood, and others sat on banquettes, drinking juice, smoking joints, and chatting in subdued tones. A few had passed out and were lying on the floor, crumpled up like old blankets. All of a sudden, I felt someone tap me on the shoulder. When I looked up, it was Robert. "Where have you been?" he asked, sitting down. "I've been looking for you. You look tired." "I am," I said, glad to see him. He had brought me here and had danced with me until we got separated. He had been coming for years and was showing me the ropes.

"What did you think of the party?" he asked.

"I had a good time. What about you?"

"I had a fabulous time! The music was good, the energy was high, and the crowd was hot. Every circuit queen was here. It was a real gathering of the tribe."

This chapter combines the dissertation research with an earlier article, "Gay Ghetto," published in the *Journal of Homosexuality* 4 (4), Summer 1979 (ed.).

"The tribe? Circuit queen? I don't understand," I said, looking a bit confused.

"I guess you wouldn't," he answered, grinning amusedly. "You haven't been around long enough. This scene is a man's world. These guys have nothing to do with 'straights.' They run around with each other — in cliques. These cliques are real tight, sort of like a clan. They hang out together, go out together, and some even work together. And every Saturday night the cliques meet here. That's why I called it a gathering of the tribe."

Cliques? Tribes? Circuits? What was going on here? How did gay men organize their social lives in the urban gay neighborhoods of the 1970s? How did they recognize each other? How did they provide the social supports necessary to sustain individual and social life?

There is no doubt that the clone was an urban phenomenon; he depended upon an institutional infrastructure and networks to facilitate the expressions of gay masculinity he intended. And the emergence of the clone was facilitated—indeed, made possible—by the emergence of visible gay neighborhoods in America's major cities. These "gay ghettoes" were themselves responses to both stigma and gay liberation—to the fact that stigmatized groups need social support networks and institutional mechanisms to survive in a hostile world, and that after Stonewall, gay men and lesbians were able to overtly build and nurture community institutions of their own. This chapter will investigate the development of these gay ghettos in the 1970s, and then describe the structured social interaction patterns that gay men used to establish clone culture.

The Gay Ghetto

Most sociologists consider a ghetto to be an area of the city housing a segregated cultural community. Historically, the term was first used only of the Jewish community (Wirth 1928, 4). In the 1920s, sociologists from the Chicago school, notably Robert E. Park (1928, vii–ix) and Louis Wirth (1928, 1–10), began to use the word to describe any urban neighborhood inhabited by a people who possess a distinctive culture and are socially segregated from the larger community. Noting that the circumstances of immigrant groups often fit these requisites, Park and Wirth applied the term to neighborhoods inhabited by Poles, blacks, and Italians, as well as by Jews. They also suggested its suitability to describe areas dominated by such moral deviants as bohemians, hobos, and prostitutes (Park 1928, vii–viii; Wirth 1928, 6, 20, 286). Contemporary usage has, in some instances, restricted the concept to communities inhabited by racial and ethnic groups, particularly those which are poverty stricken and socially disorganized (Butler 1977, 121; Kerner Commission 1968, 12). In other cases, the word "ghetto" has been applied to any area inhabited by a minority group (Fischer 1976, 13; Theodorson and Theodorson 1969, 174). Even affluent communities are said to live in "gilded ghettos" (Michelson 1970, 65).

Park and Wirth's notion translates ghetto from its historical connotation into a construct useful to urban ecology. A ghetto, Wirth argues, epitomizes ecological segregation and is a spatial indicator of the extent to which a community is isolated from the surrounding society. (Other interpretations that stress racial or ethnic features reduce the salience of the term for comparative urban studies.) The classic exposition of their formulation appears in Wirth's well-known study, *The Ghetto* (1928) in which he specifies four key features: (1) institutional concentration; (2) culture area; (3) social isolation; and, (4) residential concentration. "Institutional concentration" means the centralization of the ghettoized people's gathering places and commercial establishments. (For example, large numbers of synagogues, religious schools, ritual bath houses, kosher butchers and restaurants, and Yiddish theaters and bookstores are concentrated in the Jewish ghetto.) "Culture area" signifies that the culture of a particular people dominates the geographic area, a dominance reflected in the spatial centralization of the ghettoized people's cultural traits. "Social isolation" denotes the segregation of a ghettoized group from meaningful social relations with the larger community, an isolation produced by prejudices against ghettoized people or by the social distance differing cultural practices create between the group and the larger community. "Residential concentration" signifies that the ghetto is a residential area with a concentration of the homes of the ghettoized people.

Accordingly, an urban neighborhood can be termed a "gay ghetto" if it contains gay institutions in number, a conspicuous and locally dominant gay subculture that is socially isolated from the larger community, and a residential population that is substantially gay. By that definition, some metropolitan subcommunities are, indeed, gay ghettos.

Let's look at the ecological patterns of several cities known to house large concentration of gay men: Boston, New York, Chicago, San Francisco, and Los Angeles. To locate neighborhoods where significant numbers of gay institutions concentrate within these cities, I plotted the addresses of gay establishments on maps of each city. (The data came from a national directory of gay gathering places, *Bob Damron's 1976 Address Book*.) Oriented mainly towards cruising places, the directory contains the names and addresses of bars, bookstores, steam baths, churches, restaurants, and movie houses catering to the gay community, as well as of indoor and outdoor places (such as public restrooms, parks, or street corners) where gay men go to meet each other.[1] The maps contain street indices and are labeled by neighborhood and house number. The position of every directory listing was plotted on the appropriate map. Institutional listings such as bars, restaurants, and steam baths were indicated by solid black dots; cruising areas were marked by solid black lines. The street maps were then simplified and reduced to spot maps (see Figures 2.1–2.5).

Institutional Concentration

These spot maps indicate a definite distribution pattern of gay gathering places in these cities. Large numbers of these places are concentrated in small areas, usually in the inner city; none or very few are found in other city areas. The map of New York City omits Staten Island because the directory contains no listings there. (Other authors have noted similar concentrations in these areas: Newton (1972, 22) in New York and Chicago; Weinberg and Williams (1974, 41, 46, 56–61) in New York and San Francisco. Although Hooker (1967) and Warren (1974, 20) do not specify areas of institutional concentration, they acknowledge the phenomenon.) The first concentration measure represents the proportion of gay institutions or cruising places within the concentrated areas, compared to the total number of such places in each city. This measure was calculated by summing the number of gay institutions in all concentration areas and then relating this sum to the total number of such locations for a particular city. The second measure represents the ratio of the total sum of the land masses of each concentrated area to the total land mass of each city. This ratio was calculated by (a) converting each concentrated area into a rectangular

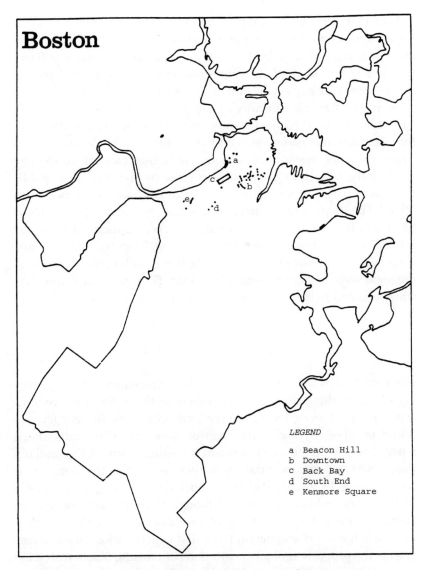

Figure 2.1. Boston: Spot Map of Gay Establishments, 1976

form, by connecting the outermost gay places; (b) figuring the area of each rectangle; (c) summing all these areas; and (d) computing the percentage of each city's total land mass represented by this sum.

Using these measures of concentration, I found that in Boston 83

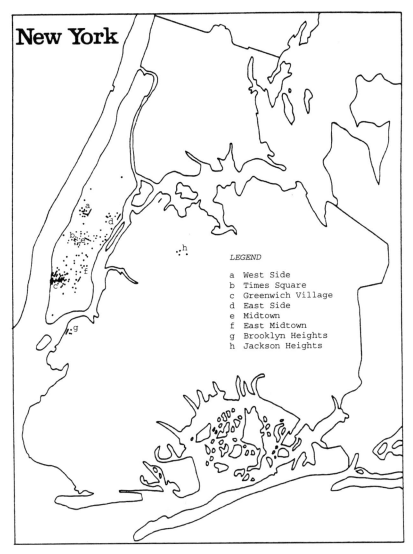

Figure 2.2. New York: Spot Map of Gay Establishments, 1976

percent of the gay locations are situated on less than 2 percent of the
city's total land mass; in New York, 86 percent on less than 2 percent;
in Chicago, 64 percent on less than 1 percent; in San Francisco, 64
percent on less than 1 percent; and in Los Angeles, 78 percent on less
than 3 percent. The spot maps demonstrate clearly that gay institu-

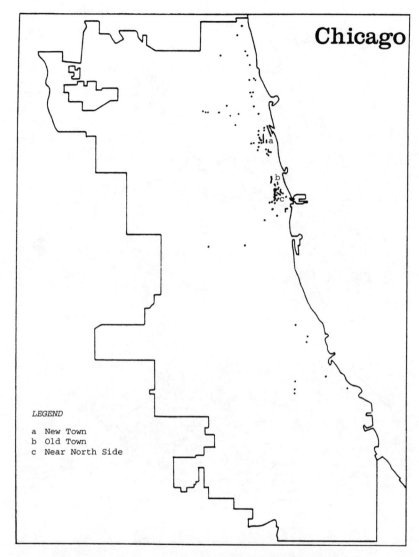

Figure 2.3. Chicago: Spot Map of Gay Establishments, 1976

tions and cruising areas are not distributed randomly but are concentrated in specific city districts. The majority of these are comprised mainly of restaurants, cruising areas, and bars. A few, however, shelter places that cater to a specialized interest within a gay community. Gay-oriented movie theaters and bookstores, and bars or street corners

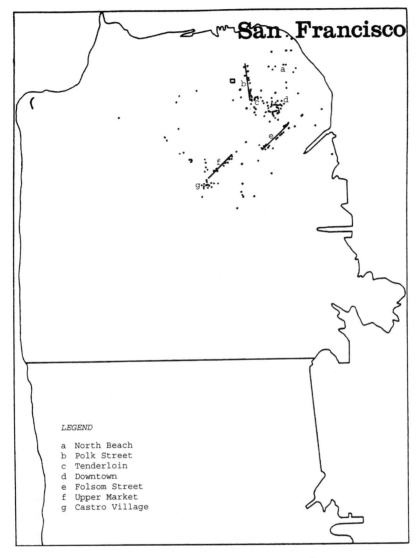

Figure 2.4. San Fransciso: Spot Map of Gay Establishments, 1976

frequented by male prostitutes, tend to concentrate in only one of these districts (e.g., Times Square in New York or the Tenderloin in San Francisco). Bars catering to western or sadomasochistic gay men are also centralized, usually in an industrial warehouse area (e.g., Folsom Street in San Francisco).

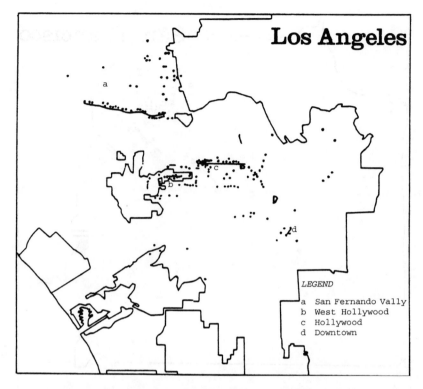

Figure 2.5. Los Angeles: Spot Map of Gay Establishments, 1976

Culture Area

Only certain sections of seven districts (the West Side and Greenwich Village in New York; New Town in Chicago; Polk Street, Folsom Street, and The Castro district in San Francisco; West Hollywood in Los Angeles) are truly gay culture areas. The boundaries are ambiguous, but generally these sections are defined as the streets housing a cluster of gay locations and the blocks proximate to them. For example, on New York's West Side, the culture area consists of the blocks surrounding the concentration of gay places between Broadway and Central Park in the mid-West Seventies; in Greenwich Village, the culture area consists of the blocks encircling the cluster of gay establishments near Christopher Street. In Chicago's New Town, the intersection of Broadway and Clark Street; in San Francisco, on Polk Street, between Eddy and Broadway; on Folsom Street, between 4th and 12th Streets and in Castro Village, the intersection of Castro and 18th Streets; in West Hollywood, Los Angeles, on Santa Monica Boulevard between Doheny Drive and La Cienega Boulevard.

These areas are typified by an extraordinarily high concentration of gay men and their cultural institutions. Large numbers of gay men are present on the major commercial streets, while women and children are conspicuously absent. Streets are lined with bars, bookstores, restaurants, and clothing stores catering to homosexual males. Many stores are gay owned (Shilts 1977, 20–22; Thompson 1976, 12–13). Gay language is widely used: I frequently heard conversations between men in which they referred to each other, or to other men, by female names and pronouns. Billboards, posters, and store signs also utilize the argot. For example, two oversized billboards towering above the intersection of Christopher Street and Seventh Avenue South formerly advertised a gay steam bath by showing a drawing of a cowboy and the message, "Come! to Man's Country." The billboard used concepts common to gay men, the sexual implications of the word "come," and the western motif (cf. Humphreys 1972) to imply that sex with especially desirable partners was available at the steam bath. Elsewhere, there are bars named Boot Hill, Numbers, Chaps, and stores called Boys' Market and Spike Liquors.

Gay fashion is ubiquitous in these sections of town. The vast majority of men on the streets are dressed in the "butch" style favored by the clone. This includes four principal looks: working man, lower-class tough, military man, and athlete (cf. St. Clair 1976). To illustrate, a variant of the lower-class tough look demands a tight black tee shirt; faded, skin-tight, straight-legged Levis; work boots; and a black leather motorcycle jacket. All of these styles call for short hair, muscular bodies, mustaches, closely cropped beards, and accessories such as key chains and handkerchiefs. A few men wear the attire of sadomasochism, complete black leather outfits. Gay fashion is sold in many of the local retail establishments.

Many social conventions within these areas are distinctly homosexual. Gestures of affection, eye contact, and other signals of sexual interest are exchanged openly. For example, men are frequently seen walking with their arms around each other's waists or holding hands. For the most part, people either accept or ignore these displays of affection. Even police patrols pay little attention to such behavior. In light of the aversion to homosexuality evident in other locations, this tolerance is remarkable.

The "scene" in the gay culture areas shifts with the time of day. Relatively quiet on weekday mornings and afternoons, bars and streets are crowded at night and on weekends, because participation in the gay world, for most homosexual males, occurs after normal working hours (cf. Achilles 1967; Hooker 1967; Warren 1974). At such times, the areas are flooded with residents as well as with gay men from surrounding neighborhoods and suburbs who travel in to participate in the local gay scene.

Gay people recognize the culture areas as their own quarters and have given special names to each area, names that are part of the gay argot. For example, the gay culture area in West Hollywood is called Boy's Town (Stone 1977, 24). As one San Francisco man put it, "I feel like an alien in other places. But in the Castro, I feel like I belong because I do." A New Yorker commented that for him, "leaving the Village means pulling myself together and straightening up my act."

Social Isolation

To cope with stigma, gay men often withdraw from the larger society and restrict their social life and primary relation to other gay people. Some of the men I interviewed told me that their interaction with heterosexual society was restricted to their jobs or to sporadic family visits. Their friends and acquaintances were usually gay residents of the district in which they lived. Roommates, if they had them, were also homosexual. A few informants had even less contact with the heterosexual world. These individuals managed to live within an almost exclusively gay world by limiting their social relations to fellow homosexual men and women and by working in either stereotypically gay jobs or businesses catering to a gay clientele.

At work, men used various strategies to negotiate their way through potential social stigma:

> I think everyone at work knows I am gay but we never talk about it. I never throw it in their face and they never ask me about my sex life. But I don't pretend I am straight. I don't make up stories about girl friends.

A San Franciscan commented that:

The people at work are real friendly, always asking me out for drinks or inviting me to parties. I never go. It's too much of a hassle. They don't know I am gay so I avoid seeing them outside of work. I'd much rather spend my free time with other gay men, hanging out on Polk Street.

And a New Yorker noted:

I live on the West Side with two gay men, work in a gay restaurant, and spend my summers on Fire island. I never relate to straight people.

While still another New Yorker observed:

I rarely spend time with "straight" people. The only "straight" friends I have are from college. I like them but see as little of them as possible. They don't know about me, and would be horrified if they did. I don't like pretending I am "straight," and they do stupid things like trying to set me up, and pestering me about girl friends.

Such fears were not groundless. The men routinely reported discrimination and ostracism. "My folks are Southern Baptists and believe all that religious stuff," noted one man. "When they found out I was gay, it was over between us. They told me they would pray for me but until I gave up my sinful ways, they would have nothing to do with me."

Clones also withdrew from these relationships for other reasons. They knew most people disapproved of promiscuity and drugs, and thus they shunned contact with both heterosexuals and homosexuals who did not participate in the clone lifestyle:

Everyone in my office is real cool about my being gay. But I don't hang out with them. They're down on drugs and would freak if they knew I got high.

Still others rejected these relationships because they had less in common:

I used to be very close with this pair of lovers, Dick and Seth. When I began "partying," we drifted apart. I was hitting the bars and getting "high," neither of which they did. We no longer had anything in common.

Such forces segregated clones from the broader gay as well as straight society.

Residential Concentration

Based on the available materials, it appears that certain districts house significant numbers of homosexual men. In the gay magazine *The Advocate*'s articles on life in these cities, reference is made to the large gay populations in a few districts. The article on Boston, for example, asserts that large numbers of homosexual males live in Beacon Hill, Back Bay, and South End (Brill 1976, 27). Similarly, articles report that in New York substantial numbers of gay men reside in the East Side, West Side, Greenwich Village, and Brooklyn Heights (Kantrowitz 1975, 48; Russo 1975, 47; Stoneman 1975, 44; Whitmore 1975, 45); in Chicago, in the Near North Side, Old Town, and New Town (Aiken 1976, 27–28); in San Francisco, in Castro Village (Shilts 1977, 21); and in Los Angeles, in the West Hollywood district (Stone 1977, 22). Academic authors cite the same residential districts. Bell and Weinberg (1978, 234), Newton (1972, 22), Starr and Carns (1973, 282), and Weinberg and Williams (1974, 41–46, 60–61) concur with *Advocate* articles with regard to neighborhoods in New York, Chicago, and San Francisco. In addition, Weinberg and Williams (1974, 46, 60) find similar concentrations in New York's East Midtown and Jackson Heights in Queens, and on San Francisco's Polk Street. The overwhelming majority of my informants lived in these neighborhoods. Some of them—the West Village of New York, The Castro in San Francisco, and Boy's Town in West Hollywood seem to have the largest concentrations of homosexual residents. In fact, these may even be predominantly gay, as entire blocks and buildings are inhabited exclusively by gay men (Shilts 1977, 21; Stone 1977, 22).

At the time of this research, then, three communities within the cities studied (West Village, Castro Village, and Boy's Town) fulfill all the requisite characteristics of a full-fledged ghetto. These communities are characterized by large numbers of gay institutions and cruising places, a marked gay culture, socially isolated gay residents, and a substantially gay population. Nine more neighborhoods partially satisfy the requisites for a ghetto. Three (West Side, Greenwich Village; New Town; Polk Street) house a concentration of gay locations, a gay culture area, and socially isolated gay residents, but lack a markedly gay population. Nine more (Beacon Hill, Back Bay, South End, East Side, Brooklyn Heights, East Midtown, Jackson Heights, Old Town, Near North Side) contain large numbers of gay institutions and socially isolated gay residents, but lack a predominant gay culture area and a substantially gay populace. The remaining twelve spot map districts are probably not ghettos, because they meet only one requisite: institutional concentration.

When considered together, it is possible to see all these communities as representing different stages in the development of ghettos born of societal antipathy towards homosexuality. Conditions of total suppression and zealous persecution inhibit ghetto development, but, with a modicum of tolerance, the process begins. At first, gay institutions and cruising places spring up in urban districts known to accept variant behavior. A concentration of such places in specific sections of the city, as shown on the spot map, results. This concentration attracts large numbers of homosexual men, causing a centralization of gay culture traits. Tolerance, coupled with institutional concentration, makes the areas desirable residential districts for gay men. At this stage, the areas have become partially developed gay ghettos.

Social Life within the Gay Ghetto

How, then, did gay men live in this increasingly gay social world of clone culture in the 1970s? In the gay New York of the 1970s, social life for gay men relied less on workplace contacts, since the workplace was inconsistent as a source of other gay friends, and more on friendship networks and sexual contacts.

The Clique. Same-sex friendship circles or "cliques" were probably the most central of these network groupings. Cliques were organized friendship networks that proved remarkably stable over time, in which individual members felt safe, comfortable, and relaxed, and in which they found social and emotional supports for their identities. In a world isolated from their biological families and in which they were legally excluded and temperamentally uninterested in forming lasting monogamous romantic dyads, the clique was the clone surrogate for the nuclear family.

Cliques gathered at particular meeting places (e.g., bar, home, gym, street corner) and met basic material, social, and psychological needs (LeMasters 1975; Suttles 1968; Kornblum 1974, 69; Warren 1974; Newton 1972; Hooker 1965). The cliques tended to be similar in life style and social status (LeMasters 1975; Sonenschein 1968, 71; Warren 1974, 80–90). (A few homosexual cliques included lesbians, "fag hags," or "wise"—nonhomophobic straights [Hooker 1956, 224; Warren 1979; Cotton 1972].)

Clone friendship circles replicated the general patterns. These groups clustered in particular neighborhoods and provided the basis for collective life, performing the functions and aping the format of a family. The names given these cliques (e.g., "boys," "sisters," or "family") reflected this status. Without the clique, social life for clones would be rather limited, structured only around the pursuit of sex.

Often, the cliques would emerge from anonymous sexual contacts known as "tricking." (Gay men use the term differently from prostitutes, although its origin is similar. To gay men, tricking simply refers to the anonymity of the sexual encounter, not to the exchange of money.) The men became friendly with each other after an initial sexual relationship, and gradually introduced one another to mutual friends and acquaintances over the course of their friendship. Those men who were compatible coalesced into a clique.

Cliques shared similar social characteristics. Most cliques resided in such downtown neighborhoods as the West Village, East Village, Soho, and Chelsea. The West Village and Chelsea had the highest concentration of cliques, leading some men to call them clone neighborhoods. A few cliques clustered on the Upper West Side in the West 70s and 80s. Members of cliques typically lived near one other which facilitated getting together and going out. As one man put it:

> All my sisters live in the West Village or Chelsea which is great. We can easily see one another and we're close to the bars and clubs.

Most men lived alone. Some were roommates who lived together because they were either lovers or best friends. Others lived together because they could not afford to live alone.

Most men in the clique came from similar social backgrounds. Cliques were stratified along racial, religious, and class lines. Most were overwhelmingly white. Black and Hispanic men belonged to only a handful of cliques. In addition, the cliques were either predominantly Christian or Jewish. However, a sizable number contained men from different faiths. The cliques were generally middle-class, but there were some upper-middle and working-class cliques. And finally, and perhaps most significantly, the cliques were almost exclusively male. The few women who belonged to cliques joined because they found the life style exciting. As one woman put it, "I run with this group because I like to party and they party the hardest."

Before the AIDS crisis, membership in the clique remained quite stable, often lasting for years. What gay men may have lacked in terms of the stability of the monogamous romantic couple they sustained in the friendship network. Turnover usually occurred among peripheral members, who were typically "boyfriends" or acquaintances of someone in the group. The clique accepted these men only for the duration of the relationship:

> Howie was part of our "family" only while he was dating Frank. Once they broke up, we stopped seeing him. He kept calling us but none of us saw him. It wouldn't have been right, since Frank was our friend.

Once the clique was firmly established, some men assumed roles paralleling those found in other homosexual cliques. Generally, these seem to have imitated roles within the nuclear family, again suggesting that the clique was the clone equivalent for the nuclear family. Though clone argot lacked specific terms for these roles, they appeared widely. I came to think of them as: nurturer, social director, leader, big brother, and kid brother. Nurturers and social directors assumed some of the duties traditionally associated with wives. Nurturers were found both in clone and other gay cliques (Bell and Weinberg 1978, 246) and specialized in mothering, providing emotional support to everyone in the group. Whenever the men needed a shoulder to cry on, nurturers listened attentively, offering comfort and advice. Whenever the men argued, the nurturers mediated disputes and smoothed things out. Social directors orchestrated the clique's recreational activities, planning and coordinating what the men did during leisure time:

> John planned Halloween. He had us over for dinner earlier that night. Then we got dressed in costumes he designed. After this, he gave us drugs. Around midnight, we piled into the limo he rented, and went off to the parties he lined up.

Frequently, these two roles merged with that of leader, often called the "queen" in other homosexual cliques (Leznoff and Westley, 1956).

Leaders typically lacked lovers or best friends and were involved in clique affairs, which gave them great influence in the clique's decision-making process. Observed one man:

> Our group spins around Tom. He arranges our house on the Island, hosts the parties before going out, and calls us every day to see if we're O.K. We all sort of follow after him.

The cliques often were named after leaders, as in "Bob's family," or "I hang with Tony's clique."

The "best friend" role appeared in most of the gay and clone cliques (Sonenschein 1968). Best friends acted like devoted brothers or cousins and frequently lived together. The men were constant companions and were emotionally close and supportive. "These two are not lovers but best friends," was the way I was introduced to two members of a clique. "You never see one without the other. They work out together, live together, and hit the bars together."

Cliques served all the functions of the family, except, of course, that of biological reproduction. But all the others—emotional support, socialization, economic cooperation, social control and sexual regulation—were adequately maintained (Smelser 1981, 281–83; Persell 1984, 333–71). The cliques provided emotional support—affection, acceptance, intimacy, nurturance, and sociability. The cliques fulfilled their needs because the men were close friends who cared for and accepted and helped one another:

> The family took good care of me after Jim left. I had fallen apart. I felt suicidal and had stopped going to work. Then my friends stepped in. At night, they would sleep over, holding me when I cried. In the morning, they made me get up, get dressed and go to work. In the evening, everyone would come over, make me dinner, and cheer me up. On weekends, they would force me to go out instead of sitting home depressed.

These friendships also provided companionship. The men avoided loneliness by spending free time together, socializing at home or in gathering places. "I don't like being alone so I make sure I see my sisters every night," said one man.

Big and kid brothers took on many of the responsibilities associated with a family's oldest and youngest son. Both roles appear in other homosexual cliques but were named differently (Bell and Weinberg

1978, 246). Big brothers were labeled "gay mothers," and kid brothers were called "twinkies" (Hoffman 1968, 22, 66–68). Big brothers were usually the group's oldest member and socialized younger men into the clone life style, teaching them the tricks of the trade and offering them counsel and advice. Kid brothers were typically the clique's junior members who had just arrived in New York and were new to the scene. They had been out for a few years but were new to the life style. They were treated like mascots and were pampered and indulged while learning the ropes. They were socialized through mentoring and role modeling. In mentoring, big brothers took them under their wings and showed them how to be a clone:

> Eric showed me the ropes when I got to the Village. He belonged to this crowd I got involved with. God, I was so dumb then. I didn't even know how to wear Levi 501s. Eric taught me how to buy and shrink them. He took me to all the "hot" clubs and parties. I spent my first summer in the "Pines" with him. He even took me to the gym and showed me how to lift weights.

Kid brothers mimicked the other men's behavior, language, and style:

> Right after I moved to the City, I started running with a group I met at the tubs. At first, they made fun of my clothes and haircut. They really needled me! To get them off my back, I started to change. I looked at what they were wearing and listened to what they said. I started to dress the way they did and talk the way they did. All the teasing stopped after this.

Clique socialization helped heal damaged identities. Novice clones devalued themselves for being gay while growing up, but participation in the clone life style erased these feelings:

> I came out in a small town in the Midwest. Although I liked being gay more after meeting other gay people, I still had regrets. The scene in my home town was so awful that it made me sad to be gay. Gay life seemed so weird and underground. All the men were either "screaming queens," dirty old men, or trolls, and the bar was a raunchy dive in the wrong part of town. Nothing about it was attractive.

But another man noted that:

> My "family" made me proud to be gay. They taught me how gay men could be hot and masculine, and how gay life could be exciting and chic.

Cliques also furnished material assistance, mainly in the form of loans and job leads. When a man was broke, someone in the clique was likely to lend him money and at times even paid his expenses, although as a circle of friends and not a family, they did not pool resources, and each man was expected to support himself. They also helped each other find jobs:

> I was working as a busboy making lousy money. I really wanted a job as a waiter. Then Tom, a guy in my "family," told me about an opening where he worked. He took me there, introduced me to the manager, who hired me on Tom's recommendation.

Finally, the cliques also acted as agents of social control, enforcing normative standards through informal sanctions. They rewarded compliance with approval, praise, and admiration, and punished disobedience with criticism, ridicule, and ostracism:

> Last week I had some friends in from out of town. We decided to go the Flamingo but had to go early because their flight was at noon the next day. My friends dished me to death for this.

These sanctions were quite effective. The men knew that admission and continued acceptance in the clique depended upon conformity to group norms, which was also the case in other gay friendship circles (Hooker 1956, 221). The clique fulfilled too many basic needs for them to risk rejection. Hence, they closely conformed to normative dictates.

The men also conformed to the norms regulating sexual behavior. These norms proscribed sex between clique members except for those men who were lovers or boyfriends, and tricking—a ban that exists in most homosexual scripts. They also influenced the men's choice of erotic partners. The men picked tricks on the basis of clique approval.

Crowds. Just as nuclear families are embedded within kinship networks of extended families and also articulate with larger neighborhood associations, so too did the clone clique. Cliques merged into broader social groupings known as crowds. Each crowd contained a cluster of cliques that knew each other either personally or by sight.

Crowds emerged in two distinct ways. Some crowds arose through tricking. Clones regularly had sex with men from other cliques because group norms forbade sex between men who were friends within the same clique. These contacts led clones to become acquainted with men in different cliques, who were then introduced to people in their respective cliques. These introductions formed the basis for a crowd.

At times, crowds evolved through social contacts. Men from different cliques either became acquainted or began to recognize each other from attending the same gathering spot (e.g., gym, bar, resort). These contacts caused them to introduce one another to their respective cliques. Often the introductions were limited to verbal identification without face-to-face contact, simply by pointing others out.

Crowds allowed for larger residential and neighborhood arrangements, and frequently included men belonging to cliques that did not live in New York. These men might live in either neighboring Northeast cities (Boston, Washington, Philadelphia, etc.), West Coast (San Francisco and Los Angeles), or Texas. They came to New York to participate in the clone life style, and commonly tricked with men living here. These tricks occasionally became friendships, with the men visiting one another and meeting each other's friends.

Crowds functioned to provide companionship in meeting places. The men would socialize with people from both their clique and crowd in the gathering places. As one man pointed out, "for me, the Saint is very social. The crowd I know goes there, and I spend most of my time dishing with friends." Crowds commonly coalesced around a particular meeting place—by which they became known. Thus the "Flamingettes" gathered at the Flamingo, an exclusive, private dance club and the "Pines Boys" were so named after the beach resort located in the Fire Island community.

The Circuit. Most crowds came together around a particular set of meeting places known as the "circuit." The circuit describes the institutions that together compose the gay ghetto, especially its social, sexual, and recreational scenes. Different circuits may have been organized around socializing and being "seen," at, for example, bars and restaurants, favorite spots for brunches and parties. Others might include sexual contacts and social locations such as gyms, while others may have been exclusively organized around sexual contacts such as bath houses, parks, streets, public restrooms, and pornographic movie theatres and bookstores. In New York, circuit spots were located mainly in lower Manhattan and catered to the clone life style. Many clustered along Christopher Street and the waterfront blocks known as the "Dock Strip" in the West Village and Chelsea. Some were found in the East Village and Soho. Others were located in the "Pines" during the summer.

"Circuits" first appeared in New York during the 1950s (Gooch, 1984), although George Chauncey's research seems to suggest nascent circuits as early as the turn of the century. This original circuit included such bars as the Blue Parrot, Golden Pheasant, and Swan, which were all located on Third Avenue in the East 50s. It was, for obvious reasons, dubbed the "Bird Circuit."

The social life of clones revolved around the circuit. The men frequented the gathering spots on a regular basis. White's (1980,271) description of the lives of some upscale New York clones aptly illustrated this pattern:

> All week they stay in or work out at the gym and put in long hours at their demanding jobs where they often are loners in a straight world. Friday night they have a quiet supper with friends, Saturday they perform their chores and clean house, Saturday night they boogie, Sunday they sleep.

Clones called these men "circuit queens."

The popularity of circuit meeting places fluctuated widely over time. A spot might be "hot" one season but "tired" or "played" the next year:

> When the Bodycenter first opened it was "hot." Everyone left the New York Health Club on Thirteenth Street for the Bodycenter. The crowd now has moved to the Chelsea Gym and the Bodycenter is tired.

Many circuit gathering spots were gay owned and operated. The men preferred to socialize in exclusively gay surroundings, and therefore felt more comfortable in gay-run places:

> I don't like eating in straight restaurants. It makes me nervous. I never have to worry about being treated poorly in gay establishments.

And circuit ambience reflected the clone life style. Most of the men dressed in accordance with clone fashion codes. The men resented intrusions by those who violated these norms. One afternoon, I was talking to some men at Ty's, a popular circuit bar. A group of suburban homosexuals walked in. These men wore designer jeans, LaCoste shirts with the collars flipped up, and reeked of cologne. They were obviously *not* clones. As they passed by, the man I was chatting to

TABLE 2.1
Circuit Gathering Places: 1977–1983

Purpose	Name
Social	
Bars	Ty's, Boots and Saddles, Keller's, Badlands, The Ramrod, The Spike, The Eagle's Nest, The Seventeenth Street Saloon, Rawhide, Pipeline, Boot Hill
Restaurants	Tiffany II, Pennyfeathers, Jeanne's Patio, Homer's, The Commissary, Claire, Christopher's, Red Star, Clyde's, Company, Trilogy, One Potato, Pershings
Recreational	
Gyms	Sheridan Square, Chelsea Gym, The Bodycenter, The McBurney YMCA
Discos	Cockring, Underground, Pavilion, Sandpiper, Moonshadow, Botel, Kamikaze, River Club, Le Mouche, The Saint, Flamingo, 12 West
Sexual	
Bath houses	Everard, The New St. Marks Baths, Man's Country
Backroom Bars	The Strap, Candle, Anvil, J's, The International Stud
Sex Clubs	Mineshaft, Glory Hole, Seventh Floor Studio, The Loft

nudged me and said, "Look at those trolls! They must be Tunnel and Bridge. What are they doing here? Who let them in?" To the clones, these gay men were anachronisms, throwbacks to another era of male homosexuality, of blowdried bouffant hairdos, gold pinky rings, and fey demeanor. As my confidant implied, they impaired the "hotness" of a place. "They're visual pollutants," he said, "disrupting the erotic beauty of a room full of hot men."

The gathering spots included places that served either social, recreational, or sexual purposes. Table 2.1 lists these places for the period between 1977 and 1983 by the functions they performed. I compiled this list by asking men which circuit places were hot and why people went to them. Almost all the places with social purposes were bars and restaurants, where men went to hang out with friends. They went there to chit-chat, to get something to eat, to see and be seen, and to hear music:

> I hang out at Ty's a lot. I guess I do it to escape being lonely. I live by myself in a tiny studio apartment. Staring at those four walls drives me crazy, so I come down here to bullshit, to get into someone's head, for social intake, and maybe find a trick.

While other commentators described the chief function of gay bars as places for meeting sexual partners, this did not seem to be the case in clone bars. Although cruising took place, it was not the predominant activity. Most men went there to socialize:

Honey, you don't go to the Eagle if you're horny. You go there to hang
out, to stand and model, to hear Jim's music. If you want sex go to the
tubs.

Bars and restaurants attracted divergent crowds. The "Village crowd"
frequented the bars along Christopher Street. "Chelsea boys" gathered
in the bars along the "Dock Strip." Working-class cliques favored
coffee shops, such as Tiffany II, which was called the "clone" coffee
shop. Middle-class cliques ate only breakfast or lunch in coffee shops.
They went to restaurants, such as Christopher's, Company, or Trilogy,
for dinner.

The men frequented similar recreational places for exercise and
entertainment. These places included primarily health clubs, discos,
and resorts. Those men who pursued rigorous body building went to
the "heavy" gyms, such as Sheridan Square or Chelsea Gym. These
men tended to use free weights to build "pumped up" physiques.
Many of them belonged to the clone demimonde of hustlers, bartenders, and porn stars. Men who were concerned only with maintaining
"tone and definition" went to the "fluff" gyms, such as the Body-
center. These gyms specialized in Nautilus training. The "hard core
party" set danced at exclusive private clubs such as The Saint which
were open only to members. Everyone else went to the nonmembership dance clubs. The more affluent men summered in the Pines.
Those who could not afford to go there sunned on the West Village
Docks, which were dubbed "the poor man's Pines."

Erotic locations were important places on every clone's circuit; this
was where the men went to find impersonal, often anonymous, sexual
contacts. These places included bath houses, backroom bars, and sex
clubs. Particular areas in each of these places were set aside for anonymous sex. In bath houses, sex took place in private rooms, dormitories,
and wet areas. Each private room included a bed, clothing hook, and
small stand. The men typically brought their sex partners into the
room. Dormitories contained several beds and were dimly lit. They
were called "orgy rooms" because sex occurred throughout the space.
Wet areas consisted of showers, saunas, and steam rooms. Sex usually
took place in the last two areas. In backroom bars, sex occurred in
poorly lit spaces or rooms located at the back of the bar. In sex clubs,
sex took place in specially designed rooms situated behind the bar
and coat check. These rooms included slings for anal fisting (fist

fucking) and bathtubs for urophilic activities ("water sports"). As one journalist described one scene:

> In the basement of the Mineshaft, a circle of men stand around a bath tub, urinating upon a semi-nude man who fondles his penis and moans, "Piss on me, Yeah, piss on me."

The men who frequented the sex clubs belonged to a crowd called "pig circles." These men engaged in "sleaze sex"—impersonal sex with multiple partners, often in group settings, in public places, and engaged in anal fisting and urophilia.

Clones frequented "circuit" gathering places in accordance with a fixed schedule dubbed "circuit hours." These conformed to general cultural standards for leisure time activity; men gathered in the places at the end of the working day and on weekends.

The Ramrod is hot on circuit nights. But on the other nights it is boring and empty. No one goes there and whoever does is a troll.

But unlike middle-class conventional norms, circuit hours stretched much further into the early morning; bars and discos on weekends rarely began getting crowded before midnight, and continued until dawn. Disco hours became progressively later over the years, especially for "hard partyers":

> We used to go to the Tenth Floor at 1:00 [A.M.] Every season after that we would go out dancing later. We would go to Flamingo and 12 West at 2:00 [A.M.] When the Saint came along, we would go at 4:00 [A.M.] And this summer, people are going to the Pavilion at 6:00 [A.M.].

The clone community was a somewhat closed community in the 1970s—a gay ghetto organized around a set of socially isolated friendship cliques and crowds, which coalesced around a series of meeting spots known as the circuit. The cliques, crowds, and circuit provided the men with commonality, companionship, community, and contacts. These were the basis for social life. Taken together, they define the structural parameters and the institutional locations for the articulation of gay masculinity in the 1970s.

NOTES

1. Urban spatial patterns are usually determined by analyzing census data through spot maps, social area analysis, or factorial ecology (Timms 1971). We

cannot use such methods for gay people, because we lack the crucial data: the addresses of all homosexual men and women. Since the census does not inquire into sexual orientation, it does not supply such information. Other potential sources (e.g. police files, psychiatrists' records, homophile organizations) are inadequate because they are patently misrepresentative (Weinberg 1970). *Bob Damron's Address Book* is one of several gay directories, all of which vary in the accuracy of their listings. This was chosen because, at the time, it was considered the most current and accurate (Sage 1975, 17; Weinberg and Williams 1974, 41n., 58n.).

Chapter Three

"(I Wanna Be a) Macho Man"
The Masculinization of Clone Social Life

"As far as I'm concerned, being any gender is a drag."
—Patti Smith

A gorgeous Sunday afternoon was rapidly fading away as I left the Morton Street pier, heading toward the Dock Strip bars. Owing to the beautiful weather, "Tea Stand" was mobbed, with men spilling out of the bars onto the sidewalks. Scanning the crowd, I saw a group of acquaintances near the side entrance to Badlands. After quick hellos and kisses, I joined them, and we started to chat about people we knew. During a lull in the conversation, one of the men went to buy the next round of drinks, returning a short while later with a handful of beers. As we drank our beers, another man lit a joint and passed it around.

By now I had become engaged in a discussion with the man standing next to me, whom I had met once before. A little older than the rest of the group, he was a seasoned veteran of "Circuit" life. We began to talk about how the "Island" had changed. After telling me what it was like when he first came out, he then looked me in the eyes, and said in a voice dripping with sarcasm, "Just look at these clones dear. With their pumped up bodies and thick mustaches, they all look so 'butch.' But I remember them when everyone was 'nelly.' What a joke!"

Perplexed by his remark, I asked him what he meant. With a warm smile and a wink, he replied, "Honey, when you have been around as long as I have, you get to know a lot of men. Over the last few years, I have watched many of these girls change as the times changed. A couple of years ago, they had puny bodies, lisping voices, and elegant clothes. At parties or Tea Dances, they came in dresses, swooning over Garbo and Davis. Now, they've 'butched up,' giving up limp wrists and mincing gaits for bulging muscles and manly handshakes, giving up fancy clothes and posh pubs for faded jeans and raunchy discos."

Here was a neat summary of the changes in gay male culture from the 1950s to the 1970s. Prior to gay liberation, gay male closet culture sanctioned "swish" presentational styles (Kleinberg 1978), but during the 1970s, clone culture adopted more hypermasculine affect. What was this look, and where did it come from?

Like everyone else, gay men constructed their images and presentational styles from the materials of the broader culture. Neither "butch" nor "swish" styles are innate in gay physiology, neither is genetically encoded, nor is one style carried in a special center of the brain. These styles represent the construction of a gay male identity from the artifacts and materials that gay men find in their culture. We may create our own identities, to paraphrase Marx, but we do not do it just as we please, but rather we do it from the materials we find around us.

"Closet" culture built this image out of the older "homosexual role"—that is, closeted gay men accepted the equation of homosexuality with effeminacy, and thus viewed feminine presentational strategies as a means of expressing their identity as gay men. Hence, they feminized their presentational imagery by adopting womanly mannerisms and interests. Many displayed stereotypically feminine interests in fashion, and wore smart, elegant, trendy, well-tailored clothes (Henry 1955; West 1977). Others adopted the feminine expressions and postures associated with swishing. Still others did "drag" and wore feminine apparel and makeup. They often donned haute couture female apparel and grooming for attendance at "drag balls." Feminization also characterized the presentational styles of their homes and gathering places. These places tended to be overly decorated and filled "with fancy frills, froufrou, bric-a-brac and au courant kitsch" (Fischer 1972, 69; White 1980; Henry 1955, 304).

Of course, not everyone bought this equation—even in the 1950s. Some participants in the closet culture rejected this image and its association of effeminacy with homosexuality. They equated same-sex love instead with hypermasculinity, and organized their presentational strategies along the lines of traditional masculinity. They wore the attire of such masculine icons as workers, bikers, and cowboys (Fischer 1972). Some even donned the uniforms of sailors, who were popular erotic ideals (Cory and LeRoy 1963). They furnished their gathering places similarly, decorating them with assorted biker and Western gear (Delph 1978; Achilles 1967; Bell and Weinberg 1978, 250–68).

Folkloric assumptions about macho masculinity lay at the heart of the manly presentational strategies. The term "macho" implied overconformity to the traditional male gender role. This role was generally regarded as more masculine than the modern male gender role (Stearns 1979). Manly homosexuals imitated the macho role (Newton 1972; Warren 1974). Homosexuals dubbed these men "butch." In the gay world, the term "butch" has multiple meanings (Rodgers 1972, 39). As an adjective, it denoted a mannish appearance and demeanor. As a noun, it signified a man playing the male role either socially or sexually. A butch homosexual thus looked and acted masculine—*very* masculine.

There was significant tension between butch masculinity and more feminized homosexuality. Many members of the closet culture regarded butch presentational strategies as deviant (Warren 1972, 1974; Helmer 1963). They felt this image was socially unacceptable in mainstream homosexual circles. Men who displayed this look belonged to the marginal leather and Western communities (Goldstein 1975). To the feminized homosexual, what mattered was that one was a homosexual who happened (however inconveniently) to be a man. To the butch, by contrast, one was a gay man—neither was inconvenient, and both were necessary to create gay male identity.

The emergence of the gay liberation movement in the early 1970s resolved this tension among mainstream gay men, and reorganized the presentational strategies of the closet culture. Activists rejected the belief that gay men were womanly, claiming that to believe so was a symptom of internalized homophobia (self-hatred based on the dominant culture's view of homosexuality as deviant or immoral). Gay men were simply men who loved men. They were not deviant, were not failed men. They were real men—and in their presentational styles they set about demonstrating their newfound and hard-fought conformity to traditional norms of masculinity.

Other men developed presentational styles from different parts of the emerging culture of the 1960s and 1970s. But virtually all played with gender ideation. Gender is, after all, the chief determinant of style. Closeted men adopted feminine affect while butch men embraced traditional masculinity. In between, men used gender display as a way of signaling their own emerging identities. Some used "gender fuck" styles—deliberately combining masculine and feminine clothing and style to toy with and challenge rigid gender differentiation. Some would wear frilly dresses with cowboy boots and heavy beards. Others adopted more androgynous styles, blending gender affect in a more countercultural mode, seeking liberation from gender restrictions altogether and the gradual melange of flowing styles.

By the early 1970s, trendy New York homosexuals regarded none of these existing presentational styles as satisfactory. Most of these men worked in such trend-conscious professions as fashion and the arts and were aware of the liberationist contention that homosexuals were manly. This belief led them to reject effeminate camp and gender fuck presentational styles. They eschewed the hip masculine look because it appeared dated. Countercultural androgyny would not cut it in the worlds of work and public presentation. So, they set about creating a new presentational style to convey their sense of manliness—a manliness that was distinctly gay, and yet no less manly for it. So the clone look was born, by embracing the presentational imagery of the butch style, and modifying it into a more stylized uniform. By the end of the 1970s, the clone look was *the* look for the postcloset urban denizen of the gay ghetto.

Presentational Styles of the Clone

Two general processes define the presentational strategies of the gay clone. Presentational rhetorics refer to a cluster of traits that function "to communicate a particular set of meanings, directed towards the representation of a specific image of impression" (Ball 1967). Gay clones employed two rhetorics of exaggerated manliness: (1) "butch" rhetoric, which fostered a masculine look through the verbal and visual symbols of macho manhood; and, (2) "hot" rhetoric, which projected manly sexuality through the verbal and visual signs of macho eroticism.

Goffman's (1959) concept of impression management was used to describe how the rhetorics conveyed these images. Goffman defined this concept as the process through which individuals manipulate the interpretation of a social situation. Individuals and institutions routinely presented particular images of their social identity, which were known as fronts, in an attempt to convey a particular definition of a situation. These fronts were fashioned from image-evoking traits called sign-vehicles and were broken down into three parts: (1) appearance; (2) manner; and (3) setting. Appearance denoted those sign-vehicles which signified social status, such as attire, physical looks, age, sex, and race. Manner referred to those sign-vehicles which conveyed attitudes, mood, and temperament. Some of these included facial expressions, speech patterns, and bodily gestures. Finally, setting denoted those sign-vehicles located in the site of social interaction, e.g., decor, furniture, and physical layout. Goffman defined sign-vehicles as impression-creating or image-evoking attributes.

Butch Rhetoric

Butch rhetoric used various hypermasculine sign-vehicles to project a butch front. These sign-vehicles were stylized (reworked) to express butchness, which often borrowed a sense of play from "gender fuck" styles, and a "camp" sensibility (Altman 1982, 13; Newton 1972). In the past, camp had caricaturized stereotypically feminine sign-vehicles; now, though, butch rhetoric expressed camp by its self-conscious appropriation of traditionally macho sign-vehicles. As one man put it:

> I look at clone drag as play clothes, just like when I would come home from school as a boy, have cookies and milk, change and go out to play. Now I come home from work, change into clone "drag," and go out and play on the circuit.

What mattered was the doubleness of clone style—its self-conscious, almost parodying references to stereotypically traditional masculinity, and its self-conscious embracing of that very stereotype at the same time. Clone style was both parody and emulation.

The physical appearance of the clone was the first signal of a new type of gay masculinity. Clones used such stereotypically macho sign-vehicles as musculature, facial hair, short haircuts, and rugged, functional clothing to express butchness. Clones developed "gym bodies," which denoted the physique associated with weightlifters. A gym body included tight buttocks, washboard stomachs, and "pumped-up" biceps and pectorals. Clones favored this physique because they

TABLE 3.1
Butch Sign-Vehicles in Clone Fashion

Butch Image	Sign-Vehicles
Western	Cowboy hat, denim jacket, cowboy shirt. Western belt, leather chaps, Frye or cowboy boots, farmer bandanas, rawhide thongs
Leather	Black leather motorcycle cap, jacket, pants, and boots. Black or white tee-shirt, studded black leather belt and wrist band, chains, tattoos
Military	Green army cap, flight jacket, red belt, and fatigues. Brown leather bomber jacket, khaki army shirt, combat boots
Laborer	Hard hat, denim jacket, plaid flannel shirt, painter's pants, construction boots, keys
Hood	Black leather jacket and belt. White tee-shirt, torn faded jeans, sneakers
Athlete	Team jacket, sweatshirt, LaCoste shirt, tank top, sweatpants, gym shorts, jock straps, white crew socks, running shoes
Woodsman	Down vest, plaid wool shirt, thermal undershirt, Levis, hiking boots
Sleaze	Washed-out denim jacket, ripped flannel or T-shirt, faded Levis
Uniforms	Policeman, fireman, highway patrol

felt it was the most macho male build. "Society sees musclemen as more masculine, so I work out putting in long hours in the gym pumping iron," one body builder told me in a local gym. "The results make me feel butch."

The men also wore the sturdy, utilitarian clothing associated with traditional macho icons. Table 3.1 lists the butch sign-vehicles in clone fashion. The men favored the hood, athlete, and woodsman looks for everyday leisure attire. They wore the Western, leather, military, laborer, and uniform looks for going out or partying. Lastly, they favored the sleaze look for cruising. All these looks called for short hair, thick mustaches, or trimmed beards. (For a clearly coded and deliberate stylizating of these styles, take a look at any album by The Village People.)

All clone fashion was a fashion of class as well as gender. (Of course, class cultural codes are decidedly gendered in the first place.) Whereas traditional closeted homosexual culture imitated the affect and pretensions of an aristocratic upper class, the clone found his masculine identity in the working class. Like most middle-class men before him, the gay male middle class found the upper class feminized and effeminate; if he was going to prove his masculinity, he needed to embrace the rougher, coarser masculinity of the common laborer. The gay fop of the 1950s wanted to be Lord Chatterley; the gay clone wanted to be the gardener. After all, he got all the good sex.

It is important to note that clones fashioned these looks differently from those of heterosexual men. Straight men might wear these fashions in a less self-conscious, and therefore more disheveled way. Their garments might not fit or match, their facial hair might not be perfectly trimmed. In that sense, straight masculinity reflected conformity to traditional male norms concerning nonchalance about appearance (Farrell 1975). Clones rejected this nonchalance and stylized these looks. They kept their hair short, beards and mustaches clipped, and clothing tailored and matched. In a sense, the clone brought a gay sensibility to a gendered attire.

Take Frank, for example, one of my informants. Frank looked like a well-groomed lumberjack. Everything he wore was tailored and matched. His jeans and plaid Pendelton shirt fit perfectly. His black, wool, watchman's cap matched his black Levis and the black in his shirt. His red thermal undershirt matched the red in his shirt. The brown in his leather belt matched the brown in his hiking boots. No real lumberjack ever looked so well put together, so coordinated in color, his outfit fitting so perfectly. Frank, then, *signified* the lumberjack—appropriating the gender conformity that is traditionally associated with lumberjacks, but not actually having to cut down trees to do it.

The popularity and constituent elements of these looks changed over time. In the 1970s, clones favored butch costuming and athletic attire, denoting the jock, Western, leather, laborer, military, and uniform looks. The men dressed as cowboys, bikers, construction workers, and soldiers in "circuit" bars and clubs. They also cropped their hair closely, right to the scalp, and wore mirrored aviator sunglasses. Some pierced their nipples with gold rings or studs. Others tattooed their arms or buttocks. For street wear, gay clones mixed athletic and laborer apparel, with construction boots, straight-legged, button-fly Levi 501s, plaid flannel shirts, and hooded sweatshirts under brown leather flight jackets in cold weather. In warmer weather, they wore green-striped, Adidas running shoes, button-fly Levis, and either LaCoste shirts, tank tops, or T-shirts.

By the early 1980s, strict butch costuming fell out of favor, as clones mixed butch elements for circuit and street wear. They wore either black cowboy boots or black leather Patrick sneakers, black or blue button-fly Levis, plaid flannel shirts, tank tops, or T-shirts, and black leather or down jackets. They also wore their hair longer—down to, but not over, the ears.

The manner of clones expressed masculinity through such typically macho sign-vehicles as spatial distance, facial inexpressiveness, and loudness. Again, like the working-class men they imitated, gay clones displayed reserve, aggression, and coarseness in their motions, speech patterns, and facial gestures (Frieze and Ramsey 1976). At the same time, they self-consciously differentiated themselves from straight men who might look similarly.

There was always a delicate interplay between a straight imitation and variation to make certain that others would know they were not only real men, but real *gay* men. After all, those very men that the clone imitated also manifest the most sharply homophobic attitudes and were perhaps the most likely to be feared for physical violence and gay bashing. One might want to imitate that presentational style of masculinity, but one may not have wanted to confront it in real life. That might be dangerous. Plus, one wanted to attract other *gay* men, so the "right" men needed to notice the visual cues. The delicacy of imitation without inappropriate signaling required significant impression management skills—using traditionally masculine styles in the service of obviously gay purposes. (The potential confusion between gay clones and the working-class men they imitated also provides the origins of "gaydar" or gay radar that gay men were said to possess, enabling them to look at a man and determine whether or not he is gay from one glance.) Thus, the clone would stand at a bar, posed with casual indifference, apart from other men, taking up as much space as possible, but with his crotch thrust forward in a way that exaggerated sexual interest. They touched only to greet acquaintances, to good-naturedly poke each other in the ribs, or to playfully slap one another on the back. Playful jostling and occasional smacks on the rear were the only contacts deemed appropriate between them. They spoke loudly and roughly, using coarse expressions and working-class idioms. And they walked slowly, with long deliberate strides (Frieze and Ramsey 1976).

The men also employed butch sign-vehicles while "posing," which was also called "standing and modeling." "Posing" involved standing alone, with a blank expression, in a conspicuous spot, like near the dance floor in discos or under spotlights or aside the pool table in bars. This stance conveyed such butch attributes as asociality, affectlessness, and confidence, and was used to obtain erotic affirmation. While I was in the Ramrod one Sunday afternoon, for example, I noticed a man standing by himself, leaning against the pool table in the middle of the bar. He was tall and good-looking, and clutched his jacket in one hand and a Bud in the other. He stood there for over an hour, alone, aloof, and expressionless, and ignored all "cruises." I asked one of the men I was with about his behavior. He told me that this man was "posing," which meant that he was acting "butch" and waiting to be "admired."

Clones abandoned some of these butch sign-vehicles at informal clique get-togethers or in noncruising situations. The men manifested instead some camp speech patterns in these circumstances. Then, they typically used cross-gendered nouns and pronouns, often referring to each other as "girl" or "she":

> *Tony:* Did you see Allan at 12 West last night?
> *Brad:* God was she a mess. That girl was ripped to the tits. I think she did too much MDA.

The persistence of this argot again belies masculine identification, and suggests that while some clones still might have equated homosexuality with effeminacy, clones were equally adept at both genres of gender display. Both masculinity *and* femininity were a form of drag, a put-on, which could just as easily be taken off. And yet, as one man commented to me, "Darling," he said, "beneath all this butch drag, we are still girls."

Clone gathering places and apartments also manifested butch masculinity through the use of stereotypically macho sign-vehicles in the decor. Table 3.2 delineates the butch sign-vehicles appearing in the design of circuit meeting spots. Clones used primarily Western or leather sign-vehicles as furnishings or decorative elements in circuit bars or sex clubs. For example, the bar Badlands was furnished with wagon wheels, corrals, and sawdust, and the bartenders wore cowboy boots, shirts, and hats. Another bar, the Eagle, contained biker posters, banners, and trophies, and the bartenders wore black leather chaps, vests, and caps. The names of these establishments were also butch sign-vehicles. These names conveyed either Western, leather, or industrial images. For example, the name of the bar Boots and Saddles evoked cowboy masculinity, while the Pipeline evoked blue-collar workers.

Many of these establishments also used dress codes to ensure that their clientele fit the decor, or, rather, that both decor and clientele

TABLE 3.2
Butch Sign-Vehicles in Circuit Gathering Places

Butch Image	Gathering Place	Sign-Vehicles
Western	Badlands Boots and Saddles Boot Hill Ty's Eagle	Corrals, saddles, wagon wheels, sawdust, timber paneling, wooden plank floors, Western painting, stuffed animal heads
Leather	The Strap The Spike Cell Block Ramrod	Dangling motorcycles and helmets; biker posters, banners and trophies, whips and chains
Industrial	Flamingo 12 West The Saint Pipeline	Banquettes, track lighting, factory lights, spiral metal staircases, pipe railings, metal lockers, industrial Carpeting, Pirelli Rubber flooring

matched. These codes were typically posted near the front door, and were enforced by doormen, who generally refused entrance to anyone breaking the code. For example, the doorman at the Ramrod prohibited men wearing sandals, shorts, or dress clothes from entering the bar. Such attire violated the bar's leather image.

Clones also favored industrial sign-vehicles as furnishings or decorative elements in circuit discos and private homes. These sign-vehicles included artifacts originally intended for industrial or commercial usage. For example, the Saint used track lighting, gray metal lockers, black Pirelli rubber floor covering, and black metal pipe railing and spiral staircases. 12 West's decor consisted of spotlights, banquettes, gray industrial carpeting, and white glossy walls. Clone apartment houses were similarly appointed—painted gray and covered with industrial carpeting. In addition, they used steel shelving, movers' pads, factory lamps, wire storage baskets, and retractable extension cords.

As with many fashions, clone fashion set the trend for the rest of American culture a few years later. Interior designers came to refer to clone style as "high tech" and it became enormously popular in the 1980s, as consumers appropriated products originally created for warehouses, factories, battleships, hospitals, and offices for residential and commercial usage. (This process was, of course, equally true in sartorial fashion, as mainstream America caught up with gay men's penchant for Levi 501s, work boots, sweatshirts, flannel shirts, and leather bomber jackets—just as gay men no longer found these of much use.) High-tech accessories provided the perfect vehicle for expressing gay masculinity and butchness. Industrial artifacts suggested blue-collar workers. In addition, the stream-lined utilitarianism of these artifacts conveyed such macho traits as practicality and unembellishment.

Hot Rhetoric

Clones also used a "hot rhetoric" to convey a distinctly sexualized masculinity. "Hot" denoted physical attractiveness and erotic capability. A hot man was handsome, horny, and experienced. In this sense, he conformed to cultural expectations regarding masculine sexuality. Just as sexual capability was becoming the chief marker of heterosexual masculinity—especially with the precariousness of the breadwinner ethic—so too was sexual prowess the chief marker for gay masculinity.

Clones used butch fashion and stylization to express hotness. Like most gay men (Hooker 1965; Humphreys 1971; Sage 1975; Hoffman 1968), clones perceived manliness as attractive, a quality only heightened by butchness. Thus their gym bodies, mustaches and beards, and butch clothing signified masculinity and a distinctly masculine sexuality. Moreover, this fashion was displayed in a particularly sexual way. Form-fitting Levis and T-shirts typically hugged the body, revealing the contours of their genitals, buttocks, and musculature. They often highlighted these features by not wearing underwear, wallets, or shirts. Some men even left the top or bottom button of their Levis undone, in part to signal sexual availability, and in part to suggest that their genitals were so large they had popped a button through sheer size. Others faded the crotch of their jeans through bleaching for a similar effect. Outerwear also called attention to these areas. Clones wore waist-length down or leather jackets over Levis. The shortness of these jackets exposed the bulge of their genitals and buttocks.

Clones wore this clothing differently from heterosexual men, again so there could be little doubt about whether someone was a heterosexual macho man or a gay macho man. Straight men wore this attire loosely in order to be more comfortable. Clones wore these garments tight in order to enhance their physical attractiveness.

TABLE 3.3
The Erotic Proclivities Signified by Clone Bandanas

Color	Proclivity	
	Left Side	Right Side
Black	Heavy S & M, top	Heavy S & M, bottom
Blue, light	Wants blow job	Expert Cocksucker
Blue, dark	Fucker	Fuckee
Blue, robin's egg	69-er	Anything but 69
Brown	Spreads scat	Receives scat
Green	Hustler, selling	Trick, buying
Grey	Gives bondage/Light S & M	Desires same
Mustard	Has 8" or more	Wants big one
Olive drab	Military uniforms	Likes military
Orange	Anything top	Anything bottom
Pink	Dildo giver	Dildo receiver
Purple	Piercer/genitorturer	Piercee/etc.
Red	Fist fucker	Fist fuckee
White	Jack off, self	I'll do us both
Yellow	Water sports, top	Water sports, bottom
Light brown	Likes to be rimmed	Likes to rim

Some accessories also communicated hotness. In the 1970s, key chains and bandanas were popular. The keys were hung from the belt loops of their Levis, and the bandanas were folded and put in the back pocket of their jeans. The placement of the keys and bandanas signified working-class accessories, but also signaled sexual interest and predilection. "Tops" (the insertive partner in anal intercourse, the "master" in an S/M scene, the one who did the doing) wore them on the left side of the body; "bottoms," (the receptive partner in anal intercourse, the "slave" in the S/M scene, the one who was "done to") on the right side. In addition, the color of the bandanas also conveyed erotic proclivities. Table 3.3 lists the sexual proclivities indicated by the color of the bandanas, compiled by asking the men about their significations. Blue was by far the most popular color. Dark blue bandanas worn on the left side meant proclivity for insertive anal intercourse; on the right side, for receptive anal intercourse. Light blue worn on the left side denoted proclivity for insertive fellatio, on the right, receptive fellatio. Keys and bandanas thus facilitated cruising, as clones articulated erotic proclivities and prospective partners thus knew what others desired sexually.

Hotness could also be expressed through stereotypically butch voices, gestures, and postures. The same rhetorics of butchness also signified sexual desirability. They spoke in low, deep voices, using rough, vulgar, language. Conveying masculinity could also simultaneously convey horniness, as the stood alone, scanning the crowd, seeing to also be seen, looking to trick.

Clone meeting places and homes signified hotness just as they signified butch masculinity—in their names, furnishings, and spatial arrangements. Many circuit bars, discos, and sex clubs had names that evoked sexual experience. For example, the Cockring, a popular nonmembership dance club, was named after a device that prolonged erections. Crisco Disco was named after a widely used lubricant for anal sex. The nickname "Everhard" was given to the Everard bathhouse, which was known for multiple sexual encounters.

The furnishings and design of circuit bars also expressed hotness. Clones dubbed these places "stand-up-and-cruise bars" because their physical layout was designed for cruising. The bars were devoid of furnishings save for a few bar stools, wall decorations, and an occasional pool table and cigarette machine. The large open spaces provided ample room for circulation through the crowd and meeting potential sex partners. Some circuit gathering spots also provided sites for sexual activity. Backroom bars, bathhouses, and sex clubs set aside specific locales for engaging in erotic conduct.

Clone apartments also reflected hotness. The men typically designed their bedrooms and bathrooms for tricking. They mirrored their bedroom walls so they could watch themselves during sexual encounters. They kept drugs, lubricants, and sex toys close to their beds to avoid disrupting the spontaneity of sex. Lastly, they kept "trick" towels and toothbrushes in their bathrooms for sex partners.

Social Interaction

If butch signified masculinity—both in its erotic and affective elements—it also structured the interactions among clones. One might think that embracing masculinity as an erotic and affective presentational strategy would have hindered emotional connectedness, community, and openness that are so atypical of traditional masculinity. On the other hand, the persistence of some typically feminine backstage affect, especially when gay men gathered in private, may have preserved the capacity for emotional availability that traditional masculinity might have eschewed. Of course, some clones got carried away, and their public presentational strategy as successful men made them inarticulate, inexpressive, and unemotional; in short, gay men behaved just like any other men.

What were the dynamics of this social interaction? How did gender figure in the interactional patterns of the clone? As we have already seen, clones underwent developmental processes similar to those of other male baby boomers. These processes—masculine socialization and the self-fulfillment ethic—affected their patterns of social interaction.

The male role masculinized interactional forms among gay clones. Expressiveness and intimacy were defined as unmanly, which caused men to avoid emotional sharing and disclosure in same-sex friendships (Lewis 1978; Jourard 1974). They consequently formed affectively neutral and activity-oriented relationships with other men (Pleck 1981; Stearns 1979). Men did not "share their fears and anxieties as well as their pleasures and joys" with each other. What they did instead is drink, play ball, play cards, or talk about "politics, sports, work or sex" (Doyle 1983, 160).

Simmel (1950) calls this kind of relationship sociable. In this form of interaction, people associate for convivial purposes, without instrumental or intimate concerns. They mingle simply for the sheer pleasure of one another's company. They may participate in a recreational activity, such as watching television, going bowling, or playing softball, or they may lightly converse, exchanging entertaining or colorful "stories, jokes, and anecdotes" (Simmel 1950, 53). Sociable relationships occurred among the clones (Warren 1974; Hooker 1956; Hoffman 1968; Read 1980), which differed in context from those of heterosexual men. Male heterosexuals organized their relationships around gender appropriate activities, such as hunting, fishing, billiards, gambling, and cars (Stearns 1979; LeMasters 1975).

Traditionally, homosexuals participating in the closet culture of the 1950s organized these relationships around gender-inappropriate practices, such as art, theater, opera, movies, fashion, and gossip (Karlen 1971; Read 1980; Leznoff and Westley 1956; Stearn 1962). In addition, gay men also discussed famous homosexuals and the special qualities of same-sex love (Newton 1972, 29; Hooker 1956; Becker 1963, 38). They did retain the gender-appropriate practice of sexual banter and drinking (Hoffman 1968; Warren 1974; Hooker 1956; Karlen 1971).

Gay liberation reorganized the content of sociable relationships among gay men (Humphreys 1971). The forms of sociability prevailing in the closet culture expressed the cultural definition of same-sex love as effeminate and aberrant. Gay activists reformulated this definition, viewing manliness as a vehicle for articulating their new sense of self and therefore abandoned gender-inappropriate styles of sociability (Altman 1971, 1982). One man told me:

> I was glad when butch became in. I no longer had to fake interest in opera which I always hated. I did it only because it was socially acceptable. Now I could stop going to the opera. I gave away all my opera records.

The self-fulfillment ethic also shaped the kinds of sociable relationships occurring among gay men. These values sanctioned self-expression and self-involvement. Perhaps this can be best illustrated by describing an experience with one of my key informants.

One evening, Kirk asked if I wanted to have a drink at Ty's. I was pleased to spend more time with him and readily agreed. As one of my key informants, Kirk had already taught me much about clone life. The more time I spent with him, the more I learned about this community. And besides, I liked him — he was good-natured, outgoing, and funny.

While walking towards the bar, we ran into Kirk's friend Chuck, whom I had met before. After kissing Kirk hello and nodding to me, Chuck said, "I'm glad I bumped into you. I was going to call you when I got home. Hal told me to tell you that he is having a 'pre-party' at his house before the Saint. He wants you to bring 'MDA' and 'coke.' Larry's coming with his new beau, who I hear is 'to-die-for.' Michael also told me to tell you to call him. He needs money for our house on the Island."

"How much do I owe?' Kirk asked. "I forgot." "The first payment," Chuck replied, — $600.00. Listen, I have to run. I have to get to the gym. This 'trick' is coming over later, the one with 'the dick of death,' so let me go pump up, shower, and 'douche.' I'll see you Saturday, Kirk. Nice seeing you, Marty."

As Chuck dashed off, Kirk turned towards me and smiling mischievously said, "That, my dear, was haute clone banter."

Having never heard this expression before, I asked, "What do you mean?"

"The conversation I just had with Chuck is common among clones. We

tend to talk about what we have in common, like the Island, the gym, and of
course the 'four D's'."
    "The 'four D's'?"
    "Yeah: disco, drugs, 'dish,' and 'dick'."

The four D's define the sociability patterns among clones. They were
the expression of and the sites for manly sociability, both its form and
its content. These were the topics of conversation they hung out in
circuit gathering places or at get-togethers at home; they were also the
goal and the process of partying.

Disco

The musical tastes of clones distinguished them from other gay men.
As is the case with heterosexuals, homosexuals varied in musical
preferences, with some liking show tunes, jazz, or rock (Sage 1975; Bell
and Weinberg 1978). But clones favored disco, and it was ubiquitous in
their world. As Kopkind (1979, 10) notes, disco glued this community
together. It blared from rather sophisticated sound systems in all
circuit meeting places and in most private homes. Many bars and
dance clubs hired disc jockeys to play this music. These establishments
typically posted the name of disc jockeys in conspicuous places, and
sold prerecorded audio tapes of their music.

    Sociable relationships took place in the context of disco. The men
listened to it while socializing, having sex, or cleaning the house,
typically humming, singing, or dancing along. They also talked about
the music. The men commonly evaluated the quality of the music,
sound systems, and deejays of various night clubs. Here's one conversation I overheard:

    "Where did you go last night?" George asked. "I didn't see you at
    Flamingo."
        "I went to 12 West," Barry replied.
        "How was it?"
        "The music was off at first, but then Richie [the disc jockey] got
    cooking later. How was Flamingo?"
        "Hot all night. Tom [the disc jockey] was fabulous, but the sound
    system was off, too much bass."

They also discussed current disco records, recording artists, and record shops, and exchanged information about the stock and prices at various stereophonic and high-fidelity equipment dealers.

Drugs

The use of recreational drugs also distinguished the sociable relationships of clones from those of other gay men. Homosexuals manifested three different patterns of drug usage: (1) abstinence; (2) occasional usage; and (3) frequent usage (Warren 1974, 61–64; Burke 1969, 315; Nardi 1982). Older gay men practiced abstinence and condemned drug use. They consumed alcohol instead (Warren 1974, 63). Some gay men occasionally used drugs for erotic or sociable purposes (Warren 1974, 63). Still others habitually used drugs for these purposes. These men tended to have countercultural or self-fulfillment values (Humphreys 1971; Burke 1969).

Clones were frequent users of recreational drugs, routinely taking them in sociable relationships. They used marijuana, alcohol, cocaine, and inhalants (amyl nitrate, also known as "poppers" because they came in little glass vials whose top was "popped" off to inhale the chemical) while hanging out at bars or home. These drugs, they believed, enhanced conviviality:

> Whenever the "family" comes over, we get "stoned." We smoke a few "joints" and have a few cocktails. Give those girls some drugs and they loosen up, and start cracking jokes and telling stories.

Hallucinogens and inhalants such as LSD, MDA, mescaline, and "poppers" were used for dancing. These drugs were said to give them the energy to dance the night away and to really get into the music. They used Quaaludes, "poppers," and MDA for sex because they regarded these drugs as aphrodisiacs.

Drugs also pervaded the men's conversations. They routinely talked about the inventory and prices of different drug dealers and discussed the effects of different kinds of drugs, particularly those which were new in town:

> "Boy was I fucked up last night," said Brad.
> "What did you take?" asked Frank.

"That new rainbow blotter. Have you tried it yet?"

"No. How was it?"

"Fabulous. It's the best acid I ever did. If you get some, buy it from Sky. He has the best in the city."

Dish

In our culture, the conversational style known as "dishing" was regarded as appropriate for women (Richardson 1981). This style included bitchy retorts, vicious putdowns, and malicious gossip. Far earlier in the century, closet homosexuals adopted this style as a means of articulating their feminine identification; it was especially characteristic of homosexuals in the theatre or entertainment industry (Leznoff and Westley 1956; Hooker 1956; Hoffman 1968; Read 1980). They dubbed it "fag talk" or "chit chat" (Read 1980, 106–8). Again, clones transformed and modified dish, just as they embraced and appropriated it.

Clones developed two forms, "dirt" and "dish." In the first, the men gossiped about the personal affairs and business of other people:

"Give me all the dirt on Warren's latest fuck up," Jim pleaded.

"You should have seen her last night,' David answered. "That 'queen' is such a mess! She did so many 'ludes' that she kept passing out, right on the dance floor. Then she started to puke, and got so sick that we had to carry her home."

In the second, the men sharply criticized acquaintances behind their backs:

"You tricked with her, the tooth fairy!" Tom snorted. "It's a good thing the Lord made her a dentist, because he certainly didn't give her a dick."

"I know," Sam chirped in. "She's so ashamed of its size that she doesn't shower or undress at the gym."

The persistence of this style raised questions about the extent of masculine identification among clones. "Dirt," "dish," and the use of cross-gendered pronouns (she, her) and nouns (sister, girlfriend) might indicate remnants of feminine identification. Some men still felt that these feminine practices expressed their gayness. "I 'dish' and call my friends 'she' or 'her' because it's a gay thing to do," one man told me. And yet there was also an attempt to masculinize dish, to butch it up. This was largely accomplished through explicit sexual banter, which brings us to "dick."

Dick

Dick signified the masculinization of dish and also the goal of gay masculinity. As among heterosexual men, erotic banter typified the sociable relationships of gay men. While growing up, men learned that sex is a means of articulating their manhood to other men. Accordingly, they discussed sexual exploits with other men (LeMasters 1975; Doyle 1983).

Past accounts of erotic banter among gay men pathologized the practice, while providing no comparative psychologization of the practice among heterosexual men. Gay male sex talk was seen as the product of either sex fetishism or the release effect (Hoffman 1968; Karlen 1971). Sex fetishism was a mental disorder in which the individual was "unable to relate to the sexual partner as a total human being and related only to a part of the body or piece of clothing" (Hoffman 1968, 60). The release effect occurred when gay men came together and dropped the pretense of being straight. In these situations, they were able to openly discuss their homosexuality, and thus engaged in erotic banter. But such accounts ignored the cultural roots of sex talk, specifically the gender conformity of sex talk among gay men and straight men. The desire to demonstrate and prove masculinity influenced both straight and gay men to share sexual exploits as a means of proving their masculine prowess to other men.

Clones expressed this typically male pattern in their sociable relationships. Erotic banter revolved around tricks, boyfriends, and homosexual erotic practices, such as douching and lubricants. They also shared jokes with sexual themes. "How do you get four queens on a bar stool?" posed one joke. "Turn it upside down." Erotically tinged stories were also a verbal currency among gay men. Such stories resembled the graphic accounts of female sexual conduct told by straight men in locker room conversations. Each story contained a thumbnail sketch of a person's erotic proclivities and occupational background, and publicized the most intimate details of an individual's private life:

> "See the tall blond near the jukebox?" Sean asked, elbowing Randy.
> "Oh her! She's been around for years," answered Randy.
> "What's her story?"
> "Big cock, loves to get fucked, waits tables."

Stories, truncated sexual histories with added commentary, emerged through tricking. Clones learned about each other's sexual prowess and predilections, as well as occupational status during the course of a one-night stand. They then reported this information in the form of a story, to friends who then passed it along to other people. As stories spread, they often became inaccurate, as all forms of gossip tend to do:

> "Do you know the dark-haired man, sitting alone in the back booth?" asked Carl.
> "The one reading the paper."
> "Oh her! She's been around since day one," replied Seth.
> "What's her story?"
> "A hairdresser who likes to fuck twinkies."
> "What!" Bill chimed in. "You got it all wrong. I know him. We met on the Island years ago. His name is Chad, he's a commercial artist, has a loft on the Bowery, and likes to fuck muscle numbers."

Erotic banter also occurred during boy watching, which was the homosexual equivalent of girl watching. Here the men evaluated the sexual attractiveness of passersby, and also might exchange "stories" about the ones they knew. They talked about the "Island" and gym, discussed past summers and current plans for taking a house in the "Pines," focusing primarily on where and with whom they lived. They also talked about the quality of the facilities and crowd at various gyms. One day, I observed this in action as the overflow from the Dock Strip bars pushed out into the street. The men lining the street were drinking beers, smoking joints, and talking about the four D's. Some were also engaged in boy watching. They would comment on the physical attractiveness of other men, discussing their face, physique, basket, and buns. Occasionally they smiled or whistled when a particularly good-looking man went by, who often responded with a broad grin.

Partying

The sociable practices of clones merged together in partying—perhaps the chief nonsexual feature of clone social life. Partying took place primarily on Saturday night and in circuit night clubs, such as Flamingo and The Saint, and involved dancing to disco music while stoned on drugs, discussing the "four D's" with friends and acquaintances, and searching for tricks. Partying had its own internal organization in clone life, and unfolded in three consecutive stages: (1) the "pre-party"; (2) the "party"; and (3) the "post-party."

"Pre-parties" denoted clique get-togethers before going out. The men typically met in someone's home around midnight. Here they took drugs, listened to disco records on prerecorded audio tapes, and talked about the "four D's." LSD and MDA were swallowed with gulps of beer. After everyone became stoned, some men might begin to stare at each other or off into space, too high to talk. At this point, the leader or host remarked that it was time to head for the party since their drugs were "clicking in." The men left for the party, traveling usually by cab. Most men arrived at the party around 2:00 A.M. "Hard core partyers" came later at 3:00 or 4:00 A.M.

"Parties" were held at private, membership only, dance clubs that were typically open only on weekends. These clubs charged hefty membership fees and carefully screened potential members for looks and life style. They admitted only men who were "hot," affluent, or socially prominent, and who were "circuit queens." Parties themselves revolved around disco dancing. Drugged men danced shoulder to shoulder on jammed dance floors, moving feverishly to throbbing lights and sounds. Often they danced bare-chested with other members of their clique. Some men danced alone on raised banquettes at the edge of the dance floor. A few men might even play a tambourine as they danced.

The pacing of the music resembled that of sexual encounters (Kopkind 1979). The music was broken down into sets that lasted for twenty to thirty minutes and built slowly to a climax. Deejays opened the set playing slower-paced songs. They then gradually increased the pace until they played a fast-paced hit record, which dramatically affected movement on the dance floor. At first, the men danced slowly. As the tempo picked up, they danced more quickly, until at the peak, they danced madly, throwing their arms up, waving their fists, and yelping cheers. At the end of the set, many poured off the dance floor to get something to drink, and to rest and "dish" with friends. The pacing of the party was also tied to the effect of the drugs. Deejays played slow-paced sets at the beginning of the party because most men were still getting off. They played faster paced sets around mid-morning (3:00 to 4:00 A.M.) because the men's drugs had clicked in. Finally they played mellow but funky sets of 'sleaze' music near dawn because the men had come down, and were more interested in meeting "tricks" than dancing.

Parties frequently had special themes. These themes often reflected masculine archetypes. For example, "butch" eroticism was the theme of black parties. The men wore "leather," uniforms, or Levis and T-shirts, and the entertainment included live sex shows depicting "leather sex." The theme at military parties was the armed forces; men would wear military uniforms, and decorations included jeeps and tanks.

"Post-parties" took place after the club closed. They were typically impromptu get-togethers held in an apartment or loft, or the men might repair to an all-night diner for post-party meals. The men usually invited friends, acquaintances, and potential tricks. They did more drugs and danced to prerecorded disco music on state-of-the-art tape decks. Occasionally, these gatherings turned into orgies.

By the mid-1980s, butch imagery began to fade as the predominant presentational style, and the heavy emphasis on the four D's, had been muted. Butch presentational strategies conveyed homosexual identities that were formed at a particular historical moment. The AIDS crisis caused a shift away from purely unadulterated "butch" imagery. Some men de-eroticized "butch" fashion, and fashion-oriented and younger gay men abandoned this look. Committed relationships, safer sex, and abstinence suddenly had a new currency among former clones and the gay men who continued to come out and populate the gay ghettos.

But the clone was about nothing if he was not about sex—and a very specifically masculine form of sexuality at that.

Chapter Four

"(You Make Me Feel) Mighty Real"
Hypermasculine Sexuality and Gender Confirmation

I should have known better than to go to the baths at 6:30 on a rainy Sunday evening. Tim had warned me about this, telling me that "Bad weather always drives the girls from the 'Dock Strip' bars to the 'tubs.'" Boy was he right, the place was packed, with no rooms available and a waiting list over twenty names long, which meant at least an hour wait. But I had to do this — the research required me to observe the baths on circuit night.

Thus I glumly pocketed a number and took my place on the line snaking through the snack bar.

The line was quiet save for the softly playing disco music. Most men waited impassively, staring blankly into space. A few lucky ones sat on stools, patiently drinking coffee and smoking cigarettes. Others glanced through parts of the Sunday paper. Almost no one spoke, but if they did, it was in a whisper. Every now and then, the room clerk broke the silence, calling out numbers. When this happened, everyone perked up, and listened attentively for their number. If it was mentioned, that meant their room was ready.

After what seemed like hours, the clerk finally shouted my number. Relieved, I scrambled to the desk, checked in, and entered the main facility, being buzzed through the front door. Once inside, an attendant greeted me and showed me to my room. Closing the door behind me, I quickly stripped, placing my clothes in the drawer beneath the bed, and wrapped a towel around my waist. Dressed like every other bathgoer, I was now ready to do the research.

Taking a few minutes to gather my thoughts, I flopped down on the bed, leaving the door shut. While sitting there and thinking about the project, I heard the door to the adjacent room close. A few second later, I picked up the noises of men having sex. As these sounds continued, I heard a voice break into a "sex rap," talking dirty, in a deep rough voice.

"Yeah take a good look at that big fucking dick. Uh huh. Look at how big,

77

long, and hard that fucker is. Yeah. That fucker is going to go up your fucking asshole. Uh huh. That big fucking cock is going to be plowing your ass, ramming and ramming your manhole. Shit, you're going to be begging for more. Yeah. You want that dick, fucker, you want it."

At this point, a second voice chimed in, rasping hungrily "Give me that dick, man. Yea. Give it to me. Give me all of that man meat. Shove it down my hot throat. Yeah. Gag me with that huge tool."

The other man must have obliged because a few seconds later I heard slurps and, "Suck that dick. Yeah. Suck it. Suck that man's dick. Yeah. Suck it, cocksucker. Show me how much you like it. Come on. Show me. Chew on that rod. Yeah. Chew on it. Come on. Suck that cock.

"Come on. Lick up and down that fucking rod. Yeah. That's right. Lick that cock. Yeah. Suck those nipples. Yeah. Come on, suck them. That's right, bite those nipples. Oh, yeah. Suck those balls, come on. Suck them. Suck those balls, yeah. You want that cock up your ass. Yeah, I'll bet you do. You want that man tool plugging up your hole. Yeah."

Breathing heavily, the other man gasped, "I want it. Fuck me, man, oh fuck me. Shove that dick up that stud hole. Yeah, fill me. Give it to me."

As his partner complied, he groaned, "I'm pushing that cock slowly up your ass, giving you a little at a time, loosening that butthole up. That's it, fucker. Take it like a man. That's it, fucker, swallow that rod. Yeah, take it, fucker. Feel that big tool as it fills your ass. Feel it, fucker. Oh, yeah. You want it, fucker. Yeah, you do."

"Oh man, I do. Oh, fuck me stud. Yeah, fuck me. Ram that tool up that butt. Fuck me hard. Yeah, fuck me hard. Give it to me rough, buddy. Yeah, fuck me hard. Come on, fuck that ass."

His partner must have obeyed because I then heard bodies slapping against each other and, "Take it, fucker. Take it like a man. Yeah. Take it, fucker. Take it like a man. Yeah. Fuck that ass. Oh, yeah. Fuck that manhole. Come on, fucker, ride that cock. Come on, fucker, ride that big dick. Uh huh. Yeah. Push that hole open. Give me that ass. Ride it. Oh yeah. Take it like a man. Open that hole. Give it to me, fucker. Yeah. Take it like a man."

The rap then ceased. All I heard now was deep breathing and furious pounding. Then someone moaned, "Shoot that load. Yeah, shoot it. Shoot it, stud. Shoot it."

The other man suddenly cried, "I'm coming. Yeah. I'm coming."

Echoing his shout, his partner gasped, "I'm coming, too. I'm coming. Shoot it. Shoot it." And then I heard nothing but heavy breathing, until someone whispered, "God, that was hot." The other man grunted affirmatively.

Hot sex. Heavy sex. Rough sex. Gay sex. But decidedly *masculine* sex. The clone "took it like a man" and he also "gave" it like a man. It was in their sexual conduct—both the cruise and the contact itself—that gay men demonstrated most convincingly that they were "real men" after all.

Cruising

Cruising was the mechanism that created most sexual contact among gay men, although some sexual contact, such as glory holes or orgies, didn't require even that much initial social contact with a potential partner. Cruising was the vehicle by which the clone either signaled sexual attraction or characterized the search for erotic partners. They cruised for affirmation of their hotness as sexual contacts. Men routinely cruised each other in circuit gathering places. They "cruised" one another on West Village and Chelsea streets, in banks, laundromats, and supermarkets. They cruised each other while talking to friends or working out at the gym. Some even cruised while waiting for dates.

Masculine erotic norms and self-fulfillment values shaped the patterns of cruising. These norms called for detached, objectified, and phallocentric, sexual conduct. In other words, they told men to engage in recreational sex for orgasmic release with partners selected for physical attractiveness. They also instructed men to affirm manly prowess through sexual conquests.

Self-fulfillment values gave the gratification of erotic needs an apparent moral imperative.

Heterosexual men might give women "the eye," checking her out, surveying her body, in more or less clandestine ways. After all, with heterosexual women, one couldn't be too overtly sexual and physical, since women's erotic codes required that there be emotional and romantic contact as a precondition of sexual contact. But without the "constraining" effects of feminine erotic standards, gay men were able to focus more overtly and obviously on the sexual activities in finding sexual partners. Heterosexual men might have stolen a glance at breast size or a bit of thigh revealed by a short skirt; gay men took notice of the pectoral muscle definition and the "basket," the outline of the genitals revealed by tight jeans. Cruising, in this sense, is a most masculine of pastimes. Gay men were simply more honest—and certainly more obvious—about it.

The cruising behavior of the clones reflected these masculine norms and self-fulfillment values. The men cruised for recreational sex with tricks chosen for their handsomeness and sexiness. They also cruised for erotic affirmation and satisfaction. For example, one morning while Tony and I were eating breakfast at Tiffany's, a handsome man sat down in a booth across from us and began to read the paper. Tony looked at him, looked at me, and then licked his lips. He then looked at this man again, who caught his glance, smiled, and returned to reading the paper. Tony then looked at him again. The other man returned his look but went back to reading the paper. I asked Tony if he was trying to pick the other man up. He said that he cruised him not because he wanted to pick him up, necessarily, but because he wanted to see if he was interested, and "to let him know he was hot."

Most cruising activity involved the search for tricks, anonymous or relatively anonymous sexual partners. The men cruised for tricks primarily in circuit gathering places. The patterns of cruising differed in social, recreational, and sexual meeting places. Cruising included verbal and nonverbal behavior in social and recreational places, mainly nonverbal conduct in sexual places. Cruising typically un-folded in four sequential stages: (1) searching; (2) stalking; (3) signaling; and (4) negotiating. Similar patterns have been observed in other homosexual and heterosexual pickup scenes (Delph 1978; Weinberg and Williams 1975; Hooker 1965; Allan and Fishel 1981; Hoffman 1968).

Searching

Bars, discos, bath houses, and sex clubs were the most obvious, the most "cruisy" places to cruise for potential sexual partners. The West Village Docks and Christopher Street were also known to be "cruisy." Most meeting spots were "cruisy" only at particular times of the day (see Table 4.1). Cruising usually commenced after the men socialized with friends. Most men went to the bars and discos with friends, spent time getting high, trading stories, or "boy watching" before cruising. The latter activities frequently affected whom they later cruised. At sexual gathering places, clones kept their socializing to a minimum.

TABLE 4.1
Cruisy Hours in Circuit Gathering Places

Meeting Place	Cruisy Hours
Christopher Street Bars	During the week, from 5:00 to 7:00 P.M.; 11:00 P.M. to 1:00 A.M.
West Street Bars	Late afternoon and early evenings on Sunday
Chelsea Bars	During the week, from 1:00 to 3:00 A.M. On weekends, from 2:00 to 4:00 A.M.
Discos	From 6:00 A.M. till closing
Bathrooms	Every night from 8:00 to 11:00 P.M. On weekends, after the bars and discos closed
Sex Clubs	On weekends after the bars closed

Some chatting occurred at the bar in sex clubs or backroom bars and in the common areas of bath houses, but the men were there primarily to cruise.

A man would initiate cruising by separating from his companions in bars and discos by telling them that he was going to check the place out or take a stroll. The other men regarded these departures as totally acceptable for two reasons: First, cruising was done alone. Only couples looking for three-ways cruised together. Second, cruising was the chief reason they came here. For example, one night Bob, Tom, and I were having a drink at Badlands when Bob suddenly left, going over to talk to a man leaning against the pool table. Because I seemed surprised, Tom explained that Bob had been cruising the guy and went over to put the moves on him. I asked Tom if the abrupt departure offended him. He looked at me as if I was crazy and said, "No. After all, we're all here for dick."

The men searched for conspicuous locations for cruising. These locations were typically places from which they could see and be seen. They included the refreshment areas or dance floor sidelines in discos, corridors of bathrooms and peep shows, and brightly lit sections of bars. Often they would ignore their acquaintances as they moved from location to location. If someone they knew walked by they might smile, but rarely would they pause for a chat. Cruising was serious business, and these men did not want to leave alone. An unsuccessful cruise was a blemish on their manhood. As they moved, they checked out everyone who either stood near them or passed by. They kept searching, moving from spot to spot until they found their type—their erotic ideal, whose physical characteristics were most appealing.

The criteria by which these types were constructed were fully gendered—that is, based entirely on physical attractiveness, a trait common to both homosexual and heterosexual men (see Delph 1978, 44; Cotton 1972; Silverstein 1981, 182; Gross 1978). Objectified body parts were far more significant than, for example, eye color or smiles, let alone emotional connection or social background. While heterosexual men commonly eroticize feminine attributes, especially breast size, gay men eroticized masculine attributes. The more butch the guy, the more he would get cruised.

Butch aesthetics thus shaped the cruise. By defining manly attributes as hot, this aesthetic made the type favored by clones hypermasculine. Their erotic ideal resembled the Marlboro man or Tom Selleck. Hot men, for clones, were hung, built, and butch—young (early 20s or so), ruggedly handsome, with a mustache or trim beard and short hair, a tight well-toned body, round and firm buttocks, large genitals, and visibly distended nipples.

This standard democratized clone types. The men perceived other men as sexy as long as they were macho. Nationality and class were irrelevant. A man could be anglo or ethnic, rich or poor, educated or illiterate, but if he was butch he was hot. Even race was unimportant. Manly Latino or black men were viewed as handsome. In fact, racial minorities and working-class men might even have a higher currency in clone circles. Since gay clones were mostly middle-class white men, the air of authenticity hung around working-class men and men of color, so that these men were often more highly prized for tricks. Given racial and ethnic stereotypes as well as class-based beliefs about sexuality, black men, Latino men, and working-class men all guaranteed great sex and affirmed the masculinity of the clone with whom he tricked. They were virtually always in great demand.

Clones tailored this type to fit their own personal preferences in physical characteristics. Though all favored macho men, some preferred blonds, and others preferred "daddies" (extremely masculine older men). One man put it succinctly. "My type is butch, around 5'8" tall and has dark hair, a fair complexion, trim physique, and a big dick." He could usually get what he wanted.

Stalking

Once a type was sighted, the men put themselves in cruising range, which varied according to meeting place. In bars and discos, they attempted to stand opposite the person they were cruising, so that they could make eye contact. In sex places, they did the same. They also attempted to stand near this person in order to make physical contact, such as touching or groping. Once in place, they started signaling erotic interest.

Signaling

To signal erotic interest, the pursuer followed commonly understood verbal and nonverbal signals. At first, the message was sent nonverbally, through gestures and expressions recognized throughout the homosexual as well as the heterosexual world as indicating sexual interest (Freedman and Mayes 1976, 3–8; Hooker 1965, 97; Goldhaber 1977; Silverstein and White 1977, 74–75; Delph 1978, 123–24; Wiseman 1976, 17–29). The pursuer caught the other man's eyes, held them, and stared intensely for a few seconds. If the pursued man was not interested, he ignored the eye contact, which ended the cruise. If he was interested, he returned the stare and broke the contact after a brief moment. (Just as frequently, the pursuer broke the contact.) This procedure was repeated a few more times as reciprocal glances were passed back and forth. The men also gave each other the once over, glancing up and down one another's bodies. Winks and smiles might also be exchanged. All this occurred in a matter of less than five minutes.

Timing was crucial. Both men might lose interest if the cruising did not quickly proceed to further contact. The time they had for connecting varied. In sexual gathering spots, they had only a couple of minutes to connect, otherwise the interaction ceased. In places banning sex, the contact ended when the men did not connect after ten to twenty minutes of staring and smiling. In one nearly empty bar, early one weekday evening, I watched two men cruise each other from opposite ends of the bar. They stared at each other for nearly fifteen minutes, but made no other contact. Neither of them changed positions or tried any other overtures. Finally, one gave up and walked out of the bar, giving the other man a look of disgust as he passed him.

On the streets, there was even less time. The men walked away if no contact was made after a couple of minutes. On another occasion, I watched two men cruise each other as they passed on a street in the West Village. They kept walking in opposite directions. A few seconds later, they both looked back over their shoulders and cruised one another. Both men stopped, turned around, and continued staring at one another. They remained that way for a couple of minutes. Then one man gave up, turned around, and walked away.

In bars and discos, the men occasionally repeated this routine for a few hours before they met. They intermittently cruised each other throughout the afternoon or evening—staring, breaking contact, moving closer to one another, staring, breaking contact, and then walking away. After doing this a few times, they finally met.

What happened next depended upon where the cruising took place. In sexual places they connected through touching. The pursuer repositioned himself so that he was in reaching distance of the other man. While doing this, he continued to stare at the other man. The pursuer then rubbed an erogenous area on his or the other man's body. He either groped or tweaked his or the other man's crotch or nipples. In bath houses, he either lifted or stroked his or the other man's towel or penis. In cruising places not permitting on-the-premises sex, the men connected verbally. This also occurred when the men met in those sections earmarked for recreation in sexual gathering places (e.g. the lounge, the front bar, the locker room). The suitor usually relocated himself so that he was within talking distance to the desired man. After a few more glances and smiles, he made contact, using a line appropriate to the situation. For example, in bars he asked "Do you come here often?" or "Isn't it crowded tonight." Dancing together broke the ice in discos. The suitor asked the other man to dance if they were standing near the dance floor. If they were cruising each other while dancing with friends, the men left their companions to dance with one another.

Once in a while, the pursued man was a "cock teaser," a person who flirts and "cruises" with no intention of having sex with anybody. He led men on to affirm his desirability. Cock teasers responded negatively to any overtures. They might refuse to dance when asked or made monosyllabic replies to any overture. In extreme cases, they even turned around and walked away when approached.

If the man was not a cock teaser, which was far more generally the case, the opening move proceeded to conversation. When the pair met while dancing, this conversation took place after they left the dance floor. At first, the men introduced themselves. Since they were strangers, the discussion was strained, consisting mainly of small talk about topics they had in common such as the four D's. Other themes included the Island, where they lived, or the weather. If the conversation did not flow smoothly, the contact ended with one of the men excusing himself. In bars or discos, he typically said that he was going to the bathroom. If they were on the street, that he was in a hurry. When the conversation went well, the last cruising stage commenced.

Negotiating

To make this encounter result in sex, the men needed to concretize erotic interest and set a time and place for sexual relations. The circumstances of the encounter determined how these plans were formulated. When the pair met in sites earmarked for sex in a sexual spot, the arrangements were made nonverbally, through physical contact. Touching erogenous areas specified erotic desire, and sex took place immediately following this contact. All of this occurred in a matter of minutes. One evening, I watched two men cruise each other in the peep show arcade of a pornographic bookstore. While continuing to stare at the other man, one man entered a movie booth, leaving the door open. The other man changed his position so that he was just outside the booth's entrance, and started to pinch his nipples, causing them to protrude through his T-shirt. The second man sat down on a bench within the booth, unbuttoned his jeans, pulled out his cock, and beckoned the other man to come in. The other man entered the booth and closed the door behind him. After a few minutes, the sounds of sex emanated from the booth. Similar scenes occurred in the backroom of certain bars and sex clubs as well as in the orgy room and cubicles of bath houses.

In recreational or social meeting places, the plans were made verbally. This was also true when the men met in those sections not set aside for sex in sexual spots. The time required for formulating these arrangements ranged from as little as a few minutes to as long as a few hours. At my estimation, the average was about fifteen minutes. The plans were typically negotiated through a process that included four sequential steps: (1) offering drinks or drugs; (2) clarifying erotic interest; (3) picking a time for sex; (4) selecting a place to trick. These stages did not occur in all negotiations. Some men skipped the first step.

Offering drinks or drugs occurred only in places allowing the use of these substances (e.g., bars, discos, parties). Even in these situations, it was sometimes overlooked, usually when the men met shortly before closing. This custom kept the pair together long enough to negotiate a trick. Men who got each other drinks or shared drugs were expected to remain in one another's company, amicably chatting, while consuming these substances. Not doing this was considered a serious breach of etiquette. When these behaviors occurred with a prospective trick, they afforded the men sufficient time to put the moves on each other. The suitor usually initiated this practice a few minutes after they started talking. When the pursuer noticed that the other man was either not drinking or finished his drink, he typically offered to buy him a drink. If the reply was affirmative, which was almost always the case when the other man was attracted to the first, he then asked him, "What are you drinking?" and went to get it. In bars and discos, he got the drinks from the bar and carried them back to where they were standing or sitting. At parties, he brought them back from wherever they were being served. Occasionally, the pursued man initiated this move. Etiquette usually demanded that whoever did not provide the first round furnished the second round. Drugs were also offered early in the conversation. To do this, the suitor asked the other man, "Would you like to get high?" Sometimes his questions specified the drug to be consumed, for example, "Do you want to smoke a joint?" or, "Do you want to snort some coke?" (Once in awhile the pursued man asked these questions.) When the queried man said yes, which was often the case if he was erotically interested in the first man, the men moved to a site in which the drugs could be consumed comfortably, usually some out-of-the-way corner. At times, the men shared both drugs and drinks.

This opening step determined what happened next. Refusal of these substances frequently caused the pair to separate because it was construed as a sign of disinterest. Both men tensed up, broke eye contact, and stopped talking. One man soon left, using some socially acceptable excuse. At a party, he might say that he was going to the bathroom. In a bar, he might state that he was going to talk to some friends. Acceptance, however, signaled continued interest.

At that point, the men would clarify their erotic interest in each other. Through both verbal statements and physical contact, the men concretized erotic desire, sexual taste, and interest in tricking. In this stage, erotic interest was specified first. The pursuer typically initiated this by dropping sexual innuendoes into the small talk. For example, he might tell the other man that he was horny or compliment him on his looks. When the second man responded similarly, both men knew that the interest was mutual.

To further clarify erotic desire, the men might discreetly explore each other's bodies. One man lightly pressed his body against the second man's buttocks or thighs, or he briefly touched his arms or chest. The more brazen even groped one another. Occasionally, this contact proceeded to kissing or hugging. These behaviors rarely took place on the streets or in the gyms because these places were too public. They typically occurred only in more secluded environments like bars, discos, or parties, and they always took place if the men met in establishments allowing sexual relations. Besides communicating sexual interest, this contact allowed the men to gauge each other's physiques. Clothes often camouflaged a man's actual build. Flannel shirts hid puny arms or flabby stomachs. Jeans covered small cocks or sagging butts. As one man explained to me:

> I'm a "size queen" [a man who desires especially large penises]. Baskets often fool you. Asking someone if they have a big dick is too embarrassing. What I do instead is grope them.

The men often lost interest at this point. This might be mutual or only on one man's part. Desire evaporated because they discovered that they did not like each other's personalities or that their physiques were not up to par. It also might disappear if the men spend too much time talking. When this happened, both men became nervous, ended eye contact, and stopped talking. One man typically left with an appropriate excuse.

If the men were interested, the conversation proceeded to erotic taste. To raise this topic, the suitor generally asked, "What are you into?" This question was widely recognized as a query about preference for sexual acts and roles. The second man responded accordingly. For example, he might say that he was "into fucking" or that he liked to "suck big dicks." Sometimes the pursued man brought this topic up first. Men who were "versatile" rarely asked this question. It was also not asked if the men were wearing an emblem symbolizing erotic taste. When their preferences were incompatible, both men realized that "tricking" would not work. They tensed up, cease eye contact, stopped talking, and soon parted company. When their tastes were compatible, one man propositioned the other.

The pursuer usually made the proposal. The solicitation was rarely straightforward because blunt propositions were regarded as offensive. Explicit questions like "Do you want to fuck?" turned off most men. Instead, euphemisms were used. The proposal was disguised in a statement about location that both men construed as being about activity, that is, having sex. Such euphemisms varied according to the situation. When the pair met in a sexual spot, the suitor usually asked the other man if he wanted to go to the area earmarked for sex. At the baths, he might say, "Would you like to come up to my room?" In a sex club, "Would you like to go to the back room?" Occasionally, he communicated this message nonverbally by leading the other man to the area. In social or recreational places, the solicitation was more indirect. At bars and discos the pursuer asked, "Would you like to go home with me?" or "My place or yours?" On the streets or in the gyms, he asked, "Would you like to get together?" or "Would you like to like to come over to my place for a drink?" Variations of the latter query included coffee or a joint.

What follows depended upon the pursued man's reply. If he was not interested, the answer would produce mutual strain and discomfort. The suitor felt rejected and sometimes even irked, believing that the other man was a cock teaser. After a few awkward moments, he would excuse himself and walk away. To avoid this unpleasantness, many men said yes even if they were not interested. Affirmative replies caused the couple to begin negotiating when they would have sex.

The pursuer generally initiated this conversation and suggested that they trick right away. He picked this time because it enhanced the likelihood of an encounter. Tricks postponed to a later time rarely worked out:

> If you don't get them when you first meet, you never will. They never call you if you give them your number, and if you call them, they are not interested.

The probability that the pursued man would agree to this suggestion depended upon several factors, including the time and place of meeting, overall health, and personal timetable. He almost always consented when the men met in places allowing erotic relations. Clones who connected in these establishments expected to have sex immediately. Acceptance of a proposition in these places signified a willingness to proceed to the area earmarked for sex and tricking.

He also agreed when he was feeling well and his schedule was open. This was generally the case when they met at night—in a bar, disco, or on a cruising street. It occasionally happened if they met during the day—in the gym or the neighborhood. Men who were picked up at night were usually seriously interested in tricking. The only time they said no was when they were either too tired, drunk, or stoned, or had to get up early the next morning. Men who met during the day were typically unavailable for an immediate encounter. Often their schedules were full: They had errands to run, appointments to keep, or were en route to work. Or they might not be well enough to have sex, the result of a cold or venereal disease. Sometimes, the pursued man claimed to be busy or ill when he was not, often to avoid tricking with the other man. This usually occurred when he agreed to a proposition only out of politeness or if he changed his mind.

When the pursued man could not have sex, he generally asked the other man, "Would you like to get together another time?" Occasionally, the suitor asked this question first. The reply determined what happened next. If the man no longer desired the pursuer, he answered negatively, causing both men to become tense and uncomfortable. Perceiving the other man as a cock teaser, the suitor would now feel justifiably angry and rejected. The conversation stumbled, eye contact ceased, and the pair soon parted. To sidestep this friction, some men replied affirmatively even though they were not attracted. Of course, they responded identically when they were.

Affirmative answers caused the men to make arrangements for seeing each other later. The suitor typically initiated this move by asking the other man for his telephone number, but sometimes the pursued man made this request first. The queried man almost always agreed to give it. After the men exchanged numbers, the negotiations ceased, and they parted company. They rarely connected again.

There were several reasons for not getting together. The men might be busy with work, friends, or relationships. Or they construed the delay in tricking as rejection; or they called, but the other man had no interest in connecting. The negotiations continued when the pursued man consented to trick right away. His decision caused the men to begin discussing where they would have sex.

The suitor usually initiated the conversation about where to have sex, proposing a particular site. The place he picked depended upon the site of the initial encounter. When they met in establishments allowing erotic relations, he suggested that they go to the area reserved for sex (e.g., the backroom, the orgy room). He proposed this while propositioning the pursued man, who nearly always felt similarly. When the pair met in a setting banning sex, he suggests that they go to his apartment. The probability of the second man consenting hinged upon several factors, including living arrangements and personal preferences. He almost always agreed if the suitor's apartment was nearby and offered privacy. The men preferred to trick in the apartment that was closest to where they met, as long as they could be alone. He also concurred when he had a policy of always going to the other person's house. Many men did this because they believed it was easier to leave someone else's home if sex did not work out, or to extricate oneself when the sex was over. He rejected the suggestion when the suitor's apartment was too far away or lacked privacy. Most clones did not go home with men who lived outside the neighborhood, or if there was no place to be alone. He also opposed the plan when he had a policy of never going to the other person's house. Many men did this because they felt more in control when they were in their own home or because they had pets which needed to be walked or fed. Rejected proposals usually prompted counteroffers. The pursued man suggested that they go to his apartment. He proposed this only if his apartment met the requisites for proximity and privacy. The other man nearly always accepted. Sometimes neither apartment was acceptable. They both were too far away or crowded with roommates. In situations like this, the men went to a sexual establishment.

After deciding where to trick, the men got ready to leave. How they did this again depended upon where they met. If they met on the streets, they immediately proceeded to the selected site. In gyms, they usually finished their workouts, showered, dressed, and then departed. At parties, they typically said goodbye to the host and friends. In bars or discos, they generally finished their drinks and said goodnight to friends. On their way, the men made small talk. The conversation was frequently forced because the men were virtual strangers. They conversed as best they could, usually talking about the "four D's." If they were traveling by taxi or car, the men held hands or stroked each other's thighs. Those who were more forward fondled and kissed.

Sometimes one man had second thoughts during this journey. As he got to know the other fellow, he realized that he did not especially like him; one man told me:

> When I first cruised him on the streets I thought he was real hot. As we talked on the way home, I started to dislike him. He was loud, vulgar, and opinionated.

Or after getting a better look at the other man, he discovered that he was no longer attracted to him. Another said:

> He looked good in the bar but when I got him outside and saw him in better light, he turned out to be a real mess. He was flabby and had bad skin.

Occasionally both men had second thoughts.

> When one of the men changed his mind, the "turned-off" man would communicate, nonverbally at first, by withdrawing, breaking eye contact, and clamming up. Noticing these changes the other man would ask what was wrong. The first would answer nonoffensively, like, "I am sorry but it is not going to work." The rejected man usually replied with an indifferent "O.K." He acquiesced because he knew that such changes were part of the game. The norms sanctioned reneging. Occasionally, though, he would ask why. To spare his feelings, the turned-off man rarely gave the true reason, reiterating instead that it would not work.

This development made both men uncomfortable. The rejected man felt bewildered, hurt, and annoyed, and the other person regarded the situation as unpleasant. To break the tension, they quickly parted company. If they were walking, they headed in separate directions. When they were in a taxi, the driver took them to separate locations. If they were in a car, the driver let the second man off at a mutually agreeable location. What they did after parting depended upon how they were feeling. If they were still horny, they went "cruising" again, either in the place they just left or somewhere else, typically a sexual establishment. When they were tired or in a bad mood, they went home.

Most of the time, the men remained interested, and they remained together. For them cruising was finished. They were now ready to trick.

Sexual Behavior: "Taking It Like a Man"

The erotic code of clones shaped the sexual activity of these men. As we have already seen, this script included erotic prescriptions acquired during adolescence. At that time, gay men, like their heterosexual counterparts, learned that sex was detached, privatized, objectified, and phallocentric. Articulating this training as adults, they depersonalized erotic encounters, concentrated only on sexual gratification, and treated partners as simply sex objects. This explains why the men at the baths said, "suck that dick" or "fuck my ass."

To affirm their identity as men, clones masculinized their sexual script. Accepting reformist images of liberation, they regarded themselves as real men. To demonstrate this sense of self, they exaggerated male expectations during sex. Having learned that men are tough, adventurous, and daring, they engage in rough, uninhibited, experimental sex. This accounts for the gagging, ramming, and slamming occurring at the baths. They justified this erotic style on the grounds of self-fulfillment. The script sets the standards for sexual activity. Defining "hot sex" as "butch sex," it led clones to "take it like a man."

Clones actualized this script in their sexual activities. For the clone, sexual behavior was the primary way of validating his masculinity, especially in a culture that denied his masculinity by maintaining stereotypes of homosexuality as effeminacy. In this sense, cultural homophobia and male gender socialization were the two primary ingredients in clone sex. Following its dictates for hot sex, they selected tricks and performed acts in a supermasculine fashion. Taught that men detached sex from relationships, they devalued sex between intimates, preferring instead to have sex with strangers. As one many explained:

Familiarity for me kills desire. Knowing someone is a turn off because their personality ruins the fantasy I have of them. Besides sucking the same dick and fucking the same ass is a drag. Variety, after all, is the spice of life.

Having learned that men chose partners according to objectified standards, they picked tricks on the basis of physical attractiveness, ignoring social and personality characteristics. Another man said:

All that matters to me in a trick is how they look. They could be as dumb as shit or as boring as hell, but if they have a nice face, a big dick, or a good body, I'll fuck with them.

As a result of these standards, derived from gender socialization within a homophobic culture, clones had impersonal sex with men they perceived as handsome.

This practice distinguished clones from other gay men. Though most homosexuals occasionally tricked, only a minority made it the mainstay of their sex lives. Among Bell and Weinberg's (1978, 132–34) respondents, for example, with a classifiable erotic style, an estimated 39 percent had sex primarily with an intimate, another 39 percent had it mainly with a stranger, and 22 percent were asexual.

The script also governed what occurred during these encounters. Told that macho sex is rough, phallocentric, and uninhibited, clones practiced "deep throating," "hard fucking," and "heavy tit work." In the first activity, a man rammed the entire length of his penis down his partner's throat. If his partner had not learned how to overcome the gag reflex, this act caused him to choke. In "hard fucking," a man rapidly moved the entire length of his penis in and out of his partner's anus. While doing this, he often vigorously hit his partner's backside with his hands. In "heavy tit work," the men forcefully stimulated each other's nipples by pinching, biting, or sucking them, often to the point of pain.

Again, these sexual behaviors differentiated clones from other gay men. As studies of homosexual erotic conduct indicated (Bell and Weinberg 1978, 106–11; Masters and Johnson 1979, chap. 3; Spada 1979, 327–28; Saghir and Robins 1973, 50–52), most gay men performed fellatio, anal intercourse, and nipple stimulation. A few of these reports (see Jay and Young 1977, 438–39; Spada 1979, 327; Masters and Johnson 1979, chaps. 5, 6) suggested that they did so in a tender and caring fashion, a style completely opposite to that of clones, who roughed sex up. Among other gay men, analingus appears to have been relatively rare. Regarding this practice as "whorish," preliberation middle- and upper-class gay men shunned it (see Cory and LeRoy 1963; Helmer 1963). For the most part postliberation homosexuals felt similarly. Among Jay and Young's (1977, 491) respondents, only 43 percent reported positive feelings for analingus and 17 percent regularly practiced it. With clones, however, it was far more common, primarily because of the emphasis on "butch sex."

The ordering of sexual activity also reflected dominant cultural standards. According to these norms, sexual activity occurred in two consecutive phases, foreplay and orgasm. Each phase was marked by different goals and behaviors (Gagnon 1977). Focusing erotic contact on sexual arousal, the first stage typically included caressing, kissing, and breast or genital stimulation. Organized around erotic climax, the second stage entailed coition and oral-genital relations. Of course, this is the same script adopted by heterosexual men with women.

Clones would typically engage in kissing, analingus (rimming), and penile or anal manipulation during foreplay and anal intercourse to orgasm. Persistent manipulation of the nipple caused them to elongate and distend (see Delph 1978, 144). Clones considered distended nipples a badge of pride. Fellatio occurred in either stage. Occasionally, they climaxed through masturbation, typically after having performed all the other acts. As one man told me:

> To get a guy hot, I like to first play with his dick while I'm kissing him. Then I suck his cock while squeezing his tits and playing with his ass. After rimming him a while, when his hole is nice and loose, I then fuck him until I come in his ass. I like them to come by jerking themselves off while I'm fucking them.

Appropriate ordering of sexual behaviors was considered an essential component of "hot sex." Clones view any violation of the sequence as bad sex. One day, while walking with a friend on the street, my companion turned to me and said:

> See that guy we just passed? He's terrible sex. I went home with him last month. All he does is throw you on the bed and fuck you. That's it, no kissing or preliminaries.

Another time, a friend commented about a mutual acquaintance:

> Carl looks like hot sex but he isn't. All he's into is jerking off. No suckee
> or fuckee. What a waste of a big dick.

The masculine erotic script led clones to become more sexually adventurous than other gay men, to experiment with a variety of fringe
sexual practices such as S/M and leather sex. As observers of the
leather scene often noted (see Townsend 1983; Kamel 1983; Mains
1984; Weinberg and Williams 1974), homosexuals regarded this conduct as archetypically masculine, mainly because it is organized
around stereotypical male role performances (dominance, control, en-
durance) and symbols (whips, chains, leather). To butch sex up, clones
engaged in sadomasochistic practices, avoiding those entailing the
infliction of severe pain. Or, they would utilize the signifiers, the props
of S/M, without actually having to engage in the practices, wearing
some black leather, but making sure no one got the wrong idea. One
man noted that:

> To me leather sex is real butch. Now don't get me wrong, I'm not into
> that heavy stuff like whipping and hot wax. But wearing leather, doing
> a uniform scene, or tying someone up—that's hot. All that power and
> control makes me feel butch.

When they were not simply appropriating the symbols of S/M and of
working-class masculinity in their appearance and presentational
styles, clones did practice some light S/M behaviors. They included
(1) bondage (B&D), which entailed one man binding another with
rope, chains, gags, harnesses, handcuffs, blindfolds, and/or leather
restraints; (2) urophilia, dubbed "water sports" or "golden shower," it
involved a man urinating on his partner; (3) anal fisting, called "fist
fucking," consisted of a man inserting his fist and lower arm up his
partner's anus; (4) humiliation, the psychological degradation of one
man by another through verbal insults (e.g., "fucker," "faggot,"
"pussy") and performance of demeaning acts (e.g., boot licking, wearing a dog collar). These insults commonly occurred during a sex rap;
(5) light spanking, the paddling of one man by another, usually with a
thick black leather belt; (6) role playing, the enactment of dominant
and submissive roles in which the controlling partner (labeled "the
top," "master," or "S") rules the other man (called "the bottom,"
"slave," or "M"); and, (7) scenes, elaborately staged erotic fantasies
constructed around hypermasculine themes like the gym, military, or
cops. The performance of these acts required such accoutrements as

uniforms (e.g., gym clothes, military dress), sex toys (e.g., dildoes, tit clamps), and well-articulated and rehearsed sex raps.

Clones tended to disfavor "heavy S&M" which entails the imposition of intense pain. Heavier S/M sex might involve such practices as flagellation, burning with hot wax, and the piercing or torture of the nipples or genitals with needles, harnesses, and stretchers (Townsend 1983). Clones regarded these acts as too extreme. As one man put it:

> That heavy shit is just too weird. I mean enjoying being beaten up or beating someone up is pretty sick. How can a dude get off on bleeding or causing someone to bleed?

The masculine sexual script also pushed clones toward group sex. Just as the dominant sexual fantasy among heterosexual men is sex with more than one woman at a time, gay men constructed sexual activity from a desire to be sexually adventurous in groups. Clones occasionally tricked with two or more partners at a time, either in a three-way or an orgy, staged at either a baths, sex club, or home. One man described his participation in an orgy:

> Frank finally invited me to one of his orgies. Boy it was something else. The first thing you did was take off all of your clothes except for a jock strap. Then everyone drank this punch that was filled with MDA. Once everyone got off, the party started. By now everyone was hot and ready for some action. The guys that were there were hot—hung and with great bodies. At one point, I was sucking one guy's dick while another guy was fucking me and I was fucking someone else. It felt great! I must have come five times.

These sexual practices also distinguished clones from other gay men. Most homosexuals totally eschewed sadomasochistic sex (Spada 1979, 126–27; Jay and Young 1977, 553–87). Only "leather" men performed these acts, but they opted for both "heavy and light S&M" (Kamel 1983). Group sex was also rarely practiced (Jay and Young 1977, 587).

To enhance erotic responsiveness, clones typically used drugs while having sex. Believing that cocaine, Quaaludes, MDA, and marijuana were aphrodisiacs, they consumed drugs during sex. Once in a while, they mixed these drugs with alcohol.

One cannot discuss clone sexual behavior without discussing roles. In heterosexual contact, roles are fairly rigidly defined by the gender of the partner and the appropriate behavior that accompanies it. Men are cast as the active pursuer, women as the more passive responder. But what happens when gender is neutralized, when both are capable of and trained to be the active partner?

At one time, both professionals and the public believed that gay men mimicked heterosexual roles during sex, with masculine homosexuals playing the active "inserter" role and effeminate homosexuals taking the passive "receptive" role in fellatio and anal intercourse (Harry 1976–77). It was also thought that gay men never switched positions. However, as a spate of studies indicated (Spada 1979, 97; Saghir and Robins 1973, 52; Weinberg and Williams 1974), these assumptions were inaccurate. Viewing flexibility as an erotic ideal, most gay men alternated roles. For those reporting a preference, choice was based not on gender role conformity but on individual preference and it changed from time to time (Hoffman 1968, 35).

The roles clones played during sex replicated those found throughout the gay world. Some men found themselves specializing in one or the other, or found themselves with a decided preference for one role of the other. In essence, there were three roles:

1. Tops—tall, muscular, or masculine men who acted as the "inserter," actively controlling erotic manipulations, particularly in anal intercourse, where they take the insertive position. These men typically had a larger penis than their partner.

2. Bottoms—short, slender, or effeminate men who acted as receivers passively reacting to erotic manipulations, especially in anal intercourse, where they take the receptive position. These men tended to have a smaller penis than their partners.

3. Versatile—men who played both roles, alternating between stimulator and stimulated. Manly demeanor, penis size, and body build determined the part they took. With more masculine, muscular, or endowed men, they become "bottoms." With more effeminate, skinny, or unendowed men, they become "tops."

It should be noted that these roles depended far more on preference than physique, bearing, or penis size. Many slight, "nelly," unendowed men were "versatiles" or "tops," and many muscular, manly, or hung men were "bottoms" or "versatiles." One of my informants pointed to another man standing across the dance floor:

See that body builder over in the corner? He sure looks like a top but Bill said he had him last week and that he's a heavy "bottom." She's a real woman. Once you get him home, he throws his legs up in the air even before his jeans are unbuttoned.

The quality of erotic encounters hinged upon these roles. Hot sex for clones depended upon role compatibility and technique. Another man told me:

> My "trick" last night was fabulous. As you know I'm a top and the guy I picked up was a total "bottom," with a deep throat and a hot hole.

While a third said:

> The sex between Mark and me was terrible, mainly because we're both "bottoms." It was like two "sisters" bumping pussy.

Interestingly, the gender appropriateness of these roles imitates heterosexual norms, but inverts the norms of S/M sexuality. Within the S/M community, it is seen as highly masculine to be a superb bottom, to be able to take an enormous amount of sexual activity and pain. In addition, it was the bottom who ultimately controlled the situation, deciding how far the scene would progress, how much he could stand. From the perspective of the self-fulfillment ethic, S/M scenes might last for hours, during which time all energy and attention would be focused on the bottom, administering to his desires and testing his limits. This gave rise to the popular expression in gay circles that "a good top is hard to find."

The pervasiveness of "cruising" gave the clone scene an erotic tinge. Always on display, the men strove to present an attractive front, going to great lengths to look "hot." Thinking of themselves as "meat in the market", they pumped iron, dieted, and dressed "butch," all for an approving glance or wink. By butching sex up, clones had sex in a rough, nonintimate, and uninhibited fashion. As a result, they "tricked" primarily with strangers and experimented with "light S& M," practices eschewed by other homosexuals.

This pattern affirmed desirability, enhancing a man's opinion of his virility. The successful clone was truly, in his own eyes and in the eyes of his fellows clones, "a man among men." Butch sex also provided unlimited sexual freedom, which allowed the men the opportunity to explore and gratify all erotic urges. But, on the other hand, it was also dehumanizing. After a while, the men reported wanting to be appreciated as a human being, not just for their "tits" and "cock."

Their sexual conduct exposed them to venereal diseases and criminal victimization, leaving them vulnerable to syphilis, gonorrhea, or, later, to AIDS, as well as to rip-offs or violent attacks by tricks. Sexual behavior also generated a desire for more personalized and permanent relationships.

Chapter Five

"Midnight Love Affair"
Gay Masculinity and Emotional Intimacy

As Carl and I walked along the boardwalk, on our way to the party at the Sandpiper, I realized how lucky I was to be on the Island for Memorial Day weekend. Marking the opening of the Pines' summer season, this weekend was a key circuit event. And the Sandpiper's party was the high point of the weekend. Thanks to Carl's invitation to spend the weekend at his house I was able to observe these events.

The party was going full blast when we walked through the door, the music blending into an ever-mounting crescendo of rhythmic beats. What appeared to be all the city's reigning circuit queens crammed the dance floor, and they were obviously flying high on drugs. Carl was eager to party and pushed me towards the dance floor, where we pulled our off T-shirts, hung them from the back pockets of our jeans, and danced until drenched with sweat.

After what seemed like hours, Carl nudged me off the dance floor and suggested that we take a breather. Tired and thirsty, I heartily agreed, and recommended that we grab some beers and go outside. We pushed our way through the crowd, got the drinks, fought our way to the porch, and found a spot close to the railing. We stood there shivering in the sea air and staring at the harbor, which shimmered under white moonlight.

Carl began to softly coo the lyrics to the song we danced to last. Looking really sad, he sang:

> *Midnight love affair*
> *How can I make you stay*
> *Midnight love affair*
> *Please don't run away*

Sighing deeply, Carl stopped singing and stared dejectedly off into space. Edging closer, I asked, "What's wrong?"

"Nothing," he replied. "It's just that this song always brings me down."

"Why?"

"Because it's the story of my life."

"What do you mean?"

"My life consists of one midnight love affair after the next. I'm constantly trying to get my tricks to stay but it just never works out. We have sex and then they leave. That's it, nothing more. Forget about seeing them again. Most don't even remember who you are when you call. And if they do, they're too busy to get together. Others don't even say hello to you the next time you see them."

"How do you feel about this?"

"I hate it. It makes me feel so empty and lonely. I want something more; a boyfriend or a lover. But I can't seem to find one. Nothing I do seems to work. So I settle instead for hot tricks and good friends. But that's not what I want."

Many men felt similarly to Carl. They frequently bitterly complained about their string of "midnight love affairs." They talked about being "fagged out" from tricking and their lack of meaningful relationships. They spoke, often movingly, about their desire for boyfriends or lovers. But they found it difficult, or nearly impossible, to develop long-term intimate emotional relationships with the men with whom they had sex. In their patterns of sociability and intimate relationships, too, the clones were real men.

Traditionally, psychiatric literature on homosexuality had viewed this pattern as deviant, as a manifestation of homosexual pathology. Bayer (1981, 32) aptly captured this perspective when discussing the findings of the New York Society of Medical Psychoanalysts' report on male homosexuality:

> Because of the pathological basis of the homosexual adaptation, the possibility of establishing a stable and intimate homosexual relationship is precluded according to Bieber. Fear of intimacy combined with a fear of retaliation on the part of other excluded males make homosexual couples relatively volatile. The hostility and competitiveness of such relationships bring to even the most apparently satisfactory among them a quality of ambivalence leading ultimately to impermanence or transience. Hence the ceaseless, compulsive, and often anonymous pattern of homosexual cruising.

Empirical verification of such notions was minimal or nonexistent. In their massive survey of Bay Area homosexuals, carefully matched to heterosexual controls, Bell, Weinberg, and Hammersmith (1981) failed to corroborate any of the most basic analytic theories on the origin of homosexual preference. Other surveys reported that gay men do indeed form long-lasting relationships (Bell and Weinberg 1978, 91–103; McWhirter and Mattison 1984).

What appeared to be different about gay men's social and sexual relationships was not that gay men did not form friendships—they did. And they were highly functional sexually. What appeared to be different was the relationship—or, rather, the absence of relationship—between sexual contact and emotional intimacy. As Edmund White put it in his survey of gay male America (1980, 287), "[s]ex is performed with strangers, romance is captured in brief affairs, and friendship is assigned to friends."

I believe that sexual orientation was far less important in the development of this pattern than was gender. Masculine prescriptions shaped the sociosexual relationships of clones. (Lesbian relationships look quite different.) These norms caused them to eschew intimacy, dependency, and emotionality in relationships and to objectify sex. They experienced some difficulty in creating intimate relationships. Accordingly, men formed sociable and companionate relationships, had difficulty coupling, and engaged in recreational sex.

The most common and important sociosexual relationships for clones were friendships. There were two kinds of friendships, both of which typically occurred within the same friendship clique. "Sisters" functioned as good friends. The men's social lives revolved around their sisters. They went out or hung out with their sisters. They also depended on their sisters for comfort and material aid. "Best friends," by contrast, acted like lovers except one did not have sex with them. The men were inseparable, and often described the feelings between them as love. Acquaintances treated them as a couple, and invited and seated them together at social events. The men did not have sex with each other but with tricks or dates.

Both friendships were remarkably stable. They typically lasted as long as the men remained romantically uninvolved. Lovers and boyfriends usually compromised friendships because they drew time and affection away from the friends. These relationships made the neglected sister or best friend feel hurt, angry, and rejected, and they often provoked bitter fights and the dissolution of the friendship. The emotional fallout accompanying these breakups was similar to that occurring when "lovers" separated.

Another type of sociosexual relationship was that based primarily on sexual contact. Here, again, there were two types, "tricks" and "fuck buddies." As was the case in the broader homosexual community (Rodgers 1972), clones used the term "trick" as a noun, as in reference to a man with whom one had an impersonal sexual encounter:

> See that guy in the gray T-shirt near the cigarette machine. He's the trick I told you about, the one I did last weekend.

or as a verb:

> I was horny last night, so I went to the baths and tricked four times.

Although tricking was fairly common in the homosexual world, gay men differed in the extent to which they performed this act (Weinberg and Williams 1974; Bell and Weinberg 1978; Saghir and Robins 1973). Although many homosexuals have sex mainly in the context of ongoing relationships, the opposite was true for the clones. They had sex primarily with tricks because they were not involved in romantic affairs. The men relied on tricking for erotic gratification.

Past accounts of tricking misrepresented or misunderstood the practice. These accounts treated tricking as simply an erotic contact stripped of any of its social components (Saghir and Robins 1973; Humphreys 1971; Hoffman 1968; Karlen 1971). In these accounts, tricking included "just enough time for a nod to social preliminaries, ejaculation, and some form of closure" (Bell and Weinberg 1978, 80). But to the clone, tricking also involved companionship, affection, and warmth (Altman 1982; Tripp 1975). Several surveys also showed that tricking frequently involved friendly, nonsexual kinds of interaction (Lee 1978, 12; Spada 1979, 68–80; Jay and Young 1977, 246–53).

Many clones felt that tricking entailed not only erotic gratification but also tenderness, affection, and companionship:

> Most of my tricks are nice men. We spend a lot of time talking about our jobs, families, and pasts. The sex is often playful, loving, and affectionate.

And it also carried the possibility of romantic relationships. In the homosexual world, relationships frequently evolved from tricking

(Harry 1984; McWhirter and Mattison 1984; Blumstein and Schwartz 1983; Spada 1979). Clones used tricking as a means to initiate romantic affairs. For them, a trick might also be a potential boyfriend or lover:

> I met all my lovers in bars. I took hundreds of tricks to get four lovers.

The degree to which clones tricked depended upon erotic drives and schedules. Men with high erotic drives tricked more often than those with low drives, sometimes as much as three or four times a weekend. Men whose schedules fit circuit hours tricked more often than those whose schedules did not match their hours. These men usually did not have to get up for work the next morning and could stay out late, picking up tricks in bars and other meeting spots. They were typically freelancers, actors, waiters, or unemployed. Rich said:

> I really enjoyed being unemployed. I went out all the time, every after-noon and evening, and constantly tricked, sometimes two or three times a day.

Some men who worked nine-to-five occasionally tricked during the week, but they paid a price for it. As Tom explained:

> Sometimes I think my penis controls me. I'm tired and have a lot to do at the office the next day. But then my cock starts throbbing, demanding satisfaction. So I get up, get dressed, and go out, cruising the bars. By the time I pick up a trick, get him home, and do it, it is one, two or three in the morning. Boy do I feel it the next day. I stagger around, feeling tired and exhausted.

As we saw earlier, tricking maintained its own ritual code, beginning and ending in certain routinized ways, with a clearly articulated nor-mative structure and process. Rarely did tricking lead to any lasting sexual relationship, let alone a more emotional one. Partly, this was the result of the decided emphasis on great sex. Men were constantly rating their tricks. Sex was hot if their partner had a large penis, a hot body, and good technique. They also felt sex was hot when their erotic proclivities matched. Hot sex was lengthy and passionate.

Alas, sex was rarely hot. Penises were not big enough, bodies not built enough, technique not good enough. Proclivities often did not match. Sex in these circumstances tended to be quick and mechanical. Occasionally, the men even ended the encounter, usually by telling their partner that "It's not working" or "I'm not into this," which caused the other man to quickly get dressed and leave. As Roy told me:

Boy, did I have a bum trick last night. I picked this guy up at the Ramrod. He looked real good in the bar. But once I got his clothes off I lost interest. He was flabby, and had a sagging butt and a small cock. And to top it all off, he scraped my cock with his teeth as he was sucking me off. So I just told him it wasn't working and left.

The "relationship," such as it was, commonly ended after tricking. In sexual places, the men climaxed and then separated, frequently without saying anything except thanks. When the encounter occurred at home, the men usually exchanged telephone numbers and addresses before departing, which typically took place shortly after orgasm.

A decision to actually sleep together hinged upon several factors. In the broader homosexual world, tricks usually spent the night (Bell and Weinberg 1978, 21). But among clones, tricks left as often as they stayed. When the sex was good, tricks might spend the night. They sometimes stayed because they were too drunk or high to leave. Men who preferred to sleep alone, were in a relationship, or were busy the next morning almost always left.

The men rarely saw each other again. Tricking implied a commitment for only one erotic encounter. As a result, most men had sex once and never again. The pervasiveness of this practice made many clones cynical about exchanging telephone numbers. As Jeff said:

> I don't know why we do this. No one ever calls each other. Most of the time you trick with them and they don't even say hello to you the next time you see them.

The second erotic relationship, the "fuck buddy," was unique to the clone community. There is no evidence that it existed in other segments of the homosexual world. Fuck buddies related sexually but not romantically. They repeatedly rendezvoused for erotic contact. A fuck buddy was a long-standing trick, and this relationship therefore involved neither commitment nor emotional attachment. Fuck buddies were extremely important to clones. Because the men were mostly single, sexual gratification and companionship were constant needs. By merging sex with friendship, fuck buddies conveniently met these needs. As Arnie put it:

> I try to turn my tricks into fuck buddies whenever I can. Fuck buddies make it so much easier to get laid. Cruising takes too much time and energy, and often you go home alone. Fuck buddies mean instant sexual satisfaction. You can also do things with them, like go out for dinner,

see a movie, or watch TV. It's sort of like boyfriends but with no strings attached.

In a sense, then, Arnie aptly described the contradictory nature of the fuck buddy system. On the one hand, the fuck buddy removed the anxiety and possible rejection from cruising, insuring that one would have sex on any given night. On the other hand, the fact that fuck buddies were essentially long-term tricks meant there was little emotional relationship, little romantic sensibility, and little intimacy. Fuck buddies were, for gay clones, what heterosexual men often suggest that they are looking for: beautiful sex partners who are always sexually willing and available, but make no emotional demands on them whatsoever.

Fuck buddy relationships varied widely in duration and continued as long as the men remain sexually interested and romantically uninvolved. Because clones regarded anonymity as hot, they usually tired quickly of their fuck buddies, causing this relationship to cease after a few weeks. Boyfriends and lovers also destroyed these relationships because they took time and sexual energy away from fuck buddies.

Perhaps the least common kind of sociosexual relationship among clones was that based on romantic affection, a relationship that fused companionship, sexuality, and affection. Among clones, there were three kinds of romantic relationships.

Dating was the least serious form of romantic involvement. It was not even mentioned in prior accounts of homosexual life. Affective feelings within these relationships consisted of mild infatuations dubbed "likings":

> When you date someone, you like them, but the feeling is not intense.
> It's much milder than love. You're fond of them but don't love them.

Companionship and sexual contact were limited to periodic meetings. The dating patterns of clones conformed to prevailing cultural standards. Dates in the broader culture involved shared recreational activities and sex. Couples typically socialized first, then had sex. Clones behaved similarly. The men typically spent time with their dates before they had sex. They often went to the movies, restaurants, or dancing and then had sex in one of their apartments. Dates generally spent the night.

Dating entailed no commitments and lasted as long as the men remained interested. The men were free to "trick" with or see other people. "What you do when you are apart from the person you're dating is your own business," Alan told me. They also dated until they became either sexually or socially incompatible or involved with someone else, as in:

> I dated Tony until the sex got boring.
>
> I dumped Tom once I discovered that I couldn't stand him.
>
> Barry and I dated until he became boyfriends with Ken.

The demise of these affairs provoked little emotional turmoil because the men were not deeply attached.

"Boyfriends," the second romantic affiliation, entailed serious, emotional, social, and sexual commitments. This relationship was also not recorded in the existing literature. Gay men regarded "boyfriends" as a primary relationship. Affective feelings between boyfriends were described as fondness or affection. In addition, boyfriends spent most of their free time together:

> I am quite fond of Paul. We see each other three or four times a week, and usually spend the weekend together.

Acquaintances treated boyfriends as a couple. They invited the men to come to parties or other get-togethers as a pair.

Boyfriends were not necessarily monogamous. Just as sexual relationships were independent of emotional relationships on the side of sexual gratification, so too was emotional intimacy independent of sexual fidelity. The men might rely on each other for sexual gratification but did not expect their relationship to be purely monogamous. In most cases boyfriends were free to trick with or even date other men, provided those affairs remained secondary to their primary boyfriend relationship. Clones expected their boyfriends to spend most of their social time, and have most of their sexual contacts with them. As Mike told me:

> I don't mind when Sam fools around as long as it doesn't interfere with our relationship. But I draw the line when his tricking starts cutting into our time. It's simply not acceptable.

The men stayed together as long as they fulfilled these expectations. Frequent violations of these agreements provoked heated quarrels and often led to breakups:

> Steven's constant tricking ended our relationship. We agreed to trick
> only when we weren't getting together. But he wouldn't do this. He
> tricked all the time, sometimes before he was coming over. Then I
> would want sex and he would be all fucked out. We fought about this
> constantly, but he didn't change, so I left.

As in heterosexual relationships then, clones faced the problem of
men's sexual fidelity often. When new and potentially exciting sexual
opportunities arose, few clones could resist them. And why should
they? After all, sexual encounters had nothing to do with emotional
intimacy, which was reserved for the boyfriend. Surely, their boyfriends would understand what so many girlfriends and wives have
been unable to understand: "It was just sex, that's all."

Boyfriends also parted because of social or emotional incompatibility. Emotional turbulence accompanied the end of these affairs. Many
men felt depressed and lonely after leaving a boyfriend.

The most significant romantic relationship occurred among lovers.
This relationship implied deep emotional, erotic, and social ties and
was found throughout the gay world (Fischer 1972; Schofield 1965;
Brown 1976; Hooker 1956, 1965). Many gay men called these relationships marriages, and referred to lovers as husbands or wives. Lovers
could either be "closed-coupled" or "open-coupled" (Bell and Weinberg 1978); differences between them lay in their treatment of sexual
and social involvement. Closed-coupled lovers cohabited, socialized
together, and were monogamous. Open-coupled lovers lived apart,
had separate social lives, and had sex with other people (Harry and
Lovey 1979; Warren 1974; Silverstein 1981; Peplau 1981). For obvious
reasons, among clones, open-coupled relationships were more pervasive than closed-coupled affairs (McWhirter and Mattison 1984;
Blumstein and Schwartz 1983). Many clones were openly contemptu-
ous of closed-coupled relationships, which they saw as outmoded and
inappropriately binding. One man told me:

> Monogamous lovers make me sick. You know, the kind that cling to
> each other and never trick with anyone else. There was this couple that
> wanted to get into our house on the Island. But none of us wanted them
> because they kept cooing at each other and fought about cruising other
> people.

Lovers among clones differed in regard to how they handled extrane-
ous sex. Most couples prohibited sexual contacts with acquaintances.

They perceived such encounters as threatening to their relationships. Many couples allowed outside affairs that do not impinge upon the primary relationship. The men could "date" or "trick" with anyone they wanted provided these affairs remained secondary relationships. Jeff described his lover:

> Charles and I see other men. Our relationship comes first and the others are secondary. If I get overly involved with someone, seeing them too often, Charles tells me, and I cool it down or cut it off.

Other couples restricted outside contacts to particular situations. The men could trick either at the baths or sex clubs or when the other lover was out of town (on a business trip or family visit). They also could have three-ways or orgies that included both lovers.

Lovers generally separated because of violations of these agreements or incompatibility. These breakups caused tremendous pain. Bill recalled that:

> Jack and I agreed we wouldn't date other people. But he kept seeing men on the side. Each time I found out he promised me he would stop. But he didn't and I split because I felt I couldn't trust him. He hurt me too much. I felt lonely and sad afterward.

Sociosexual relationships were an area of deep concern for most clones. The men deeply desired lovers, a feeling they shared in common with other gay men (Schofield 1965; Hooker 1956; Sage 1975). They spoke movingly about being dissatisfied with tricking. They were tired of being alone and wanted more permanent relationships. Carl said:

> I'm burnt out on one-night stands. I'm sick of waking up next to strangers. I want someone to share my life with.

These desires often provoked them to become hastily involved with other men. They frequently became lovers or boyfriends overnight. Needless to say, these relationships rarely lasted. The men became involved for all the wrong reasons. They thought hot sex or physical beauty could be the foundation for a lasting emotional relationship. Like heterosexual men, gay clones were far more likely to believe in love at first sight than women are.

Like heterosexual men, clones also lacked the skills for being in a relationship. They did not know how to merge intimacy and sexuality, or how to become emotionally vulnerable. Clones, therefore, had difficulty forming lasting romantic relationships. They settled for hot tricks and good friends.

EDITOR'S NOTE

The original ethnography concluded with a brief theoretical reprise, suggesting that social constructionist theories of sociosexual patterns among gay men better explained the emergence of the gay male clone and his affective and sexual styles. Of course, there was another epidemiological conclusion to the work, as the early 1980s found the gay community responding to the ravages of the AIDS crisis. It was the clone, after all, who seemed to be at highest risk for contracting the HIV virus, and in part this risk was based on those same social and sexual patterns that clones had used to confirm their masculinity. Just as Marty's original research explored the creation of a masculine subculture, his subsequent work charted the response of that subculture to the AIDS crisis. In that sense, the second part of this book serves as the conclusion to the first part.

References to Part One

Achilles, Nancy. 1967. "The Development of the Homosexual Bar as an Institution." In John H. Gagnon and William Simon (eds.), *Sexual Deviance*. New York: Harper and Row.

Adam, Barry D. 1978. *The Survival of Domination: Inferiorization of Everyday Life*. New York: Elsevier.

———. 1979 "The Social History of Gay Politics." In Martin P. Levine (ed.), *Gay Men: The Sociology of Male Homosexuality*. New York: Harper and Row.

Aiken, D. 1976. "Chicago." *Advocate* 198:27–28.

Alfred, Randy. 1982. "Clones: A New Definition." *Advocate* 338 (March 18):22–23.

Allan, Natalie, and Diane Fishel. 1981. "Singles' Bars as Examples of Urban Courtship." In Peter J. Stein (ed.), *Single Life: Unmarried Adults in Social Context*. New York: St. Martin's.

Altman, Dennis. 1971. *Homosexual: Oppression and Liberation*. New York: Avon Books.

———. 1977. "Letter from Australia." *Christopher Street* 1 (January):35–37.

———. 1982. *The Homosexualization of America: The Americanization of the Homosexual*. New York: St. Martin's.

Anderson, Elijah. 1978. *A Place on the Corner*. Chicago: University of Chicago Press.

Ball, Donald W. 1967. "An Abortion Clinic Ethnography." *Social Problems* 14:293–301.

Balswick, Charles. 1972. "Attitudes of Lower Class Males toward Taking a Male Birth Control Pill." *Family Coordinator* 21:195–199.

Bayer, Ronald. 1981. *Homosexuality and American Psychiatry*. New York: Basic Books.

Becker, Howard S. 1963. *Outsiders: Studies in the Sociology of Deviance*. New York: Free Press.

Bell, Alan, Martin S. Weinberg, and Sue Hammersmith. 1981. *Sexual Preference: Its Development in Men and Women*. Bloomington: University of Indiana Press.

Bell, Alan P., and Martin S. Weinberg. 1978. *Homosexualities: A Study of Diversity among Men and Women.* New York: Simon & Schuster.

Bell, Arthur. 1977a. "Looking for Mr.Gaybar." *Village Voice* (January 24):19–20.

———. 1977b. "The Sixties." *Christopher Street* 1 (July):33–35.

Bell, Daniel. 1976. *The Cultural Contradictions of Capitalism.* New York: Basic Books.

Bergler, Edmund. 1957. *Homosexuality: Disease or Way of Life.* New York: Hill and Wang.

Berlandt, Konstantin. 1972. "My Soul Vanished from Sight: A California Saga of Gay Liberation." In Karla Jay and Allen Young (eds.), *Out of the Closets: Voices of Gay Liberation.* New York: Douglas.

Bieber, Irving. 1962. *Homosexuality: A Psychoanalytic Study.* New York: Basic Books.

Blachford, Gregg. 1981. "Male Dominance and the Gay World." In Kenneth Plummer (ed.), *The Making of the Modern Homosexual.* Totowa, N.J.: Barnes and Noble Books.

Blumstein, Phillip, and Pepper Schwartz. 1983. *American Couples.* New York: William Morrow.

Brill, D. 1976. "Boston." *Advocate* 184:27.

Brown, Howard. 1976. *Familiar Faces, Hidden Lives: The Story of Homosexual Men in America Today.* New York: Harcourt Brace Jovanovich.

Burke, Tom. 1969. "The New Homosexuality." *Esquire* 72 (December):178ff.

Butler, E. W. 1977. *The Urban Crisis: Problems and Prospects in America.* Santa Monica, Calif.: Goodyear Publishing.

Chafetz, Janet Saltzman. 1974. *Masculine/Feminine or Human?* Itasca, Ill.: F. E. Peacock.

Chicago Gay Liberation. 1970. Working paper for the Revolutionary Peoples' Constitutional Convention. *Gay Flames Pamphlet No. 13.* New York: Gay Flames.

Cicourel, Aaron V. 1972. "Basic and Normative Rules in the Negotiation of Status and Role." In David Sudnow (ed.), *Studies in Social Interaction.* New York: Free Press.

Cory, Donald W. 1951. *The Homosexual in America: A Subjective Approach.* New York: Greenberg.

Cory, Donald W., and John P. LeRoy. 1963. *The Homosexual and His Society: A View from Within.* New York: Citadel Press.

Corzine, Jay, and Richard Kerby. 1977. "Cruising the Truckers: Sexual Encounters in a Highway Rest Area." *Urban Life* 6:171–72.

Cotton, Wayne L. 1972. "Role-Playing Substitutions among Homosexuals." *Journal of Sex Research* 8:310–23.

———. 1975. "Social and Sexual Lesbians." *Journal of Sex Research* 11:129–48.

Dank, Barry. 1971. "Coming Out in the Gay World." *Psychiatry* 34:180–97.

———. 1974. "The Homosexual." In Erich Goode and Richard Troiden (eds.), *Sexual Deviance and Sexual Devianta.* New York: William Morrow.

David, Deborah S., and Robert Brannon. 1976. *The Forty-Nine Percent Majority: The Male Sex Role.* Reading, Mass.: Addison-Wesley.

Davis, Nanette. 1975. *Social Constructions of Deviance: Perspectives and Issues in the Field.* Dubuque, Iowa: William C. Brown.

DeLamater, John. 1981. "The Social Control of Sexuality." *Annual Review of Sociology* 7:263–90.

Delph, Edward. 1978. *The Silent Community: Public Homosexual Encounters.* Beverly Hills, Calif.: Sage.

D'Emilio, John. 1983. *Sexual Politics, Sexual Communities: The Making of a Homosexual Minority in the United States 1940–1970.* Chicago: University of Chicago Press.

DeVall, Bill. 1973. "Gay Liberation: An Overview." *Journal of Voluntary Action Research* 1:24–35.

Diaman, Tony. 1970. "The Search for the Total Man." *Come* (December–January):22–23.

Douglas, Jack. 1972. *Research on Deviance.* New York: Random House.

Doyle, James A. 1983. *The Male Experience.* Dubuque, Iowa: William C. Brown.

Duberman, Martin. 1982. "Gay in the Fifties." *Salmagundi* 58–59:42–75.

Dyer, Richard. 1977. *Gays and Film.* London: British Film Institute.

Ellis, Albert, and Albert Abarbanel. 1973. "Homosexuality." *The Encyclopedia of Sexual Behavior.* New York: Jason Aronson.

Erikson, Kai T. 1962. "Notes on the Sociology of Deviance." *Social Problems* 9:307–14.

———. 1976. *Everything in Its Path: Destruction of Community in the Buffalo Creek Flood.* New York: Simon & Schuster.

Farrell, Ronald A., and Thomas S. Morrione. 1974. "Social Interaction and Stereotypic Responses to Homosexuals." *Archives of Sexual Behavior* 3:425–42.

Farrell, Ronald A., and James F. Nelson. 1976. "A Causal Model of Secondary Deviance: The Case of Homosexuality." *Sociological Quarterly* 17:109–20.

Farrell, Warren. 1975. *The Liberated Man: Beyond Masculinity: Freeing Men and Their Relationships with Women.* New York: Bantam.

Fein, Sara Beck, and Elaine Neuhering. 1981. "Intrapsychic Effects of Stigma: A Process of Breakdown and Reconstruction of Social Reality." *Journal of Homosexuality* 7:3–13.

Feinbloom, Deborah Heller. 1977. *Transvestites and Transsexuals.* New York: Dell.

Feldman, M. P., and Malcolm J. MacCulloch. 1971. *Homosexual Behavior: Therapy and Assessment.* New York: Pergamon.

Fernbach, David. 1975. "Toward a Marxist Theory of Gay Oppression." *Socialist Revolution* 6:29–41.

Fettner, Ann Guidici, and William A. Check. 1984. *The Truth about AIDS: Evolution of an Epidemic.* New York: Holt, Rinehart & Winston.

Fischer, Claude S. 1976. *The Urban Experience.* New York: Harcourt Brace Jovanovich.

Fischer, Peter. 1972. *The Gay Mystique.* New York: Stein and Day.

Flacks, Richard. 1971. *Youth and Social Change.* Chicago: Markham.

Ford, Clellan S., and Frank A. Beach. 1953. *Patterns of Sexual Behavior.* New York: Harper and Row.

Freedman, Mark, and Harvey Mayes. 1976. *Loving Man: A Photographic Guide to Gay Male Lovemaking.* New York: Hark Publishing.

Frieze, Irene, and Sheila Ramsey. 1976. "Nonverbal Maintenance of Traditional Sex Roles." *Journal of Social Issues* 32:133–42.

Gagnon, John H. 1973. "Scripts and the Coordination of Sexual Conduct." In James E. Cole and Richard Dienstbier (eds.), *Nebraska Symposium on Motivation.* Lincoln: University of Nebraska Press.

———. 1977. *Human Sexualities.* Glenview, Ill.: Scott, Foresman.

Gagnon, John H., and William Simon. 1968. "The Social Meaning of Prison Homosexuality." *Federal Probation* 32:23–29.

———. 1973. *Sexual Conduct: The Social Sources of Human Sexuality.* Chicago: Aldine.

Garfinkel, Harold. 1972. "Studies of the Routine Grounds of Everyday Activities." In David Sudnow (ed.), *Studies in Social Interaction.* New York: Free Press.

Glenn, Weaver. 1977. "Attitudes toward Premarital, Extramarital and Homosexual Relations in the U.S. in the 1970's." *Journal of Sex Research* 15:108–18.

Goffman, Erving. 1959. *Presentation of Self in Everyday Life.* New York: Anchor Books.

———. 1963. *Stigma: Notes on the Management of Spoiled Identity.* Englewood Cliffs, N.J.: Prentice-Hall.

Goldhaber, Gerald M. 1977. "Gay Talk: Communication Behavior of Male Homosexuals." In William Arnold and Jerry Buley (eds.), *Urban Communication: Survival in the City.* Cambridge, Mass.: Winthrop.

Goldstein, Richard. 1975. "S&M: The Dark Side of Gay Liberation." *Village Voice* (July 7):10–13.

Gooch, Brad. 1984. "Cruising the San Remo: Such Good Friends: Artists and the Gay Life in 50's New York." *Advocate* (May 15):26–30.

Goode, Erich, and Richard Troiden. 1980. "Correlates and Accompaniments of Promiscuous Sex among Male Homosexuals." *Psychiatry* 43:51–59.

Gould, Meredith. 1979. "Statutory Oppression: An Overview of Legalized

Homophobia." In Martin P. Levine (ed.), *Gay Men: The Sociology of Male Homosexuality.* New York: Harper and Row.

Gouldner, Alvin. 1968. "The Sociologist as Partisan: Sociology and the Welfare State." *American Sociologist* 3:103–16.

Greenberg, David F., and Marcia H. Bystryn. 1982. "Christian Intolerance of Homosexuality." *American Journal of Sociology* 88:515–48.

———. 1984. "Capitalism, Bureaucracy, and Male Homosexuality." *Contemporary Crisis* 8:33–56.

Gross, Alan. 1978. "The Male Role and Heterosexual Behavior." *Journal of Social Issues* 34:87–107.

Hammersmith, Sue Kiefer, and Martin S. Weinberg. 1973. "Homosexual Identity: Commitment, Adjustment and Significant Others." *Sociometry* 36:56–79.

Harry, Joseph. 1976–77. "On the Validity of Gay Males." *Journal of Homosexuality* 2:143–53.

———. 1982. *Gay Children Grown Up: Gender, Culture and Gender Deviance.* New York: Praeger.

———. 1984. *Gay Couples.* New York: Praeger.

Harry, Joseph, and William B. DeVall. 1978. *The Social Organization of Gay Males.* New York: Praeger.

Harry, Joseph, and Robert Lovey. 1979. "Gay Marriages and Communities of Sexual Orientation." *Alternative Lifestyles* 2:177–200.

Hatterer, Lawrence. 1970. *Changing Homosexuality in the Male.* New York: McGraw-Hill.

Helmer, William, J. 1963. "New York Middle Class Homosexuals." *Harper's* 226 (March):85–92.

Henry, George W. 1955. *All the Sexes: A Study of Masculinity and Femininity.* New York: Rinehart.

Hoffman, Martin. 1968. *The Gay World: Male Homosexuality and the Social Creation of Evil.* New York: Basic Books.

———. 1979. "The Male Prostitute." In Martin P. Levine (ed.), *Gay Men: The Sociology of Male Homosexuality.* New York: Harper and Row.

Holleran, Andrew. 1982. "The Petrification of Clonestyle." *Christopher Street* 69 (October):14–18.

Hooker, Evelyn. 1956. "A Preliminary Analysis of Group Behavior of Homosexuals." *Journal of Psychology.* 42:217–23.

———. 1957. "The Adjustment of Overt Male Homosexuality." *Journal of Protective Techniques.* 21:18–31.

———. 1965. "Male Homosexuals and Their World." In Judd Marmor (ed.), *Sexual Inversion: The Multiple Roots of Homosexuality.* New York: Basic Books.

———. 1967. "The Homosexual Community." In John H. Gagnon and William Simon (eds.), *Sexual Deviance.* New York: Harper and Row.

Humphreys, Laud. 1970. *Tearoom Trade: Impersonal Sex in Public Places.* Chicago: Aldine.

―――. 1971. "New Styles in Homosexual Manliness." *Transaction* 8:38ff.

―――. 1972. *Out of the Closets: The Sociology of Homosexual Liberation.* Englewood Cliffs, N.J.: Prentice-Hall.

―――. 1979. "Exodus and Identity: The Emerging Gay Culture." In Martin P. Levine (ed.), *Men: The Sociology of Male Homosexuality.* New York: Harper and Row.

Humphreys, Laud, and Brian Miller. 1980. "Identities in the Emerging Gay Culture." In Judd Marmor (ed.), *Homosexual Behavior: A Modern Reappraisal.* New York: Basic Books.

Irwin, Patrick, and Norman L. Thompson. 1978. "Acceptance of the Rights of Homosexuals: A Social Profile." *Journal of Homosexuality* 3:107–21.

Jay, Karla, and Allen Young. 1977. *The Gay Report.* New York: Summit.

Jourard, Sidney M. 1974. "Some Lethal Aspects of the Male Role." In Joseph H. Pleck and Jack Sawyer (eds.), *Men and Masculinity.* Englewood Cliffs, N.J.: Prentice-Hall.

Kamel, G. W. Levi. 1983. "Leathersex: Meaningful Aspects of Gay Sadomasochism." In Thomas Weinberg and G. W. Levi Kamel (eds.), *S and M: Studies in Sadomasochism.* Buffalo, N.Y.: Prometheus Books.

Kantrowitz, Arnie. 1975. "I'll Take New York." *Advocate* 175:48–51.

―――. 1978. "The Boys in the Back Room." *Advocate* 242 (May 31):40–41.

Kaplan, Helen Singer. 1985. *Comprehensive Evaluation of Disorders of Sexual Desire.* Washington, D.C.: American Psychiatric Press.

Karlen, Arno. 1971. *Sexuality and Homosexuality.* New York: W. W. Norton.

―――. 1978. "Homosexuality: The Scene and Its Student." In James M. Henslin and Edward Sagarin (eds.), *The Sociology of Sex: An Introductory Reader.* New York: Schocken.

Katz, Jonathan. 1976. *Gay American History: Lesbians and Gay Men in the U.S.A.* New York: Thomas Y. Crowell.

Kelly, James. 1977. "The Aging Male Homosexual: Myth and Reality." In Martin P. Levine (ed.), *Men: The Sociology of Male Homosexuality.* New York: Harper and Row.

Kerner Commission. 1968. *Report of the National Advisory Commission on Civil Disorders.* New York: Bantam Books.

Kinsey, Alfred C., Wardell B. Pomeroy, and Clyde E. Martin. 1948. *Sexual Behavior in the Human Male.* Philadelphia: W. B. Saunders.

Kitsuse, John I. 1962. "Social Reaction to Deviant Behavior: Problems of Theory and Method." *Social Problems* 9:247–56.

Kitsuse, John I., and Aaron V. Cicourel. 1963. "A Note in the Use of Official Statistics." *Social Problems* 10:131–39.

Kleinberg, Seymour. 1978. "Where Have All the Sissies Gone?" *Christopher Street* 2 (March):13–16.

Komarovsky, Myra. 1964. *Blue Collar Marriage*. New York: Random House.

Kopkind, Andrew. 1979. "The Dialetic of Disco: Gay Music Goes Straight." *Village Voice* 24 (February):iff.

Kornblum, William. 1974. *Blue Collar Community*. Chicago: University of Chicago Press.

Laner, Mary Riege. 1978. "Growing Older Male: Heterosexual and Homosexual." *Gerontologist* 18:496–501.

———. 1979. "Growing Older Female: Heterosexual and Homosexual." *Journal of Homosexuality* 4: 267–75.

Lasch, Christopher. 1979. *The Culture of Narcissism*. New York: W. W. Norton.

Lee, John Alan. 1977. "Going Public: A Study in the Sociology of Homosexual Liberation." *Journal of Homosexuality* 4:49–78.

———. 1978. *Getting Sex*. Don Mills, Ontario: Mussan.

Lehne, Gregory K. 1976. "Homophobia among Men." In Deborah S. David and Robert Brannon (eds.), *The Forty-Nine Percent Majority: The Male Sex Role*. Reading, Mass.: Addison-Wesley.

LeMasters, E. E. 1975. *Blue-Collar Aristocrats*. Madison: University of Wisconsin Press.

Levine, Martin P. 1979a. "Employment Discrimination against Gay Men." *International Review of Modern Sociology* 9:151–63.

———. 1979b. "Introduction." In Martin P. Levine (ed.), *Gay Men: The Sociology of Male Homosexuality*. New York: Harper and Row.

———. 1979c. "Gay Ghetto." In Martin P. Levine (ed.), *Gay Men: The Sociology of Male Homosexuality*. New York: Harper and Row.

———. 1980. "Annotated Bibliography: The Sociology of Male Homosexuality and Lesbianism: An Introductory Bibliography." *Journal of Homosexuality* 5:149–275.

Levitt, Eugene E., and Albert D. Klassen. 1974. "Public Attitudes towards Homosexuality: Part of the 1970 National Survey of the Institute for Sex Research." *Journal of Homosexuality* 1:29–43.

Lewis, Robert A. 1978. "Emotional Intimacy among Men." *Journal of Social Issues* 34:108–21.

Leznoff, Maurice, and William A. Westley. 1956. "The Homosexual Community." *Social Problems* 3:257–63.

Liebow, Elliot. 1967. *Tally's Corner: A Study of Negro Streetcorner Men*. Boston: Little, Brown.

Long, Judith Laws, and Pepper Schwartz. 1977. *Sexual Scripts: The Social Construction of Female Sexuality*. Hinesdale, Ill.: Dryden Press.

Magee, Bryan. 1966. *One in Twenty: A Study of Homosexuality in Men and Women.* London: Secker and Warburg.

Mains, Geoff. 1984. *Urban Aboriginals: A Celebration of Leathersexuality.* San Francisco: Gay Sunshine Press.

Manosevitz, Martin. 1972. "Development of Male Homosexuality." *Journal of Sex Research* 8:31–40.

Marotta, Toby. 1981. *The Politics of Homosexuality.* Boston: Houghton Mifflin.

Masters, William, and Virginia Johnson. 1979. *Homosexuality in Perspective.* Boston: Little, Brown.

Matza, David. 1969. *Becoming Deviant.* Englewood Cliffs, N.J.: Prentice-Hall.

McIntosh, Mary. 1968. "The Homosexual Role." *Social Problems* 10:182–92.

McWhirter, David, and Andrew Mattison. 1984. *The Male Couple: How Relationships Develop.* Englewood Cliffs, N.J.: Prentice-Hall.

Meissner, William. 1980. "Psychoanalysis and Sexual Disorders." In Benjamin Wolman and John Money (eds.), *Handbook of Human Sexuality.* Englewood Cliffs, N.J.: Prentice-Hall.

Mendelsohn, J. 1996. "We're Here! We're Queer! Let's Do Lunch!" *New York* (May).

Michelson, William M. 1970. *Man and His Urban Environment: A Sociological Approach.* Reading, Mass.: Addison-Wesley.

Miller, Brian. 1978. "Adult Sexual Resocialization: Adjustment toward a Stigmatized Identity." *Alternative Lifestyles* 1:297–324.

Miller, Brian, and Laud Humphreys. 1980. "Lifestyles and Violence: Homosexual Victims of Assault and Murder." *Qualitative Sociology* 3:169–85.

Monteflores, Carmen, and Stephen J. Schultz. 1978. "Coming Out: Similarities and Differences for Lesbians and Gay Men." *Journal of Social Issues* 34(3):59–72.

Morris, Aldon, D. 1985. *Origin of the Civil Rights Movement.* New York: Free Press.

Murray, Stephen O. 1979. "The Institutional Elaboration of a QuasiEthnic Community." *International Review of Modern Sociology* 9:164–87.

Nardi, Peter M. 1982. "Alcoholism and Homosexuality: A Theoretical Perspective." *Journal of Homosexuality* 7:4–25.

Nassberg, Jay. n.d. *Revolutionary Love.* Gay Flames Pamphlet.

Newton, Esther. 1972. *Mother Camp: Female Impersonators in America.* Englewood Cliffs, N.J.: Prentice-Hall.

Nyberg, Kenneth, and Jon P. Alston. 1976. "Analysis of Public Attitudes toward Homosexual Behavior." *Journal of Homosexuality* 2:97–107.

Opler, Marvin K. 1965. "Anthropological and Cross-Cultural Aspects of Homosexuality." In Judd Marmor (ed.), *Sexual Inversion: The Multiple Roots of Homosexuality.* Basic Books: New York.

Park, R. E. 1928. "Foreword." In L. Wirth, *The Ghetto*. Chicago: University of Chicago Press.

Pattison, E. Mansell, and Myrna Pattison. 1980. "Ex-Gays: Religiously Medicated Change in Homosexuals." *American Journal of Psychiatry* 137: 1553–62.

Peplau, Letitia Anne. 1981. "What Homosexuals Want in Relationships." *Psychology Today* (April):28–38.

Peplau, Letitia A., and Steven Cochran. 1981. "Value Orientations in the Intimate Relationships of Gay Men." *Journal of Homosexuality* 6:1–19.

Perkins, Kenneth, and James K. Skipper. 1981. "Gay Pornographic and Sex Paraphernalia Shops: An Ethnography of Expressive Work Settings." *Deviant Behavior* 2:187–99.

Persell, Caroline. 1984. *Understanding Society: An Introduction to Sociology*. New York: Harper and Row.

Pietropinto, Anthony, and Jacqueline Simenauer. 1977. *Beyond the Male Myth: What Women Want to Know about Men's Sexuality*. New York: Signet.

Pleck, Joseph H. 1981. *The Myth of Masculinity*. Cambridge, Mass.: MIT Press.

Plummer, Kenneth. 1975. *Sexual Stigma: An Interactionist Account*. Boston: Routledge and Kegan Paul.

———. 1981a. "Building a Sociology of Homosexuality." In Kenneth Plummer (ed.), *The Making of the Modern Homosexual*. Totowa, N.J.: Barnes and Noble Books.

———. 1981b. "Homosexual Categories: Some Research Problems in the Labelling Perspective of Homosexuality." In Kenneth Plummer (ed.), *The Making of the Modern Homosexual*. Totowa, N.J.: Barnes and Noble Books.

Polsky, Ned. 1967. *Hustler's Beats, and Others*. Chicago: Aldine.

Ponte, Meredith. 1974. "Life in a Parking Lot: An Ethnography of a Homosexual Drive-In." In Jerry Jacobs (ed.), *Deviance: Field Studies and Self-Disclosures*. Palo Alto, Calif.: National Press Books.

Read, Kenneth E. 1980. *Other Voices: The Style of a Male Homosexual*. Novato, Calif.: Chandler and Sharp.

Reich, Charles A. 1970. *The Greening of America*. New York: Random House.

Reiss, Albert J. 1961. "Social Integration of Queens and Peers." *Social Problems* 9:102–12.

Richardson, Laurel W. 1981. *The Dynamics of Sex and Gender: A Sociological Perspective*. Boston: Houghton Mifflin.

Riecken, Henry W. 1969. "The Unidentified Interview." In McCall and J. L. Simmons (eds.), *Issues in Participant Observation: A Text and a Reader*. Reading, Mass.: Addison-Wesley.

Rodgers, Bruce. 1972. *Gay Talk*. New York: Putnam's.

Rubin, Lillian B. 1975. *Worlds of Pain: Life in the Working-Class Family*. New York: Basic Books.

Russo, Vito. 1975. "The Village." *Advocate* 175:47.

Rutter, Elliot. 1982. "An Exploration of Intimacy between Gay Men." (Unpublished doctoral dissertation, The City University of New York.)

Sagarin, Edward. 1976. "Prison Homosexuality and Its Effects on Post-Prison Sexual Behavior." *Psychiatry* 39:245–57.

Sage, Wayne. 1975. "Inside the Colossal Closet." *Human Behavior* 4:16–23.

Saghir, Marcel T., and Eli Robins. 1973. *Male and Female Homosexuality*. Baltimore: William Wilkens.

Sale, Kirkpatrick. 1973. *SDS*. New York: Vintage.

Schatzman, Leonard, and Anselm L. Strauss. 1973. *Field Research: Strategies for a Natural Sociology*. Englewood Cliffs, N.J.: Prentice-Hall.

Scheff, Thomas J. 1968. *Being Mentally Ill: A Sociological Theory*. Chicago: Aldine.

Schneider, William, and I. A. Lewis. 1984. "The Straight Story on Homosexuality and Gay Rights." *Public Opinion* 7:16–20, 59–60.

Schofield, Michael. 1965. *Sociological Aspects of Homosexuality*. Boston: Little, Brown.

Schur, Edwin M. 1965. *Crimes without Victims: Deviant Behavior and Public Policy: Abortion, Homosexuality, Drug Addiction*. Englewood Cliffs, N.J.: Prentice-Hall.

———. 1971. *Labeling Deviant Behavior: Its Sociological Implications*. New York: Harper and Row.

———. 1972 "Sociocultural Factors in Homosexual Behaviors." *National Institute of Mental Health Task Force on Homosexuality: Final Report and Background Papers*. Bethesda, Md.: National Institute of Mental Health.

———. 1976. *The Awareness Trap: Self-Absorption Instead of Social Change*. New York: McGraw-Hill.

———. 1979. *Interpreting Deviance: A Sociological Introduction*. New York: Harper and Row.

———. 1984. *Labeling Women Deviant*. New York: Random House.

Shilts, Randy. 1977. "Mecca or Ghetto? Castro Street." *Advocate* 209:20–23.

Silverstein, Charles. 1981. *Man to Man: Gay Couples in America*. New York: William Morrow.

Silverstein, Charles, and Edmund White. 1977. *The Joy of Gay Sex*. New York: Crown.

Simmel, George. 1950. *The Sociology of George Simmel*. New York: Free Press.

Simmons, John L. 1965. "The Public Stereotypes of Deviants." *Social Problems* 13:223–32.

Simon, William. 1973. "The Social, the Erotic, and the Sensual: The Complexities of Sexual Scripts." In James K. Cole and Richard Dienstbier (eds.), *Nebraska Symposium on Motivation*. Lincoln: University of Nebraska Press.

Simon, William, and John H. Gagnon. 1967a. "The Lesbians: A Preliminary Overview." In John H. Gagnon and William Simon (eds.), *Sexual Deviance.* New York: Harper and Row.

———. 1967b. "Homosexuality: The Formulation of a Sociological Perspective." *Journal of Health and Social Behavior* 8:177–85.

———. 1969. "On Psychosexual Development." *Transaction* 6(5)(March):9–23.

———. 1973. "Sexual Scripts: Permanence and Change." Paper presented at American Sociological Association, Detroit.

Smelser, Neil J. 1981. *Sociology.* Englewood Cliffs, N.J.: Prentice-Hall.

Socarides, Charles. 1968. *The Overt Homosexual.* New York: Grune and Stratton.

Sonenschein, David. 1968. "The Ethnography of Male Homosexuals' Relationships." *Journal of Sex Research* 4:64–83.

———. 1969. "The Homosexual's Language." *Journal of Sex Research* 5:281–91.

Sorenson, Robert C. 1973. *Adolescent Sexuality in Contemporary America.* New York: World Publishing.

Spada, James. 1979. *The Spada Report.* New York: Signet.

Spector, Malcolm. 1977. "Legitimizing Homosexuality." *Society* 14:52–57.

Starr, R., and D. E. Carns. 1973. "Singles and the City: Notes on Urban Adaptation." In J. Walton and D. E. Carns (eds.), *Cities in Change: Studies on the Urban Condition.* Boston: Allyn and Bacon.

St. Clair, S. 1976. "Fashion's New Game: Follow the Gay Leader." *Advocate* 186:18–19.

Stearn, Jess. 1962. *The Sixth Man.* New York: MacFadden.

Stearns, Peter N. 1979. *Be a Man: Males in Modern Society.* New York: Holmes & Meier.

Stein, Peter. 1976. *Single.* Englewood Cliffs, N.J.: Prentice-Hall.

Stone, C. 1977. "West Hollywood. Where the Boys Are." *Advocate* 214:23–24.

Stoneman, D. 1975. "East Side." *Advocate* 175:44–45.

Styles, Joseph. 1979. "Outsider/Insider: Researching Gay Baths." *Urban Life* 8:135–52.

Sufleski, Bill. 1979. "Clone Boggie: Wrestling with Alligators." *Coast to Coast Times* 29 (November):12.

Sutherland, Edwin H. 1937. *Professional Thief.* Chicago: University of Chicago Press.

Suttles, Gerald D. 1968. *The Social Order of the Slum: Ethnicity and Territory in the Inner City.* Chicago: University of Chicago Press.

———. 1972. *The Social Construction of Communities.* Chicago: University of Chicago Press.

Sweet, Roxanne Thayer. 1975. *Political and Social Action in Homophile Organizations.* New York: Arno.

Szasz, Thomas S. 1961. *The Myth of Mental Illness.* New York: Dell.

Taub, Dane G. 1982. "Public Sociability of College-Aged Male Homosexuals: The Gay Bar and Cruise Block." *Sociological Spectrum* 2:291–305.

Teal, Donn. 1971. *The Gay Militants.* New York: Stein and Day.

Theodorson, George A., and Achilles G. Theodorson. 1969. *A Modern Dictionary of Sociology.* New York: Thomas Y. Crowell.

Thompson, Mark. 1976. "Small Business Owners Experiencing a Natural Progression of Liberated Consciousness." *Advocate* 192:12–13.

Timms, Duncan. 1971. *The Urban Mosaic: Towards a Theory of Residential Differentiation.* New York: Cambridge University Press.

Tipmore, David. 1975. "Homosexual Cult Figures: A Sunday Kind of Love." *Village Voice* 204 (January):72ff.

Townsend, Larry. 1983. *The Leatherman's Handbook II.* New York: Modernismo Publication.

Tripp, C. A. 1975. *The Homosexual Matrix.* New York: McGraw-Hill.

Troiden, Richard R. 1975. "Homosexual Encounters in a Highway Rest Stop." In Erich Goode and Richard Troiden (eds.), *Sexual Deviance and Sexual Deviants.* New York: William Morrow.

———. 1979. "Becoming Homosexual: A Model for Gay Identity Acquisition." *Psychiatry* 142:362–73.

Tuller, Neil R. 1978. "Couples: The Hidden Segment of the Gay World." *Journal of Homosexuality* 3:331–45.

Vining, Donald. 1983. "Cruising: The Art and Artifice." *Advocate* 364 (March).

Ward, Russell A. 1979. "Typifications of Homosexuals." *Sociological Quarterly* 20:411–23.

Warren, Carol A. B. 1972. "Observing the Gay Community." In Jack D. Douglas (ed.), *Research on Deviance.* New York: Random House.

———. 1974. *Identity and Community in the Gay World.* New York: John Wiley & Sons.

———. 1977. "Fieldwork in the Gay World: Issues in Phenomenological Research." *Journal of Social Issues* 33:93–107.

———. 1979. "Women among Men: Females in the Male Homosexual Community." In Martin P. Levine (ed.), *Gay Men: The Sociology of Male Homosexuality.* New York: Harper and Row.

———. 1980. "Homosexuality and Stigma." In John Marmor (ed.), *Homosexual Behavior: A Modern Reappraisal.* New York: Basic Books.

Way, Peggy. 1977. "Homosexual Counseling as a Learning Ministry." *Christianity and Crisis* 37(9, 10):123–31.

Weinberg, Martin S. 1970. "Homosexual Samples: Differences and Similarities." *Journal of Sex Research* 6:312–25.

Weinberg, Martin S., and Colin J. Williams. 1971. *Homosexuals and the Military: A Study of Less Than Honorable Discharge.* New York: Harper and Row.

————. 1972. "Fieldwork among Deviants: Social Relations with Subjects and Others." In Jack D. Douglas (ed.), *Research on Deviance*. New York: Random House.

————. 1974. *Male Homosexuals: Their Problems and Adaptions*. New York: Oxford University Press.

————. 1975. "Gay Baths and the Social Organization of Impersonal Sex." *Social Problems* 23:124–36.

————. 1980. "Sexual Embourgeoisement? Social Class and Sexual Activity: 1938–1970." *American Sociological Review* 45:33–48

Weinberg, Thomas S. 1978. "On Doing and Being Gay: Sexual Behavior and Homosexual Self-Identity." *Journal of Homosexuality* 4:143–56.

West, D. J. 1977. *Homosexuality Re-Examined*. Minneapolis: University of Minnesota Press.

Westwood, Gordon. 1960. *A Minority: A Report on the Life of the Male Homosexual in Great Britain*. London: Longmans, Green.

White, Edmund. 1980. *States of Desire: Travels in Gay America*. New York: E. P. Dutton.

Whitmore, George. 1975. "West Side." *Advocate* 175:44–45.

Whyte, W. F. 1943. *Street Corner Society*. Chicago: University of Chicago Press.

Wirth, L. 1928. *The Ghetto*. Chicago: University of Chicago Press.

Wiseman, Jacqueline P. 1976. *The Social Psychology of Sex*. New York: Harper and Row.

Wittman, Carl. 1972. "A Gay Manifesto." In Karla Jay and Allen Young (eds.), *Out of the Closets: Voices of Gay Liberation*. New York: Douglas.

Wolf, Deborah G. 1979. *The Lesbian Community*. Berkeley: University of California Press.

Wolfe, Tom. 1979. "The Sexed-Up, Doped-Up, Hedonistic Heaven of the Boom-Boom '70s." *Life* 2 (December):103–14.

Yankelovitch, Daniel. 1974. *The New Morality: A Profile of American Youth in the 70's*. New York: McGraw-Hill.

————. 1981. *New Rules: Searching for Self-Fulfillment in a World Turned Upside Down*. New York: Random House.

Young, Allen. 1972. "Out of the Closets, Into the Streets." In Karla Jay and Allen Young (eds.), *Out of the Closets: Voices of the Gay Liberation*. New York: Douglas.

Part II

The Death of the Gay Clone

The cover of *Newsweek* magazine from August 10, 1987, featured photographs of twenty-four people who had died of AIDS the previous year. Seven were women (two of these were older women), two were children, and three appeared to be men over 50. The eighth cover story about the AIDS epidemic since 1983, the magazine announced that the photo spread inside would show "a gallery of 302 men women and children struck down by the epidemic" in the twelve previous months. They ranged in age from "an infant of one to a widow of 87," and they came "from every walk of life from mailman to banker, from housewife to superstar" (Liberace). Here, they promised, was "the real face of AIDS."

The cover montage looked very little like the photo spread inside. Inside, the efforts at inclusion fell to the demographic realities of the epidemic. Page after page was filled with small photographs of young handsome men, virtually all of them between 28 and 40, with short hair, mustaches, and wide smiles.

When the issue first appeared, Marty and I talked about what it meant. One of the photographs was of Marty's companion, Michael Distler, who had died in August 1986, at age 35. Writ larger, we thought of the issue as a memorial for the gay clone. Like the Vietnam War Memorial in Washington, it provided a visceral experience of the social consequences of the disease.

By the late 1980s, Marty's research had shifted away from documenting the successful articulation of masculinity among gay clones. Now he set about trying to understand the ways in which the AIDS epidemic was working itself out in the community, even as he also tried to explain to the gay community what he knew. He became increasingly active as a scholar and an activist, devoting his skills as a researcher and as a community advocate finding ways to respond to AIDS.

The essays in this section represent much of his collaborative work from the later part of Marty's scholarly life. Three earlier, more polemical, papers begin the section. "Bad Blood" appeared early in the history of the epidemic, in *New York Native,* a gay community newspaper, and drew analogies to the government's notorious Tuskegee syphilis experiments. "Fearing Fear Itself" appeared in one of the earliest issues of the *GMHC Newsletter* where Marty advised a community response of concern and cautious defiance. Finally, "Men and AIDS" is an essay that Marty and I co-authored originally for a text-anthology I co-edited, *Men's Lives.* It was subsequently published as an op-ed piece in both the *San Francisco Chronicle* and the *Los Angeles Times.* Here we draw upon our complementary expertise in sociology of gender and sexuality to locate AIDS within a discourse of masculinity, suggesting that, among other things, AIDS was a demonstration that gay men were real men after all.

We were only partly right. As the epidemic has progressed, gay men have also demonstrated the ability to combine a most compassionate caring for those with the disease, and a resilience and resistance to those forces that would celebrate their pain. If only all men could exhibit such a combination of traits!

In "The Myth of Sexual Compulsivity," co-authored with another sociologist, Rick Troiden, Marty used that defiance to confront the cultural reaction against sexuality itself that began to sweep the nation. If gay men could not be pathologized as failed men, perhaps they could be "treated" for the newly minted condition known as sex addiction. Levine and Troiden demonstrate that such pathologies reveal more about cultural squeamishness about sexuality than they do about those who seek sexual gratification.

Marty's last research projects were collaborations with Karolynn Siegel and her colleagues at Memorial Sloan-Kettering Cancer Research Center. Here, Marty's attention turned to understanding what would enable these men to take the HIV test and to practice safer sex.

Chapter Six

Bad Blood

The Health Commissioner, the Tuskegee Experiment, and AIDS Policy [1983]

They say we have bad blood. Nearly forty years ago, they told some black men they had bad blood. Some experts believe, largely on the basis of Centers for Disease Control speculation, that our blood contains an unknown agent which causes acquired immune deficiency disease, or as all know it, AIDS.

Believing that AIDS pollutes our blood, the Public Health Service asked all blood suppliers to bar donations from gay men suspected of carrying the disease. Heeding the Service's call, the American Red Cross and blood banks across the nation are discouraging donations from all of us.

The Public Health Service is the parent organization of the Centers for Disease Control.

Forty years ago, believing that there were racial differences in the ravages syphilis causes, the Venereal Disease Branch of the Public Health Service began the Tuskegee Syphilis experiment, a nontherapeutic study of the effects of syphilis on a group of poor, illiterate, black men in Macon County, Alabama. All the men participating in the experiment were suffering from the later stages of syphilis. Throughout the entire course of the study, these men were denied any treatment for the disease. In addition, they were never told what they had nor did they ever consent to be part of the experiment. The men participated because they thought the government was giving them free treatment for their bad blood.

Due to public outcry, the experiment ended in 1972. In its closing days, it was lodged in the Division of Venereal Disease Control, a bureau within the Centers for Disease Control.

This same organization has played a central role throughout the march of the AIDS epidemic. When the disease first broke, the Centers for Disease Control created the Task Force on Kaposi's sarcoma and Opportunistic Infections. The Task Force had two major functions—to investigate AIDS' cause and to act as a clearinghouse for information about the disease. The Task Force was staffed mainly with people from the Venereal Disease Control Division. Later on, the Task Force was renamed the Task Force on Acquired Immune Deficiency Activity or the AIDS Activity group. The staff and functions have remained largely the same throughout the name changes.

Bad blood, AIDS, syphilis, gays, blacks, the Division of Venereal Disease Control, the Centers for Disease Control. A remarkably similar cast of characters.

The similarities first dawned on me while reading James H. Jones' *Bad Blood: The Tuskegee Syphilis Experiment* (The Free Press, 1981, $7.95). Jones' book is widely regarded as the definitive study of the experiment. It is must reading for all who are concerned about AIDS.

The book had been on my reading list for quite a while. When it was first published, it was acclaimed as an important addition to the fields of bioethics, socio-history, and race relations. It was my professional interest in the latter that drew me to the book. I am a sociologist who teaches, among other things, race and ethnicity. I have also done research on urban gay communities. Because of this work I have been contacted by Dr. William W. Darrow, a research sociologist attached to the AIDS Activity group.

When I started the book, I had no idea that the story Jones tells would raise serious questions about the Centers for Disease Control's role in AIDS. But before I can detail these questions, we need a clearer picture of what took place in Tuskegee.

The Division of Venereal Disease Control conceived, implemented, and administered the Tuskegee Syphilis Experiment. The study ran from 1932 until 1972. Since 1957, the Venereal Disease Division has been housed in the Centers for Disease Control.

The Tuskegee Syphilis Experiment rose upon the ruins of a syphilis control demonstration program. In the late 1920s, the Rosenwald Fund, a private philanthropy with a long-standing concern in black affairs, approached the Public Health Service for aid in formulating a plan to improve the health of blacks living in the rural South. While negotiating this plan, the Service convinced the Fund to sponsor a syphilis treatment program in Mississippi. The Service's Venereal Disease Division had uncovered high rates of syphilis among blacks laboring for the Delta and Pine Land Company. The Fund's moneys paid for the treatment of these men with the primitive remedies of the day, numerous doses of arsphenamine and neo-arsphenamine, administered periodically over the course of a year. The doses had to be supplemented with applications of mercury and bismuth ointments.

The project's success inspired its expansion. Drawing upon the Mississippi experience, a number of high-ranking Public Health Service officers, including the director of the Venereal Disease Division, produced a plan calling for syphilis control demonstration projects in other Southern black communities. In each area, the Wasserman test would be used to detect the disease, and all those found to be infected would be treated.

The Rosenwald Fund reacted favorably to the plan. With financial backing provided, the Mississippi project was expanded to five other communities, each representing a different aspect of black life in the rural South.

Macon County was chosen as one of the new sites. The county typefied the worst in Southern black living. Located deep in the heart of Alabama's "black belt," cotton was king, and the overwhelmingly black populace worked as sharecroppers for the ruling white minority. They were uneducated and poor as well as inadequately fed and sheltered.

The project began in the County during 1930. A syphilis control team arrived with a two-step plan of operation. There would first be a Wasserman survey. This would then be followed by a one-year treatment program.

The plan obviously required cooperation from the community. The Wasserman test for syphilis involved examining samples of human blood for the presence of the disease-causing microbe. Somehow blood had to be taken from Macon County's blacks.

The treatment, too, required cooperation. The painful shots had to be frequently administered over the course of a year. Mercury ointments had to be rubbed daily into the injected area. Some enticement was needed to get syphilitic blacks to undergo the unpleasant and time-consuming treatment.

In the end, the social conditions of the County guaranteed the community's participation. Ever since slavery, blacks had unquestioningly obeyed white landlords. This tradition meant that if the planters ordered their tenants to cooperate, they would. The Public Health team won the planters' support. The landlords instructed the sharecroppers to participate because they knew a healthy field hand was a better worker than a syphilitic one.

Blacks cooperated also because they were eager for free medical care. The project team offered them no-cost testing and treatment for "bad blood." The team used this term because they felt it meant syphilis in rural black jargon. It was their understanding that the exact medical word, syphilis, would be incomprehensible to illiterate blacks.

But bad blood meant far more than syphilis. Blacks used it as a catchall expression for a bevy of ailments. Bad blood denoted headaches, indigestion, pellegra, sores, fatigue, general aches and pains, and numerous other maladies.

The lure of free medical treatment proved irresistable. The sharecroppers' crushing poverty cut them off from existing health care services. They simply could not afford it. It is not surprising that they flocked in droves to the project.

With cooperation ensured, the project went into full swing—testing and treating thousands of people. The Rosenwald Fund closely scrutinized the operation. While the results were impressive—35 percent of those tested had syphilis, resulting in nearly 1400 people being treated—Fund monitors reported problems: the treatments were not administered correctly, the people were completely confused as to the project's true nature, and Alabama violated Fund operating policies when it failed to provide monies for the project.

For these reasons, as well as for the financial difficulties the Great Depression engendered, the Fund decided in Spring 1931 to discontinue the project. The Public Health Service was crushed. Hoping to salvage something for all its hard work, Dr. Taliaferro Clark, the Director of the Venereal Disease Control Division, thought up a new project—a study of the effects of untreated syphilis in "Negroes." Macon County "offered an unparalleled opportunity" for this kind of research. The poverty of its black residents denied them almost any kind of medical treatment. With the incidence of syphilis so high, the researchers were bound to find blacks with untreated syphilis.

Dr. Clark circulated his ideas among the Venereal Disease Division, and later with the leading syphilologists of the day. They all thought the idea had significant scientific merit. Such a study would provide much needed empirical evidence for the prevailing belief that syphilis hit the races in different ways. In whites, it affected the neural system; in blacks, it affected the cardiovascular system.

Racist science buttressed this notion. It was widely believed that black racial inferiority made them "a notoriously syphilis-soaked race"; that their smaller brains lacked mechanisms for controlling sexual desire, causing them to be highly promiscuous; they matured earlier and consequently were more sexually active; that the black man's enormous penis with its long foreskin was prone to venereal infections; that these physiological differences meant the disease must affect the races differently.

With the import of the study firmly established, a protocol was ironed out, drawn largely from the procedures used in the prior Rosenwald Fund project and suggestions from other syphilis experts. The study would last between six months to one year. A Wasserman survey would be used to uncover syphilitic blacks. Only men over 25 would be further studied. They would be physically examined and given a number of medical tests at neighboring Andrew Hospital, part of the Tuskegee Institute.

Before the study could begin, it had to obtain approval from all concerned governmental and medical authorities—except the patients. All of them gave it save the state of Alabama. The state insisted that provision be made for treating all people discovered to have syphilis. The Venereal Disease Division agreed.

The study commenced in Fall 1932. For the most part it was a replay of the Rosenwald project. The cry of free treatment for bad blood lured blacks from all over the country to the testing site. All those found to be syphilitic received treatment. All those fitting the study's requirements were examined and tested at Andrew Hospital.

While all syphilitic blacks, including those in the study, obtained treatment, the cures were totally ineffectual. The Public Health Service lacked the funds to adequately treat all those with the disease. At best, the treatment was less than half the minimum recommended.

Toward the end of the study, Dr. Raymond A. Vonderlher, the field director, formulated a plan for continuing the research. Vonderlher thought science could learn much more about the long-term effects of untreated syphilis on blacks if the men in the study group were followed for a much longer period of time, perhaps even to death. Furthermore, this could be easily done. Public Health Service doctors could periodically examine the men. When they died Andrew Hospital would perform autopsies.

Dr. Vonderlher was in the position to implement these ideas when he replaced Dr. Clark as director of the Division of Venereal Disease Control in the summer of 1931. Drawing upon his own thoughts as well as from ideas gleaned from other division members and syphilologists, he fashioned a design for the new study, an experiment to investigate the effects of syphilis on the Negro male. The experimental group included all syphilitic men from the prior study. A control group of non-diseased men, recruited from those found not to have syphilis in previous projects, would be matched against them. Public Health Service doctors would examine both groups once a year. When the doctors were not present, Nurse Rivers, formerly employed in Dr. Clark's study, would oversee the men. Andrew Hospital would perform autopsies after their deaths.

With the protocol finished and consent obtained from all concerned parties, the experiment began. Thinking the government was giving them free treatment for their bad blood, the six hundred or so men, two-thirds of whom had syphilis, happily participated.

For the next forty years, the experiment went its merry way. Every year Nurse Rivers rounded up the men for the annual examination. Every year the Division of Venereal Disease Control studied the new reports, frequently publishing articles in leading medical journals on its findings. All the while, syphilis ate through the men's bodies.

What is remarkable in this experiment is that it was completely nontherapeutic. No provisions were ever made to treat the men, nor were they ever given information that would have motivated them to seek remedy.

The men knew only that they had bad blood—they never knew they had syphilis. Not knowing this, they never sought a proper cure. And not knowing this, they unwittingly spread it to their spouses, who unknowingly gave it to their children. (Children pick up syphilis from infected mothers while they are in the womb.)

Even if they did look for treatment, the experiment contained procedures which would prevent this. In the beginning, Vonderlher secured commitments from all medical providers not to treat the men. The Macon County Medical Society and the Macon County Board of

Health and those in neighboring counties all agreed not to provide any remedy for the men.

The nontreatment policy held for the entire course of the experiment. Even the advent of penicillin in the early 1940s did not alter this policy. Acclaimed as a miracle cure when first discovered, penicillin quickly became the standard remedy for syphilis. But no one thought to treat the men: "not treating them had become routine." The men remained untreated no matter what advances took place in syphilis therapy.

The experiment, however, contained a fatal flaw. The men in the experimental group had all received some treatment while they were subjects in Dr. Clark's study. The experiment was set up to measure the effects of untreated syphilis in Negro men. But all the men in the experimental group had been partially treated. The study was simply "bad science."

The Tuskegee Syphilis experiment quietly rolled along until a young employee of the Division of Venereal Disease Control blew the whistle in the mid-Sixties. Peter Buxton learned about the experiment while working as a venereal disease investigator in San Francisco. Disturbed because the men did not know what was going on, he wrote a letter to Dr. William J. Brown, the head of Venereal Disease Control, expressing his moral concerns. Brown was dumbfounded by the charge, and sent emissaries to lecture Buxton on the experiment's scientific merit.

A short while later, Buxton voluntarily left his job, and subsequently went to law school. Still haunted by Tuskegee, he wrote Dr. Brown again, this time pointing to how the public might react to the experiment's racist and immoral overtones.

Brown now got alarmed. He took the matter up with Dr. David Sencer, at that time the director of the Centers for Disease Control. The racial turmoil of the period convinced them they had a problem. However, it was not one of morals or race—it was a public relations problem. Unfamiliar with the procedures of medical research, the press would misconstrue the experiment, fomenting adverse political reaction.

Recognizing the study had become a political time-bomb, Dr. Sencer convened a blue-ribbon panel to discuss the experiment's future. The meeting was held at the Centers for Disease Control in February of 1969. The panel thought the experiment's scientific importance overrode any potential political liabilities. They voted to continue the study, with provisions for improving its procedures and for safeguarding the agency from negative criticisms.

Only one member raised the issue of treatment. Dr. Gene Stallerman, chairman of the Department of Medicine at the University of Tennessee, insisted that the Centers for Disease Control had a moral obligation to cure the men. But his plea fell on deaf ears. The rest of the panel thought penicillin therapy would be too medically dangerous at this advanced stage of infection, and they voted for no treatment.

The experiment's theoretical and methodological faults were never mentioned. By 1969 science had erased the theoretical rationale for the study. Anthropological and medical research had long disproven the notion that there were meaningful physiological differences between the races. Yet the belief that there was constituted the study's theoretical foundation. This point went unnoticed. The panel also ignored the problem of contamination. (All the men in the experimental group had obtained some treatment.) Moreover, they paid no attention to the fact that Tuskegee violated existing Public Health Service guidelines for experimentation on human beings.

Sencer accepted the panel's recommendations, pouring new resources into upgrading and safeguarding the experiment. (Contacted by the *Native* for comment, Sencer said that, in his view, the men should have been offered treatment, not in the 1970s, when they were elderly and treatment might have proven harmful to their health, but in the 1940s, when penicillin became widely available. "I was one of those people who believe treatment should have been given at that time," he said. "That's when it would have benefitted the individual. ... The decision not to treat in 1969 was scientifically and ethically correct but politically wrong.") The Centers for Disease Control entered the 1970s with every intention of carrying the experiment to its end—until the last man was brought to autopsy.

In 1972, Buxton and the press shut the study down. The surviving men learned for the first time that their bad blood was really syphilis, and that the governmental doctors had not been treating them. All of them responded well to penicillin therapy when it was finally administered.

The Public Health Service created an ad hoc advisory panel, comprised of prominent citizens of both races, to investigate the study. The panel concluded that the experiment was unethical because it failed to obtain the informed consent of the participants, and because it failed to provide penicillin therapy when it became available.

There are other grounds for faulting the study. The experimenters systematically lied to the men, telling them they had bad blood instead of syphilis, telling them they were being treated when they were being tested. Furthermore, it was illegal, violating public health laws in Alabama that call for the reporting and prompt treatment of venereal disease.

The Centers for Disease Control's actions in Macon County raise serious questions about its activities in AIDS. The agency's Division of Venereal Disease Control played a key role in both situations, furnishing scientists who formulated the research design and conducted the investigation. We need to know if any of the present AIDS researchers participated in the experiment. We know where one former member went. Dr. David Sencer is the Commissioner of Health in New York City.

Sencer says now that under no circumstances would he condone similar (non)treatment of AIDS patients. "I feel strongly that any medical intervention ought to be done in an atmosphere of openness and understanding," he said. "We would not enter into anything that didn't have the full understanding of the community." Sencer said that at his direction the Health Department voluntarily submits its AIDS-related projects for review by the Gay Men's Health Crisis Scientific Review Committee. "I think we've built into the system in New York more safeguards than you'll find anywhere in the country for safeguarding the rights of the patient," he said.

The parallel between the social positions of the two sets of players, however, also engenders concern. In both Tuskegee and AIDS, the socially franchised studied the socially disenfranchised. White doctors experimented upon illiterate black men. Heterosexual researchers explore a disease which usually strikes gay men, as well as Haitians, intravenous drug users, and hemophiliacs.

While there are a few gays involved in the Centers for Disease Control's work on AIDS, the overwhelming majority of the staff is straight. Consider the composition of the AIDS Activity group's full-time personnel. Those working exclusively at headquarters number ten—seven doctors, two public health professionals, and one research sociologist. All of them are straight: one is an orthodox Jew and another a deacon in his church.

What do these similarities mean? After listing them for the author of *Bad Blood* I asked what implications he thought Tuskegee had for us. Dr. Jones replied: "The Centers for Disease Control has done a lot that is wrong and a lot that is heroic. The fact that they were responsible for the Tuskegee experiment does not automatically mean they will exploit a minority group. The information in *Bad Blood* needs to be shared and raised as a note of caution. You have every right to be cautious, but don't fear conspiracy until the hard evidence is in."

Most of us involved in AIDS agree with Jones. In the last few weeks, I have discussed Tuskegee with gay people working on AIDS across the country. All reacted deeply to Tuskegee's unethical nature, racist overtones, and methodological flaws. All felt it had significant implications for AIDS. Many of the people I spoke to are not in the position to be quoted publicly.

Two were most concerned about ethics. They wondered if the researchers were again violating human experimentation regulations. "The researchers are gathering gay men's names, addresses, and sexual histories. The public disclosure of this information could potentially harm those men. I see no safeguards for protecting the men's anonymity," said a person working with AIDS victims in San Francisco. This individual further commented upon the failure of some researchers to get informed consent from the men. Another worried about the possible danger in the Centers for Disease Control's case studies. "They are going around the country collecting names and addresses of gay men. Can we trust them not to use the lists in harmful ways? What are they doing with it?"

Others wondered if the research had homophobic overtones. Racist science prompted the Tuskegee experiment. It was thought that the innate characteristics of blacks made them more sexually promiscuous, thus more prone to syphilis. Homophobic science has created a similar myth—the myth that all gay men are highly promiscuous. "This notion has become the foundation for all the Centers for Disease Control's studies. From the onset, they theorized that if AIDS hit gay men, it had to be because they were promiscuous," said a person closely connected to the Center.

A number of people criticized the Centers for Disease Control's methods. "If Tuskegee was such poor science, why not AIDS?" asked Dr. Stephen Murray, a San Francisco-based sociologist. "All they have done is taken a group of sick people and seen what they have. It is nothing more than correlations based on a sample of the sick, and all the while the relationships may be caused by a third factor. And from this they build the infectious agent theory, and panic the public into believing our blood is diseased. It's a medical counterrevolution— from the mental hospitals to the quarantine." Pondering the possibilities of methodological error, Dr. Lawrence Mass feels, now more than ever, that the Centers for Disease Control must publish its results. All of our thinking about AIDS comes from these studies. To date they have not been published. Public policy, as in the case of blood banks, is being made on these results. We've got to see them to determine their validity."

Everyone I spoke to felt it is time to be more cautious. What happened in Macon County means we cannot blindly trust the Centers for Disease Control. While none of us feels AIDS is a repeat of Tuskegee, it is high time we took a long hard look at what they are doing. The message from Macon County is simply: Be wary, be critical.

Chapter Seven

Fearing Fear Itself [1984]

Tom doesn't go out any more. Formerly a heavily drugged habitue of the Pines-Saint-Eagle circuit, he now sits home alone and very depressed. He has radically changed his lifestyle. Why? Fear of the "gay cancer".

John is a legendary figure in "pig" circles, but now he's sleazy no more. Once a regular at the Mine Shaft and the Everard, he is now celibate. Occasionally he masturbates to a Colt Studios videocassette. What happened? Two of his fuck-buddies died.

Robert maintained a butterfly's life at the Pines, but he's off the party circuit now. His social career hit an iceberg when he began a nonstop litany of self-loathing and worry. He spends his nights alone at home, wringing his hands over his health. What sank Robert's reputation? He's hysterical over the "gay plague."

A new outbreak of disorders is following the outbreak of lethal diseases grouped under the AID acronym. As a sociologist who writes about New York's gay ghetto and is very much a part of it, I have observed a wave of terror wash over our community during the past few months. Driven by an assumption that our lifestyle is responsible for these new diseases, this wave leaves in its wake much psychological turmoil. The emotionally wounded now stalk the city's streets. But the plight of these men remains, for the most part, unaddressed.

The AID outbreak—some call it the gay cancer or the gay plague, which is no help at all—undoubtedly is our community's main concern now. Wherever we gather—at our gyms, in bars, at parties— clone banter is switching from the four D's (disco, drugs, dick, and dish) to who is the latest victim of Kaposi's sarcoma. Hospital visits and funerals are becoming as commonplace as Levi's 501 jeans. Friends who never before showed the slightest interest in gay causes are now besieging us for donations to Gay Men's Health Crisis.

The pages of our periodicals continuously harangue us with the latest medical research. Since the heterosexual media's stories on the outbreak, even our families and straight friends are questioning us.

All this talk has produced a poisonous side effect. We are overcome by hysteria, afraid of the consequences to our health of the way we have been living.

The panic originates in the widespread belief that clonedom—that is, drugs and fast sex—causes the diseases. While our doctors and journalists have been meticulous to inform us about the pitfall of this notion and about other theories of cause, most gay men blindly accept the idea. Our inability to comprehend or critically evaluate all of the highly technical information being presented accounts for this acceptance.

Consider the following: In early May, Gay Men's Health Crisis sponsored a forum on the outbreak; three physicians intimately involved with diagnosing and treating these diseases spoke before more than 500 men and a few women at New York University. Each speaker carefully reviewed current medical knowledge on the problem. But the subtleties and technical minutiae of what they said escaped most of the men I spoke to afterward. Though these doctors clearly pointed out the flaws in the clone lifestyle theory, the audience left thinking that life in the gay fast lane kills.

This panic lacerates our emotions.

After watching friends and lovers die, certain that tricking and drugs killed them, many of us now regard our once-glamorous and exciting lifestyle as toxic. We are left frightened, nervous, and confused. We wonder what we have done to our bodies. Do all those years of frenzied drug orgies at the baths mean it is only a matter of time before we will be stricken? We felt guilt over our past ways. We are obsessed about our health. A minor sore throat, a slight black-and-blue mark conjures up visions of pneumonia or cancer. We *run* to our doctors.

For some, this hysteria breeds self-hatred. The threat of disease and death erases more than a decade of gay pride. Internalized homophobia steps out of the closet as "homosexuality" is blamed for the illnesses.

"I always *knew* being gay was wrong," said a leading Saint acolyte. "I knew all the drugs and sleeping-around was sinful, and now it just might kill me."

The panic also reaches very deeply into the marrow of our sexuality.

We now regard cruising and tricking as fraught with danger. Worrying that the next trick will make us ill, we resist a fast roll in the hay. "When I saw a man I liked at the Eagle, I'd go for him right away. Sometimes I'd pick him up and get him out of the bar in less than five minutes," said a much-desired top. "Now I find myself hesitating. I see a man I like, but then I think about the gay cancer and turn myself off."

Terrified, we are staying horny.

To cope with this panic, many of us are radically rearranging our lifestyles. The gay man of the 1980s is temperate, dates or has a lover, all because he believes the clone theory. If drugs and quick sex kill, then shunning both will keep him healthy. Convinced that this switch is self-protective, some of the city's hottest men are forsaking clonedom. In droves, they are abandoning legendary pleasure spots. The fashion now is not to go out, to stay away from the tubs, discos, and sex clubs. It is becoming terribly *déclassé* to be ripped to the tits.

Even the Pines is being left behind. This summer, for the whole season now there are more unrented houses than ever before. With fast tricks "out" wedding bands are "in"; men are coupling off, and lovers are popping up all over town. Even veterans of countless one-night stands are giving dating a go.

This switch in styles isn't necessarily a bad thing. It could be a positive growth experience. But the change itself may only add to our emotional disturbances. With all its bad points, clone life fulfilled some basic psychological needs. Partying was a way to relax, to see friends, and to have a good time. Tricking affirmed our desirability and satisfied our sexual urges, and it often furnished warmth and affection. Though the next lifestyle also meets these needs, far too many of us will fail in making the switch successfully. Giving up clonedom may cost us the gratification of key emotional needs.

Masculine role-playing accounts for why so many men will fail in this transition. Sociologists view clone sexuality as the product of male gender role training. Socialized into this role, we organize our interpersonal lives in accord with the dictates of masculinity. We learn that it is manly to have frequent, impersonal sex. Consequently, we cruise and trick. We are told men are emotionally cool and don't get involved in relationships. Therefore we stay unattached or only briefly involved.

What the male gender role does *not* teach us is the know-how for success in the new lifestyle of the '80s. Dating and lover relations require skill in relationship formation and an ability to integrate sexuality and emotions. But this is exactly what we have never learned. Not knowing this signifies that we will have tremendous difficulty making the lifestyle change. Pressured into changing by the perceived lethal dangers of clone life, we will alter our lifestyles. Lacking the skills to do so successfully will push many of us into an emotional void.

"I feel so lonely and miserable," a friend told me. "Dancing at the Saint and fucking at the baths . . . now I'm too scared to do it. I tried dating, but it didn't work. I'm left with nothing, just me and my hand."

Sadly enough, all this hysteria and psychological disturbance is needless. The outbreak is far from being an epidemic—even if "epidemiologists" are studying it—and it is unlikely that the clone lifestyle alone can explain what causes it.

As the AID newsletter goes to press, 373 cases of these diseases have been reported to the Centers for Disease Control in Atlanta. Only 292 of these cases were among homosexual or bisexual men. The most recent U.S. Census data lists 110 million men in the entire nation. Most experts estimate that 10 per cent of this figure is actively, openly gay. This means that we number around 11 million men; 278 cases out of a possible 11 million hardly constitutes an epidemic.

Furthermore, the clone lifestyle theory does not hold water. It is inadequate because it is based on correlational findings and fails to explain all cases, especially those among men who use no drugs (other than alcohol and nicotine) and who are sexually celibate.

The first error in the blind-panic is to assume that because two factors are related, one causes the other. Often this is not the case; a third factor is responsible for the relationship. Consider this example: The arrival of storks every year in a small Dutch village coincides with the birth of several babies. Thus storks and babies are related. Can we conclude that storks *cause* babies? It doesn't take much intelligence to realize that, while storks and babies are coincidental, one does not cause the other; a third factor is the causal agent.

Such fallacious reasoning is the mark of the clone lifestyle theory. After taking detailed life histories from the earliest victims, researchers found that many of them were frequent drug users, were highly sexually active, and had recurrent bouts of venereal diseases. But to suggest that one causes the other is poor science. The relationship between these factors could easily be due to some unknown third factor or factors, as many of the investigators are now saying.

Another flaw in the theory is its failure to account for all those suffering from these illnesses. Many of the victims practice a lifestyle far removed from clonedom. A little more than a fifth of the cases are in women or straight men. Certainly, *they* aren't clones. The same goes for many of the gay patients. These men report being faithful to their lovers, entirely monogamous.

Ill-founded or not, the panic from this problem is still washing over us. What should you do if you are feeling anxious? First, by all means, share your feelings with gay men. Don't go through this alone. Talk it over. Keep yourself posted on the latest medical information. Second, practice sound health care. Eat well and sleep well. Visit your doctor regularly, particularly when you think you have one of the symptoms.

Third, be more selective about your sexual partners. And fourth, make a lifestyle switch. Find yourself some steady fuck-buddies. Try your hand at dating and relationships. Don't try to do this alone. Do it in the context of some sort of therapeutic program.

All is not gloom and despair. This challenge also gives us the opportunity to prove that we are more than a community of men who fuck each other. We can show ourselves and the world that we are a community of men who *love* each other. In this crisis, we are family, and we have the talent, money, and concern to take care of one another.

Chapter Eight

Men and AIDS

Michael Kimmel and Martin Levine [1989]

Over 93% of all adult Americans with AIDS are men (as of December 1987), and 73% of all adult AIDS cases occur among gay men (and all cases among homosexuals are male). Eight out of every 10 cases linked to intravenous drug use are men (AIDS Surveillance Report, Centers for Disease Control, December 1987). In New York City, AIDS is the leading cause of death among men aged 30 to 44.[1] Most instances of the other AIDS-related diseases are also among men. These conditions mark earlier stages of infection with the virus causing AIDS, the Human Immune Deficiency virus (HIV). They include AIDS-related complex (ARC) and AIDS virus antibody positivity (HIV seropositivity). Although the prevalence of these conditions is presently unknown, they appear to be concentrated among male intravenous drug users and homosexual men (Institute of Medicine, 1986).

And yet no one talks about AIDS as a men's disease. No one talks about why men are so overwhelmingly at greater risk for AIDS, ARC, and HIV seropositivity. No one talks about the relationship between AIDS and masculinity. In fact, the rhetoric is more often about AIDS as a moral disease. Christian Voice leader Bob Grant says that people with AIDS are simply "reaping the results" of their "unsafe and immoral behavior" (Kropp, 1987). Evangelist Jerry Falwell calls AIDS "the wrath of God among homosexuals" (cited in Altman, 1986: 67).[2] These pronouncements enjoy some popular acceptance. Almost one-third of the respondents in one survey believed that "AIDS is a punishment that God has given homosexuals for the way they live." (Although, echoing Falwell, these respondents seem to be unaware that lesbians who are not intravenous drug users are virtually risk free.) And one-fourth of those same respondents believed that AIDS victims are "getting what they deserve" (*Los Angeles Times,* 12 December 1985). "The poor homosexuals," explained Patrick Buchanan, a conservative columnist and aid to President Reagan, sarcastically, "they have declared war upon Nature, and now Nature is exacting an awful retribution" (*The New York Post,* 24 May 1983). And almost two-fifths of the respondents (37%) to another survey said that AIDS had made them less favorably disposed toward homosexuals than they had been before (*New York Times,* 15 December 1985).

Such beliefs confuse the cause of the disease with transmission. Sin does not cause AIDS, a virus does. Homosexual intercourse and sharing intravenous needles are but two of the ways in which this virus is transmitted. Other forms include heterosexual relations, blood transfusions, and the exchange of blood during pregnancy. In fact, in Africa, most people infected are heterosexual nonintravenous drug users (Quinn, Mann, Curran, and Prot, 1986).

But in the United States, AIDS is a disease of men. The seriousness of the disease demands that we pose the question: what is it about masculinity that puts men at greater risk for AIDS-related illness? To answer that question, we will explore the links between manliness and practices associated with risks for HIV infection; that is, we will examine the relationship between masculinity and risk-taking. To do this, we will first outline the norms of masculinity, the defining features of what it means to be a "real" man in our society. Then we will look at how these norms predispose men to engage in behaviors that place them at greater risk for AIDS. And finally, we will discuss how this perspective may shed new light on strategies of AIDS prevention.

Masculinity As Social Construction

What does it mean to be a man in contemporary American society? Most experts believe that the answer to this question lies in the prevailing cultural construction of masculinity.[3] This perspective maintains that our understanding of masculinity and femininity derives less from biological imperatives or psychological predispositions than from the social definitions of what is appropriate behavior for each gender. Men acquire the scripts that define gender-appropriate behavior through socialization; the family, educational and religious institutions, and the media all contribute to this cultural definition. Such a perspective insists that the cultural definitions of masculinity and femininity are not universal, but culturally and historically specific; what it means to be a man or a woman varies from culture to culture, within any one culture over time, and over the course of one's life.[4]

What, then, are the expectations of gender behavior that men in the United States learn? What are the norms of manliness? Social scientists Deborah David and Robert Brannon (Brannon 1976) group these rules into four basic themes: (1) *No Sissy Stuff:* anything that even remotely hints of femininity is prohibited. A real man must avoid any behavior or characteristic associated with women; (2) *Be a Big Wheel:* masculinity is measured by success, power, and the admiration of others. One must possess wealth, fame, and status to be considered manly; (3) *Be a Sturdy Oak:* manliness requires rationality, toughness, and self-reliance. A man must remain calm in any situation, show no emotion, and admit no weakness; (4) *Give 'em Hell:* men must exude an aura of daring and aggression, and must be willing to take risks, to "go for it" even when reason and fear suggest otherwise.

This cultural construction of masculinity indicates that men organize their conceptions of themselves as masculine by their willingness to take risks, their ability to experience pain or discomfort and not submit to it, their drive to accumulate constantly (money, power, sex partners, experiences), and their resolute avoidance of any behavior that might be construed as feminine. The pressures accompanying these efforts cause higher rates of stress-related illnesses (heart disease, ulcers) and venereal diseases among men. The norms encouraging risk-taking behaviors lead men to smoke, drink too much, and drive recklessly, resulting in disproportionate incidences of respiratory illness, alcoholism, and vehicular accidents and fatalities. And the rules urging aggressiveness induce higher rates of violence-related injury and death among men. Over a century ago, Dr. Peter Bryce, director of a mental institution in Alabama, underscored the relationship between masculinity and mental health. "The causes of general paresis," Dr. Bryce wrote (cited in Hughes, 1988: 15):

> are found to prevail most among men, and at the most active time of life, from 35 to 40, in the majority of cases. Habitual intemperance, sexual excesses, overstrain in business, in fact, all those habits which tend to keep up too rapid cerebral action, are supposed to induce this form of disease. It is especially a disease of *fast life*, and fast business in large cities.

"Warning," writes one modern psychologist, "the male sex role may be dangerous to your health!" (Harrison, 1978).

Masculinity and Male Sexuality

These norms also shape male sexuality, organizing the scripts that men follow in their sexual behaviors. Men are taught to be rational, successful, and daring in sex: Real men divorce emotions from sexual expression, have sex without love and are concerned solely with gratification. Real men "score" by having lots of sex with many partners, and they are adventurous and take risks.

The norms defining masculinity also significantly increase men's vulnerability to AIDS. The virus causing AIDS is spread through bodily fluids such as blood, semen, and vaginal secretions. To become infected with this virus, men (and women) must engage in practices that allow these fluids to enter the bloodstream. Such practices are known as "risk behaviors" (see Frumkin and Leonard, 1987: Ch. 4).

The most common risk behaviors among adults are unprotected sexual intercourse, oral sex, and sharing needles. Heterosexual or homosexual intercourse can cause tiny breaks in the surface linings of these organs, through which infected bodily fluids can enter the bloodstream directly. In oral sex, the fluids enter through breaks in the lining of the mouth.[5] Sharing needles allows these infected fluids to enter the bloodstream directly on needles containing contaminated blood.

Fortunately, there are ways one can avoid contact with the AIDS virus. Authorities recommend avoiding risk behaviors. This can be accomplished in several ways: (1) abstinence: the avoidance of sexual contacts and use of intravenous drugs; (2) safer sex: the avoidance of all sexual behaviors in which semen or blood are passed between partners (usually accomplished by the use of condoms); and (3) safer drug use: avoidance of all unsterilized needles. Safer drug use means not sharing needles if possible; if needles must be shared, they must be cleaned (with bleach or rubbing alcohol) before each use.

Unfortunately, these types of risk-reduction behavior are in direct contradiction with the norms of masculinity. The norms of masculinity propel men to take risks, score, and focus sexual pleasure on the penis. Real men ignore precautions for AIDS risk reduction, seek many sexual partners, and reject depleasuring the penis. Abstinence, safer sex, and safer drug use compromise manhood. The behaviors required for the confirmation of masculinity and those required to reduce risk are antithetical.

Strategies of AIDS Prevention

Given this perspective, how might we evaluate the various strategies that have been developed to combat the AIDS epidemic? To what extent do they reproduce or encourage precisely the behaviors that they are designed to discourage? The procedures developed to combat the AIDS epidemic ignore the links between masculinity and risk behaviors. The battle against AIDS relies heavily upon the public health strategies of testing and education (Gostin, in Dalton and Burris, 1987). But each of these is limited by the traditional norms of masculinity, as well as other factors.

Testing. Testing involves the use of the HIV antibody test to screen the blood for antibodies to the AIDS virus, and posttest counseling. People who test positive for the HIV antibodies are regarded as infected, that is, as carrying the virus and capable of transmitting it to others. These individuals are counseled to avoid risk behaviors.

AIDS antibody testing, however, even when coupled with counseling, is not a sufficient method to deal with the AIDS epidemic. The rationale for testing has been that it will encourage safer-sex behavior among those already infected but not yet ill, and thus curtail the epidemic. Yet this rationale remains unproven. Although this procedure may have been successful in the past with other infectious diseases, Dr. William Curran of the Harvard School of Public Health argues that it does not apply to AIDS (Curran, 1986). One study found that a positive result on the AIDS antibody test does not necessarily promote safe-sex behaviors. "It is not the test that promotes safe sex," the authors write, "but education and social support for safe sex" (Beeson, Zones, and Nye, 1986: 14).

AIDS antibody testing also has negative side effects, such as psychological distress, the possibility of social sanctions such as losing one's job, loss of medical care or life insurance, or the possibility of forced quarantine, if specific public policy recommendations are adopted by voters. Thus, antibody testing is opposed by nearly all medical and epidemiological experts. The Institute of Medicine of the National Academy of Sciences recently summarized their findings that testing was

> impossible to justify now either on ethical or practical grounds ... [raising] serious problems of ethics and feasibility. People whose private behavior is illegal are not likely to comply with a mandatory screening program, even one backed by assurances of confidentiality. Mandatory screening based on sexual orientation would appear to discriminate against or to coerce entire groups without justification. (Institute of Medicine, 1986: 14)

From our perspective, as well, we must examine the ways in which the norms of masculinity impede the effectiveness of AIDS antibody testing. These rules compel men to shun stereotypical "feminine" concerns about health. "Real" men do not worry about the dangers associated with smoking, drinking, and stress—why should they worry about the risks associated with intravenous drug use and sex? Manly nonchalance will keep men from getting tested. Early reports from New York City indicate that more women than men are being tested for AIDS (Sullivan, 1987).

These norms of masculinity also impede the effectiveness of counseling. During counseling, men are warned against spreading the virus. Such warnings, however, contradict the dictates of manliness. "Real" men score, and their sexuality is organized phallocentrically, so counseling, which would encourage men to deemphasize the penis and emphasize sexual responsibility, may fall on deaf ears. To demonstrate manliness, seropositive men may actually give the virus to someone else.

Public Health Education. Public health authorities have also utilized education as an AIDS prevention strategy. The Institute of Medicine of the National Academy of Sciences recommends "a major educational campaign to reduce the spread of HIV" and that "substantially increased educational and public awareness activities be supported not only by the government, but also by the information media, and by other private sector organizations that can effectively campaign for health." For intravenous drug users, the Institute recommends "trials to provide easier access to sterile, disposable needles and syringes" (Institute of Medicine, 1986: 10, 12, 13).

Educational efforts have been developed by both public sector agencies, such as federal, state, and local health departments, and private organizations, such as local AIDS groups, and groups of mental health practitioners. These public and private efforts are each faced with a different set of problems, and each confronts different components of the norms of masculinity.

Public health education campaigns, funded by taxpayer dollars, have utilized mass transit advertisements, billboards, brochures, and hotlines to explain the medical facts about AIDS, its causes, how it affects the body, how it is transmitted, and who is at risk. Such campaigns deemphasize information about safe sex behaviors, because such information might be seen as condoning or even encouraging behaviors that are morally or legally proscribed. As Dr. James Mason, undersecretary for health in the Department of Health and Human Services said, "[w]e don't think that citizens care to be funding material that encourages gay lifestyles" (cited in Anderson, 1985). Editor and writer Norman Podhoretz criticized any efforts to stop AIDS because to do so would encourage homosexuality so that "in the name of compassion they are giving social sanction to what can only be described as brutish degradation" (cited in *New York Times*, 18 March 1986). And North Carolina Senator Jesse Helms, one of the nation's most vocal critics of education programs, sponsored an amendment that stipulated that no federal funds be used to promote or encourage homosexual activity, and emphasized that AIDS education emphasize abstinence outside a sexually monogamous marriage as the only preventive behaviors that the government would fund. The choice that Helms offers, he claims, is "Reject sodomy and practice morality. If they are unwilling to do that, they should understand the consequences" (Helms, 1987).

The content of these educational campaigns reflects the political ideology embedded within them. The pamphlet issued by the U.S. Public Health Service's Centers for Disease Control, "What You Should Know About AIDS," counsels that the "safest way to avoid being infected by the AIDS virus is to avoid promiscuous sex and illegal drugs." Teenagers, especially, "should be encouraged to say 'no' to sex and illegal drugs" (Center for Disease Control, 1987).

The effectiveness of such strategies is extremely limited by the myopic moralizing that is embedded within them. "It is too late to be prudish in discussing the crisis with youngsters," warns an editorial in

The Washington Post, urging explicit safe-sex education in the schools ("AIDS Education," 1987). But more than this, they are limited because they violate the traditional norms of masculinity. Just saying "no" contradicts the norms that inform men that "real" men score in sex, by having many sexual partners and by taking risks, or, more accurately, by ignoring potential risks in their pursuit of sex. Because of the norms of masculinity, which are especially salient for teenagers and younger men, the burden of just saying "no" will undoubtedly fall upon the shoulders of women. Efforts to halt the spread of a sexually transmitted disease by encouraging men to abstain have never been successful in American history, although such strategies have been attempted before, during the syphilis epidemic following World War I (see Brandt, 1986).

Private-Agency Educational Campaigns. Educational campaigns sponsored by privately funded agencies have developed various mechanisms that are far less negative about sexuality, and may, therefore, have far greater chances of reaching male populations. These campaigns vary in tone and effect. Some organizations that have emerged from within the gay community in major cities across the nation have given explicit information about safer sex practices. "Plain Talk about Safe Sex and AIDS" (published by Baltimore Health Education Resource Organization and also distributed in Boston) uses scare tactics:

> You must be aware that AIDS will almost certainly kill you if you get it. No fooling. It's that deadly. And at this moment it's incurable. This is no wishy washy Public Health "warning" from the Surgeon General, determining that cigarette smoking is dangerous to your health. The medical breakthrough hasn't happened yet. In other words, if you contract AIDS, the chances are that you'll be dead within a year, probably. Got it? Let's put it in plain language. If you develop AIDS, kiss your ass goodby.

The San Francisco AIDS Foundation condemns past practices among gay men, such as anonymous sex, bathhouses, backrooms, bookstores, and parks, while giving this advice:

> We do know that the long standing health problems caused by sexually transmitted diseases in the gay community could be reduced if everyone were to heed the suggestions outlined here. If, as many believe, repeated infections also weaken the immune system, these suggestions

can help you lead a healthier and safer life. If our comments sound rather judgmental or directive, understand that we, too, have and are experiencing these diseases and are trying to follow our own recommendations. . . . [W]e believe that intimacy, both sexual and emotional, is necessary as we move toward a more healthy regard for our own bodies and those we love.

Other educational efforts attempt to remain sex-positive, such as Houston's "AIDS Play Safe" campaign, whose slogan is "Adapt, Enjoy, Survive." Their pamphlet states:

You don't have to give up good times, being social, having fun, going out, or even having sex, but you can change to safe sex, accept the experience and enjoy it. The results are lower risk of AIDS, less fear and anxiety, your health, and possibly your life. Come on, let's party. Don't be left behind, don't sit at home fretting. You can still have a good time, you can still enjoy your sexuality, you can still enjoy your lifestyle, you can still party, dance, play, have sex, and get the most out of life. You don't have to deny it to yourself. Adapt, enjoy and survive. And we'll see you around next year.

This position is echoed in the "Healthy Sex Is Great Sex" pamphlet published by the Gay Men's Health Crisis in New York City. Other efforts to educate gay men about safe sex practices include safe sex videos, house parties where information and free condoms are distributed on a model of Tupperware parties, and workshops run by professionals on eroticizing safe sex encounters.

In general, these campaigns developed by local gay organizations have had remarkable success. By a variety of measures—impressionistic, comparative, and surveys—unsafe sex practices have declined sharply among those groups who have access to explicit information about safe sex behaviors. Impressionistic journalistic reports indicate that gay baths and bars are less crowded and monogamous coupling is on the rise. The rates of other venereal disease, a certain marker of promiscuity and unsafe sex practices, have plummeted among gay men across the country.

The results of survey data reveal a significant decrease in unsafe sex practices among gay men. The San Francisco AIDS Foundation found in 1984 that almost all respondents were aware that certain erotic behavior could result in AIDS, and two-thirds had stopped engaging in high risk behavior (*Advocate*, 428, 3 September 1985).

The Research and Decisions Corporation in 1985 found widespread awareness about safe sex guidelines, and a continued decline in high risk behaviors among subjects between 1984 and 1985.

Some Lingering Problems. But we are concerned not with the significant numbers of men who have altered their behavior in the face of serious health risk, but with the residual numbers who have not changed. How can we explain that one-third of those men surveyed in 1984 and one-fifth of the men surveyed in 1985 continued to engage in unsafe sex? How do we explain the conclusion of the 1985 study, which reported that the "men in these groups were uniformly well informed for AIDS risk reduction. Despite their knowledge of health directives, the men in this sample displayed discrepancies between what they believed about AIDS and their sexual behavior" (McKusik, et. al. 1985:495). It appears that a significant number of men continue to engage in high risk behavior, even though they know better.

Such continued high risk behavior cannot be attributed to homophobia, since the information provided is by local gay groups. And it is not attributable to sex-negativism, since much of the material is also sexually explicit about safe sex practices and gay-affirmative in tone. We believe that the cultural norms of masculinity compose one of the hidden impediments to safe sex education. That men's sexuality is organized around scoring, associates danger with sexual excitement, and is phallocentric limits the effectiveness of safer sex educational campaigns. In one study, 35% of the gay men who agreed that reducing the number of sexual partners would reduce risks had sex with more than five different men during the previous month (McKusik, et. al. 1985). Over four-fifths of the men who agreed with the statement "I use hot anonymous sex to relieve tension" had three or more sexual partners the previous month. And almost 70% of the men having three or more sexual partners the previous month agreed with the statement "It's hard to change my sexual behavior because being gay means doing what I want sexually."

Challenging Traditional Masculinity As Risk Reduction

Here we see the question in its boldest form: gay male sex is, above all, male sex, and male sex, above all, is risky business. Here, we believe, the social scientist can inform public health campaigns and epidemiological research. We need to recapitulate our understanding of how masculinity informs sexual behavior, and how masculinity might serve as an impediment to safer sex behaviors among men. Since there is no anticipatory socialization for homosexuality, boys in our culture all learn norms for heterosexual masculinity. This means that gay or straight, men in our culture are cognitively oriented to think and behave sexually through the prism of gender. Gay male sexuality and straight male sexuality are both enactments of scripts appropriate to gender; both have, in their cognitive orientations, "male" sex.

What this means concretely includes the meanings that become attached to our sexual scripts in early adolescence. Through masturbation and early sexual experiences, boys learn that sex is privatized, that emotions and sexuality are detached, that the penis is the center of the sexual universe, that fantasy allows heightened sexual experience, that pleasure and guilt are intimately linked, and that what brings sexual pleasure is also something that needs to be hidden from one's family. Masculinity is enacted in sexual scripts by the emphasis on scoring, by its recreational dimension (the ability to have sex without love), and by the pursuit of sexual gratification for its own sake, and by the association of danger and excitement (enacted through the link of pleasure and guilt). The male sexual script makes it normative to take risks, to engage in anonymous sex, and to have difficulty sustaining emotional intimacy, and it validates promiscuous sexual behavior.

In such a script, "safe sex" is an oxymoron. How can sex be safe? How can safety be sexy? Sex is about danger, excitement, risk; safety is about comfort, security, softness. And if safe sex isn't sexy, many men, enacting gender scripts about masculinity, will continue to practice unsafe sex. Or they may decide not to engage in sex at all. "I find so-called safe sex comparable to putting my nose up against a window in a candy store when I'm on a diet. I'd rather not go near the window at all, because seeing the candy makes me want to eat at least three or four pieces," said one man explaining his two-year voluntary celibacy as a response to AIDS ("Sex in the Age of AIDS," 1986). To educate men about safe sex, then, means to confront the issues of masculinity.

In spite of the efforts of some policy makers, whose misplaced moralism is likely to cost thousands of lives, we know that "health education is the only tool that can stem this epidemic," as the executive director of the Gay Men's Health Crisis put it. "AIDS education should have started the moment it was realized that this disease is sexually transmitted," wrote one medical correspondent (cited in Watney, 1987: 135). It would appear that a public health policy that was truly interested in reducing the spread of AIDS (instead of punishing those who are already stigmatized and at risk) would need to add two more considerations to the impressive educational efforts already underway. First, we will need to make safer sex sexy. Second, we will need to enlarge the male sexual script to include a wider variety of behaviors, to allow men a wide range of sexual and sensual pleasures.

Safer sex can be sexy sex. Many organizations are developing a safer sex pornography. GMHC in New York City offers safe sex videos as a form of "pornographic healing." In his important new book, *Policing Desire: Pornography, AIDS, and the Media,* English author Simon Watney argues that gay men "need to organize huge regular Safe Sex parties in our clubs and gay centers . . . with workshops and expert counseling available. We need to produce hot, sexy visual materials to take home, telephone sex-talk facilities, and safe sex porno cinemas" (Watney, 1987: 133).

And while we make safer sex into sexy sex, we also need to transform the meaning of masculinity, to enlarge our definition of what it means to be a man, so that sexuality will embrace a wider range of behaviors and experiences. As Watney argues, we "need to develop a culture which will support the transition to safer sex by establishing the model of an erotics of protection, succour and support within the framework of our pre-AIDS sex lives" (Watney, 1987: 132).

Conclusion

The process of transforming masculinity is long and difficult, and AIDS can spread so easily and rapidly. Sometimes it feels as if there isn't enough time. And there isn't. While we are eroticizing safer sex practices and enlarging the range of erotic behaviors available to men, we must also, as a concerned public, increase our compassion and support for AIDS patients. We must stand with them because they are our brothers. We are linked to them not through sexual orientation (although we may be) or by drug-related behavior (although we may be), but by gender, by our masculinity. They are not "perverts" or "deviants" who have strayed from the norms of masculinity, and therefore brought this terrible retribution upon themselves. They are, if anything, overconformists to destructive norms of male behavior. They are men who, like all real men, have taken risks. And risk taking has always implied danger. Men have always known this and have always chosen to take risks. Until daring has been eliminated from the rhetoric of masculinity, men will die as a result of their risk taking. In war. In sex. In driving fast and drunk. In shooting drugs and sharing needles. Men with AIDS are real men, and when one dies, a bit of all men dies as well. Until we change what it means to be a real man, every man will die a little bit every day.

NOTES

This essay is dedicated to the memory of José A. Vigo, 1950–1988.

1. New York City Department of Health, personal communication, January 11, 1988.

2. For an overview of moralistic interpretations of AIDS, see Fitzpatrick (1988).

3. Our work here draws upon the "social constructionist" model of gender and sexuality. The pioneering work of John Gagnon and William Simon, *Sexual Conduct* (1973), has been followed up by our recent work. See, for example, Michael Kimmel and Jeffrey Fracher (1987), "Hard Issues and Soft Spots: Counseling Men about Sexuality."

4. Gender norms also vary within any culture by class, race, ethnicity, and region. Although there are many masculinities or femininities in the contemporary United States, however, we will elaborate the standard for white middle-class men in major metropolitan areas, because this is the model that is the hegemonic form that is defined as generalizable and normative. It is essential to understand its universality as a power relation and not as a moral ideal (see Connell, 1987).

5. The evidence for oral sex as a mode of transmission is only speculative. To date, there are no reported instances of transmission in this way (Green, 1987).

REFERENCES

Advocate, 3 September 1985.

"AIDS Education." Editorial in *Washington Post*, 28 February 1987.

"AIDS: The Public Reacts." *Public Opinion*, 8, December 1986.

Altman, Dennis. 1986. *AIDS in the Mind of America.* New York: Doubleday.

Anderson, Jack. 1985. "Fear consigns AIDS material to the shelf." *Newark Star Ledger*, 11 November 1985.

Beeson, Diane R., Jane S. Zones, and John Nye. 1986. "The social consequences of AIDS antibody testing: Coping with stigma." Paper presented at annual meetings of the Society for the Study of Social Problems, New York.

Brandt, Alan. 1986. *No Magic Bullet.* New York: Oxford University Press.

Brannon, Robert. 1976. "Introduction." In Robert Brannon and Deborah David, eds. *The Forty-Nine Percent Majority.* Reading, MA: Addison-Wesley.

Centers for Disease Control. "AIDS Surveillance Report," December 1987.

Connell, R. W. 1987. *Gender and Power.* Stanford: Stanford University Press.

Curran, William. 1986. AIDS. Cambridge: Harvard School of Public Health.

Dalton, Harlon, and Scott Burris, eds. 1987. *AIDS and the Law: A Guide for the Public.* New Haven: Yale University Press.

Fitzpatrick, James K. 1988. "AIDS is a Moral Issue" in Lynn Hall and Thomas Mode, (eds.). *AIDS: Opposing Viewpoints.* St. Paul: Greenhaven Press, pp. 32–37.

Frumkin, Lyn, and John Leonard. 1987. *Questions and Answers on AIDS.* New York: Avon.

Gagnon, John, and William Simon. 1973. *Sexual Conduct.* Chicago: Aldine.

Gostin, Larry. 1987. "Traditional public health strategies." In Harlon Dalton and Scott Burris, eds. *AIDS and the Law: A Guide for the Public.* New Haven: Yale University Press.

Green, Richard. 1987. "The transmission of AIDS." In Harlon Dalton and Scott Burris, eds. *AIDS and the Law: A Guide for the Public.* New Haven: Yale University Press.

Hall, Lynn, and Thomas Modl, eds. 1988. *AIDS: Opposing Viewpoints.* St. Paul: Greenhaven Press.

Harrison, James. 1978. "Caution: Masculinity may be hazardous to your health." *Journal of Social Issues*, 34(1), pp. 65–86.

Helms, Jesse. 1987. "Only morality will effectively prevent AIDS from spreading." Letter to *New York Times*, November 12, 1987.

Hughes, John. 1988. "The madness of separate spheres: Insanity and masculinity in late 19th century Alabama." Paper presented at Conference on Masculinity in Victorian America, Barnard College, 9 January 1988.

Institute for Advanced Study of Human Sexuality. 1986. *Safe Sex in the Age of AIDS.* Secaucus, NJ: Citadel Press.

Institute of Medicine, National Academy of Sciences. 1986. *Confronting AIDS: Directions for Public Health, Health Care and Research.* Washington, D.C.: National Academy Press.

Kimmel, Michael, and Jeffrey Fracher. 1987. "Hard issues and soft spots: Counseling men about sexuality." In Murray Scher et al., eds. *Handbook of Counseling and Psychotherapy with Men.* Newbury Park, CA: Sage Publications.

Kropp, Arthur. 1987. "Religious right cashing in on AIDS epidemic." *Houston Texas Post*, July 20, 1987.

Levine, Martin P. *Gay Macho: The Ethnography of the Homosexual Clone.* Ph.D. dissertation, New York University, 1986.

Los Angeles Times, 12 December 1985.

McKusik, Leon, William Hortsman, and Thomas J. Coates. 1985. "AIDS and sexual behavior reported by gay men in San Francisco." *American Journal of Public Health*, 75(5). May. *New York Post*, 24 May 1983.

New York Post, 24 May 1983.

New York Times, 15 December 1985.

New York Times, 18 March 1986.

Quinn, Thomas C., Jonathan M. Mann, James W. Curran, and Peter Prot. 1986. "AIDS in Africa: An epidemiological paradigm." *Science*, 234, November 21.

"Sex in the Age of AIDS," a symposium. 1986. *Advocate*, July 8.

Sullivan, Ronald. 1987. "More women are seeking test for AIDS." *New York Times*, 23 May 1987.

Watney, Simon. 1987. *Policing Desire: Pornography, AIDS and the Media.* Minneapolis: University of Minnesota Press.

Chapter Nine

The Myth of Sexual Compulsivity

Martin Levine and Richard Troiden [1988]

Since the 1960s, sociological thinking on mental illness has undergone a radical transformation (Gallagher, 1987; Mumford, 1983; Scheff, 1984). Traditionally, sociologists accepted basic psychiatric and psychological assumptions about mental disorder; sociological inquiry focused on the social forces "relevant to the etiology, identification, distribution, incidence, and course of mental illness" (Fletcher, Manning, & Smith, 1974, p. 43). The emergence of the labeling (constructionist or interactionist) perspective on deviance, however, altered this focus (Scheff, 1984). Recognizing the cultural relativity and social control aspects of defining behavior as mental illness (Schur, 1979), the labeling perspective (Fletcher, Manning, & Smith, 1974) challenged "the traditional medical explanations of mental illness, the applicability of the disease concept to mental illness, and the efficacy and value of psychiatric institutions and treatment techniques" (p. 43).

In rejecting a medical model that treats mental problems as diseases (Gove, 1970; Mumford, 1983, pp. 415–416; Scheff, 1984), labeling theorists joined forces with psychiatrists such as Thomas Szasz (1970) and R. D. Laing (1967), who argued similarly that mental illness is the outcome of socially created and applied judgments. Pointing to the sociohistorical variability that surrounds behaviors labeled as mental illness, interactionists (labeling theorists) argued that mental illness is a metaphor or a cultural construct rather than a clinical condition which people either possess or lack, a "medicalization" of normative departures (Conrad & Schneider, 1980). In a variation of Howard S. Becker's (1963) famous summary of the labeling approach to deviance, mental illness is not a quality of the act the person commits, but rather a consequence of the application by others of rules and sanctions to an offender. The [mentally ill] person is one to whom that label has successfully been applied; [mental illness] is a behavior that people so label. (P. 9)

Antimedical-model psychiatrists and labeling sociologists also examined the kinds of behavior that are called mental illness (Schur, 1979, pp. 58–64), and concluded that behavior designated as a symptom of mental disorder almost always involves conduct or beliefs that violate cultural definitions of what is or is not normal (Mechanic, 1969, p. 2). Because the lay public and even health care providers often disagree about which behaviors are or are not mental illnesses, Scheff (1984) classifies mental illness as a form of *residual deviance*, a social category that encompasses a hodgepodge of norm violations "for which the culture provides no explicit label" (p. 37). In a similar vein, Szasz (1970) argues that mental illness is simply a pejorative label for "problems in living" that deviate from "psychosocial and ethical standards" (p. 15).

The constructionist reconceptualization of mental illness sparked a reevaluation of the role played by mental health practitioners, particularly psychiatrists and psychologists, in constructing or manufacturing mental illness (Conrad & Schneider, 1980; Davis & Anderson, 1983; Scheff, 1984; Szasz, 1980). According to this reconceptualization, mental health professionals are "imputational specialists" (Lofland, 1969), agents of social control whose function is to enforce conformity to the existing social order through the differential application of diagnostic labels (Becker, 1963, pp. 150–152; Schur, 1979, p. 63). Using conformity to existing normative standards as the measure of mental health, clinicians with a medical perspective treat departures from norms as forms of mental illness, which justifies coercive treatment and institutionalization of offenders. In the words of Thomas Szasz (1970):

Among all the medical specialties psychiatry is the only one whose job is to stigmatize people with moral judgments camouflaged as diagnoses and to imprison them under the guise of treatment. (P. 125)

This paper analyzes the newly "discovered" psychosexual "conditions" of "sexual addiction" and "sexual compulsion," using an interactionist or constructionist perspective. We argue that sexual addiction and sexual compulsion represent pseudoscientific codifications of prevailing erotic values rather than bona fide clinical entities. The concepts of sexual addiction and compulsion constitute an attempt to repathologize forms of erotic behavior that became acceptable in the 1960s and 1970s. To support our argument, we will discuss (1) the ways mental health professionals use the concepts of sexual addiction and sexual compulsion; (2) the cultural relativity of these diagnoses; (3) the social context in which these "disorders" emerged; and (4) the value laden and conceptually flawed manner in which these "conditions" are defined.

Usage of the Sexual Addiction and Compulsion Concepts

Although the definitions of what constitutes sexual addiction and compulsion are ambiguous at present (Coleman, 1986), mental health practitioners commonly use the terms to describe a "lack of control over erotic impulses" (Barth & Kinder, 1987). So defined, sex addicts or sexual compulsives are people who feel driven to engage frequently in nonnormative sex, often with destructive consequences for their intimate relationships (e.g., marriages) and occupational roles (Carnes, 1983; Schwartz & Brasted, 1985; Quadland, 1985a, Quadland & Shattls, 1987).

Mental health professionals differ, however, in how they conceptualize a lack of control over erotic impulses. Some classify it as an *addiction*, likening it to chemical or food dependencies (Carnes, 1983; Edwards, 1986; Goleman, 1984; Schwartz & Brasted, 1985). In this view, loneliness, low self-esteem, and anxiety cause individuals to lose control over their sexual behavior, which poses grave threats to ongoing relationships and careers. Despite the risks, sex addicts engage in these practices because they offer temporary relief from psychic distress. This relief is described as a sexual "fix" or "high" similar to the ones obtained from illegal drugs, alcohol, or food.

Sexual addiction appears differently among men and women (Carnes, 1983; Schwartz & Brasted, 1985); male sex addicts outnumber female addicts. Among men, the addiction is thought to cause uncontrollable promiscuity, autoeroticism, transvestism, homosexuality, exhibitionism, voyeurism, fetishism, incest, child molestation, and rape. The following case history illustrates male sexual addiction:

Don was a politically prominent lawyer with a wife and three children. His addiction drove him into multiple affairs with other women (often juggling two or three at the same time), sexual relations with masseuses in massage parlors, and homosexual encounters in movie booths at adult book stores. Don's behavior filled him with guilt and remorse because it violated his values, broke the law, and jeopardized his career and family. (Carnes, 1983, pp. 1–4)

Sexual addiction in women manifests itself in "frequent dangerous sexual encounters with strangers" (Schwartz & Brasted, 1985, pp. 103–104). The following case study illustrates sexual addiction in women:

Carrie was a well respected music teacher who moonlighted at night as a singer. Dissatisfied with her career, Carrie began to pick up customers from the bars for one night stands. At first this behavior was sporadic, but then it became routine, occurring everytime she sang. Carrie's conduct made her despondent. (Carnes, 1983, pp. 17–18)

Other mental health practitioners classify a lack of sexual control as a *compulsion,* comparing it to other disorders of impulse control (Gershoni, 1985; Mattison, 1985; Quadland, 1985a, 1985b; Quadland & Shattls, 1987). In this view, sexual compulsion is a self or therapist-defined lack of control over sexual impulses. A desire for sex is triggered by anxiety. Feelings of "anxiety, loneliness, and low self-esteem" are mislabeled as "horniness," and trigger the search for a sexual encounter. Sexual activity temporarily reduces these anxious feelings; however, a temporary boost to self-esteem is soon replaced by guilt and remorse over the sexual activity, which rekindles the feelings of anxiety and the cycle of compulsion. A typical example illustrates the pattern:

An individual is at home and experiences some agitation or restlessness. He labels this feeling "horniness" and decides to go out looking for sex. Immediately he is distracted from the anxiety-provoking stimulus, possibly loneliness in this case, by preparing to go out. This is the first reinforcer (a negative one) for the behavior, the removal of a painful stimulus. Positive reinforcement for the sexual behavior may be derived from the sexual encounter itself, the pleasure of the orgasm, but, perhaps even more importantly, from the affirmation of the individual's sexual, personal, or physical appeal. Unfortunately, such reinforcement is fleeting and is often accompanied by guilt or remorse. The anxiety-provoking stimuli return, tension builds, and the pattern is repeated. (Quadland & Shattls, 1987, p. 288)

The following case history of a male homosexual also illustrates sexual compulsion:

> Oscar, 29, entered therapy in a desperate effort to overcome his anxiety and depression about AIDS. In his early teens he had his first sexual experience. It was in a truck, out at the piers. "For years I went to the same place until I started going to the baths. I need a lot of sex and often I'd go two or three times a week. Last winter was the worst period. I was drifting along. I hated my job—it was the pits. Nothing interested me. I couldn't stand the cold weather, either. I went to the baths every other day, until I got scared. Now I go once a week or so. I have a hard time admitting that I'm hurting. I don't deal with it. Still, I don't like being alone in my apartment. When I'm alone, I immediately have the urge to take a cab and hit the baths again." (Gershoni, 1985, p. 24)

Thus, at the present time, some mental health professionals diagnose people as either sexual addicts or sexual compulsives when clients are unable to control their sexuality; that is, to stop masturbating, to stop having extramarital affairs or anonymous sex, or to stop purchasing and using pornography. Individuals use similar standards for diagnosing themselves as sexual addicts or sexual compulsives (Augustine Fellowship, 1986).

The Cultural and Historical Relativity of Sexual Conduct

The diagnosis of sexual addiction or compulsion rests on culturally induced perceptions of what constitutes sexual impulse control. Perceptions of control over erotic impulses, however, are social constructions. Definitions of "controlled" and "uncontrolled" sexuality are cultural inventions specific to particular societies at particular times. In any given society, sexual scripts provide the standards determining erotic control and normalcy. What one society regards as being sexually "out of control" or deviant, may or may not be viewed as such in another.

Sexual scripts (or erotic codes) are sets of norms, values, and sanctions that govern the erotic acts, statuses, and roles recognized by a social group (Gagnon & Simon, 1973; Laws & Schwartz, 1977, pp. 1–2).

These scripts articulate the prevailing cultural definitions of sexuality, including the purposes it serves, its manner of expression, and the normalcy or deviance of various sexual patterns (Simon & Gagnon, 1977).

Different cultures articulate different sexual scripts. These differences account for the extraordinary variation in definitions of erotic normalcy and deviance (Gregersen, 1983); the same activity is defined in different ways in different cultures. Among societies with "sex-positive" erotic codes, for example, a high level and a wide variety of erotic desire and activity are regarded as sexually normal (Gregersen, 1983). Among the sex-positive people of Mangaia, casual sex with different partners, and frequent intercourse with multiple orgasms (as many as three climaxes nightly), are perceived as sexually normal (Gagnon, 1977, pp. 10–11). In such sex-positive cultures, sexual scripts define restricted sexual contacts and low levels of erotic desire and activity as sexually abnormal.

Sexual scripts that evolve in "sex-negative" societies contain different standards for erotic normalcy or deviance. These societies regard extremely limited sexual contacts and low levels of sexual desire and activity as sexually normal. The sex-negative Irish (Inis Beag), for instance, consider abstinence and monogamy as normative and typically report low levels of sexual desire and low frequencies of sexual intercourse (Gregersen, p. 278). In such cultures, high levels of erotic desire and frequent and varied sexual activities are defined as sexually deviant, and as evidence of being "out of control" sexually.

In the United States, the nature of the prevailing sexual scripts determines whether or not a behavior is labeled as a psychosexual disorder or as sexually normal. Three competing erotic codes have emerged: the *procreative*, the *relational*, and the *recreational* (DeLamater, 1981). The procreative script, which conveys sex-negative (Judeo-Christian) norms and values, holds that sexual expression is dirty, sinful, and wrong except when it occurs in marriage and for reproductive purposes. Sexual pleasure is valued, but only in the context of marriage and in the service of procreative endeavors (Szasz, 1980). This script bans all nonmarital and nonprocreative forms of erotic expression. Casual sex and frequent sexual intercourse are defined as pathological conditions, that is, instances of being out of control sexually (see "Don Juanism" and "nymphomania" in the first edition of *The Diagnostic and Statistical Manual of Mental Disorders*, 1952).

Relational and recreational erotic codes are more sex-positive and place a higher value on erotic feelings and expression. The relational script regards sexual activity as a "means of expressing and reinforcing emotional and psychological intimacy." It prohibits sexual expression outside of committed relationships, which may or may not involve marriage (DeLamater, 1981, p. 266). Any act is appropriate in the relational context, provided that both partners mutually approve. The recreational script, which perceives mutual pleasure as the chief purpose of sexual activity, endorses sexual contacts between mutually interested partners, even if they are total strangers, and permits them to engage in any agreed-upon act that enhances sensual pleasure. Commitment is not a prerequisite to sexual intimacy.

These three scripts have different definitions of control over erotic conduct. The procreative code views any nonmarital or nonprocreative sexuality as indicating a lack of sexual control; the relational code regards nonrelational sex as indicating a lack of sexual control, whereas issues of control are irrelevant in recreational scripts, which define only nonconsensual sex as deviant.

The Context in which Addiction and Compulsion Emerged

The cultural dominance of the procreative, relational, and recreational codes has varied throughout modern American history. In the 1950s, the procreative code was hegemonic and was incorporated into basic institutions, including the family, law, education, religion, and medicine (Harris, 1981; Luker, 1984). Reflecting this institutionalization, mental health professionals viewed nonmarital and nonprocreative sex as pathological (Szasz, 1980). The first edition of *The Diagnostic and Statistical Manual of Mental Disorders (DSM: I,* 1952), for example, defined masturbation, fellatio, cunnilingus, homosexuality, and sexual promiscuity (e.g., "Don Juanism" and "nymphomania") as forms of mental illness. Other psychiatrists labeled prostitution and abortion similarly (Greenwald, 1958; Luker, 1984).

The rise of the counterculture and the sexual revolution of the 1960s and 1970s challenged the hegomony of the procreative ethic (Harris, 1981; Schur, 1976; Yankelovich, 1974). The libertarian ethos of the counterculture loosened normative constraints on sexuality and self-actualization, giving rise to the self-fulfillment ethic of the 1970s (Yankelovich, 1981). Many young, urban, college-educated, and middle-class Americans abandoned procreative scripts for relational or recreational scripts (Bell, 1976; Reich, 1970; Yankelovich, 1981), which changed the cultural meanings of erotic control and deviance.

As a result, the sociosexual landscape was altered fundamentally. An entire generation of men and women was exposed to sexual standards that legitimized erotic experimentation. Many Americans came to view nonmarital sex, mate swapping, one-night stands, homosexuality, and the use of pornography as viable sexual options (Edwards, 1986). Legalized abortion, advances in contraceptive technology, and the availability of potent antibiotics for the treatment of sexually transmitted disease weakened further the procreative code by eliminating or reducing the risk of unwanted pregnancy or sexually transmitted disease.

Against the backdrop of a (briefly) sex-positive culture, mental health professionals and sexologists re-evaluated professional definitions of erotic control and deviance. Influenced by the more sexually permissive relational and recreational scripts, they depathologized nonmarital and nonprocreative sex. The *DSM: III* (1980) no longer listed masturbation, fellatio, cunnilingus, homosexuality, Don Juanism, and nymphomania as psychosexual disorders.

Sexually permissive values, however, also provided grounds for adding new psychosexual disorders to the *DSM.* "Not enough" sex and "inappropriate" sexual response became pathologized. A number of problems of living were transformed into sexual dysfunctions (Szasz, 1980), and were regarded as clinical conditions amenable to therapeutic intervention. The terms "anorgasmia" (not having orgasms), "inhibited sexual desire" ("low" levels of sexual desire), "sexual aversion" (fear of sex), "ejaculatory incompetence" (ejaculating "too soon"), and "erectile insufficiency" (the inability to have or maintain an erection) were coined to describe the newly discovered sexual dysfunctions.

By the late 1970s, however, people began to abandon recreational scripts essentially for four reasons. The medical risks posed by genital herpes, hepatitis B, and later by AIDS, and the widespread stigmatization of those infected, were two reasons. The rise of the commitment ethic (Yankelovich, 1981, 1984) also weakened people's attachment to nonrelational patterns. Dissatisfied with the "me first-ism" implicit in the self-fulfillment ethic, many individuals adopted an ethic celebrating commitment, which placed a greater value on connectedness to other people, institutions, and occupational structures. In the sexual realm, the new ethic led people to value obligations, fidelity, and romance between (and within) the sexes.

Finally, the radical religious right also contributed to the demise of the recreational code. Embracing Judeo-Christian standards of morality, the various factions of this movement (the Moral Majority, Citizens for Decency, and "right-to-life" groups) vigorously attacked nonprocreative forms of sexuality and mounted campaigns against pornography, abortion, contraception, homosexuality, premarital intercourse, and sex education in the schools. The political and economic power of these right-wing religious groups has created a social climate that is increasingly hostile toward nontraditional forms of sexuality, fostering the idea that sexual expression apart from marriage is both dangerous and a threat to traditional family life. The genital herpes and AIDS epidemics provided further legitimacy to these claims.

Thus by the 1980s, "too much sex" rather than "not enough sex" began to emerge again as an issue of concern both to the lay public and to mental health professionals. In the permissive climate of the 1970s, it had been unthinkable to argue that there were people who were "addicted to sex" or "out of control sexually." Mattison (1985), for instance, stated that he first saw sexual compulsives in the 1970s but failed to diagnose them as such at the time. Carnes (1983) also writes that he first observed sex addicts in the 1970s, but did not publish his work because sexual addiction "was an idea whose time had not come" (p. i). When Levine (1986) questioned Carnes about this statement during an interview, Carnes replied that he "did not actively champion the idea during the 1970s because he feared negative reactions from his colleagues." In the increasingly sex-negative 1980s, however, the time had come for the ideas of sexual addiction and compulsion.

In the context of national concern about drug use and addiction, sexually transmitted disease, teenage pregnancy, and an ethic of commitment, "sex addicts" and "sexual compulsives" were mentioned increasingly in professional publications and in mass media (Carnes, 1983; Gershoni, 1985; Goleman, 1984; Mott, 1986; Quadland, 1983, 1985a, 1985b; Quadland & Shattls, 1987; Saline, 1985; Schwartz & Brasted, 1985). Nonrelational sexual conduct that had been legitimized in the 1970s was reclassified in the 1980s as a symptom of mental disorder (Levine, 1985). "If a behavior is demedicalized [i.e., purged of pathology] but not vindicated (absolved of immorality), it becomes *more* vulnerable to moral attack" (Conrad & Schneider, 1980, p. 211).

The Conceptual Flaws of Addiction and Compulsion

The constructionist or interactionist model of mental illness provides a framework for analyzing psychosexual disorders. According to constructionists, psychosexual disorders are social constructions: that is, stigmatizing labels attached to sexual patterns that diverge from culturally dominant sexual standards (Gallagher, 1987; Szasz, 1980). There is nothing intrinsically pathological in the behavior that falls into the category of psychosexual disorders; they are defined as pathological only because they violate prevailing erotic norms. Rather than referring to actual clinical entities, psychosexual disorders denote forms of stigmatized erotic conduct. In this sense they are value judgments cloaked as pseudoscientific diagnosis (Szasz, 1980). By inventing and treating these "conditions," that is, by "medicalizing" morality, mental health professionals and sexologists pathologize nonnormative sexual practices (Conrad & Schneider, 1980); they function as social control agents, enforcing conformity to culturally hegemonic erotic standards. The concepts of sexual addiction and sexual compulsion provide examples of the "medicalization" of sexual conduct.

As used currently, the terms "sexual addiction" and "sexual compulsion" are value laden and conceptually flawed. Both terms employ prevailing cultural standards as the basis for determining erotic control or deviance. Consequently, people who engage in frequent nonrelational sex and/or sex in inappropriate places are defined as "sex addicts" or "sexual compulsives."

Sexual Addiction

The concept of sexual addiction emerged first among members of an Alcoholics Anonymous (AA) chapter in metropolitan Boston (Augustine Fellowship, 1986; Goleman, 1984). A member of this group discovered this "condition" in the mid-1970s. Taking a cue from the philosophy and ideology of AA, he reconceptualized his frequent masturbation, impersonal sex, emotional dependency, and extramarital affairs as manifestations of a "new" disease that he called "sex and love addiction." As he saw it, his "obsessive, compulsive, uncontrollable" erotic impulses meant that he was addicted to sex and love. This addiction, in turn, compelled him to engage in nonrelational sexual activities. To "cure" himself of his "illness," he modified AA's "Twelve Steps of Recovery" program to focus on sex rather than on alcohol. He began to practice "sexual sobriety" by rejecting nonrelational sex for celibacy or relational sex. After convincing other AA members that they also suffered from this affliction, he formed the first chapter of Sex and Love Addicts Anonymous (Augustine Fellowship, 1986, chs. 1–2).

Professional recognition of sexual addiction appeared shortly afterward (Edwards, 1986; Goleman, 1984) in the work of Patrick Carnes (1983), an ex-prison psychologist. According to Carnes, sexual addiction is a "progressive form of insanity" (pp. 4–6). Sex addicts become increasingly out of touch with reality (insane) and more dangerous to themselves and others as their behavior escalates from "Level One" to "Level Three." The addiction process, which originates in low self-esteem, begins with Level One behaviors; these are tolerated widely or regarded merely as nuisances, and include multiple heterosexual relationships, use of pornography, strip show attendance, use of prostitutes, and homosexual activity (pp. 28–37). The addiction then progresses to Level Two—exhibitionism, voyeurism, obscene phone calls, and indecent liberties (pp. 37–45), and culminates in Level Three behaviors: rape, incest, and child molestation (pp. 45–51). Movement from one level to the next is fueled by the need for greater sexual thrills and excitement.

Criticisms of Sexual Addiction

The concept of sexual addiction may be criticized on a number of grounds. First, sex is not a form of addiction. Strictly speaking, addiction is "a state of physiological dependence on a specific substance arising from the habitual use of that substance" (Wedin, 1984a, p. 48). Sex is an experience, not a substance. Although sexual experiences, may be "mood altering," abrupt withdrawal from sexual behavior does not lead to forms of physiological distress such as diarrhea, delirium, convulsions, or death. Vomiting induced by fear of giving up a learned pattern for dealing with anxiety (such as having sex) is not the same thing as vomiting induced by physiological withdrawal from a physically addicting substance.

In addition, as conceptualized professionally (e.g., Carnes, 1983; Schwartz & Brasted, 1985), sexual addiction is currently the only type of "addiction" in which the addict is not expected to give up her or his "drug" of choice as part of the "treatment." As long as sex is "used" in appropriate contexts (such as marriage, a committed relationship), the addict has been "cured." Note that sexual expression is condoned when it occurs in social contexts that affirm the traditional sexual order, but medicalized as an "addiction" when it falls outside existing norms.

Third, Coleman (1986) notes that research fails to document convincingly the existence of sexual addiction as a clinical condition. Recent attempts to include a new category of psychosexual disorder— "hyperactive sexual desire disorder"—in the third edition of *The Diagnostic and Statistical Manual* (1980) met with failure because of disagreements over terminology. Thus sexual addiction literally does not exist.

Fourth, Carnes (1983) likens sexual addiction to "the 'athletes foot' of the mind" (p. vii), but the analogy between sexual addiction and athlete's foot is also misleading. Athlete's foot is a disease; sexual conduct is a behavior, whose meaning is mediated through cultural filters.

Fifth, to the extent that sex addicts actually exist and are in fact insane, one would expect psychological tests to reveal clear-cut differences between the mental states of sex addicts and those of nonaddicts. Quadland (1985a) compared the psychological profiles of "sexual compulsives" to those of matched controls seeking general psychotherapy and found only one significant difference between the two groups: noncompulsives were more likely than compulsives to experience positive feelings of love and relaxation in a sexual context. In later work, Quadland and Shattls (1987) argued that:

> The research reported here supports the hypothesis that persons who have difficulties with sexual control are no more neurotic than people who present themselves for psychotherapy for other conflictual life issues. This finding challenges the many anecdotal reports which attempt to associate a lack of sexual control with neuroticism or psychoticism. (P. 291)

Sixth, moralism is another problem associated with the sexual addiction concept. A major but unmentioned common denominator links all the behaviors on all three levels: they are divorced from—or not intended for—procreation. Moreover, from a traditional perspective, none of these patterns should occur (or be necessary) in a committed, monogamous, heterosexual relationship. Carnes's notion of levels of addiction is a classic instance of moral judgment parading as scientific fact.

Seventh, subjectivity is also an issue in the question of sexual addiction. The signs of sexual addiction—secrecy, abusiveness, painfulness, and emptiness (Carnes, 1983, p. 158)—are subjective, value laden assessments rendered from a moralistic perspective toward sexuality. Most couples, for example, keep their sex lives secret. They may make love to overcome feelings of loneliness or depression. One partner may agree to an act that he or she considers degrading because he or she perceives that it is immensely meaningful to the other person. Finally, they may feel empty afterward because the lovemaking did not dispel feelings of loneliness or depression. Thus, according to Carnes's model, the behavior of many conventional people would be labeled as sexually addictive.

Finally, the characteristics that trigger and fuel the addictive process—preoccupation, ritualization, compulsive sexual behavior, and despair (Carnes, 1983, p. 9)—are equally subjective and value laden. Each of these characteristics could just as well describe the intense passion of courtship or the sexual routines of conventional couples.

For example, partners who desire sex become engrossed with thoughts of sex with their loved one. Upon retiring they kiss, touch, and drift into "their own" personal ritual for sex, which intensifies the preoccupation and adds arousal and excitement. In time they engage in sexual intercourse, the goal of their preoccupation and ritualization. If one partner does not achieve orgasm, they experience "despair." They feel powerless to do anything about their occasional, unpredictable anorgasmia. Whereas a clinician or a counselor would probably recommend sex therapy, Carnes's model would characterize this pattern as a sign of sexual addiction.

Carnes undermines the validity of his own argument when he acknowledges that "the *intoxication* of young love is what the addict attempts to capture" (Carnes, 1983, p. 10). We need only examine the books in the "Sex and Marriage" section of any local bookstore to conclude that "sex addicts" are not the only people who enjoy "the pursuit, the hunt, the search, and the suspense heightened by the unusual" in the sexual realm (Carnes, 1983, p. 10).

The concept of sexual compulsion emerged first in the professional literature in the writings of Michael Quadland (1983), a sex therapist who works with self-identified sexually compulsive gay males. Quadland (1985a) defines sexual compulsion as a "lack of control over one's sexual behavior" (p. 122). The major symptom of sexual compulsion is the individual's (or therapist's) perception that he or she is "out of control" sexually.

However, when the concept of sexual compulsion is expanded to include perceptions of control, the problems of subjectivity and moralism are created in the same fashion as the concept of sexual addiction. Thus, the boundary between "being in control sexually" and "being out of control sexually" depends on the therapist's value orientation and purposes.

Consider the following example. A young man has been unsuccessful in his attempts to stop masturbating three times a week. He read that sex can be addictive, began to worry about his behavior, and sought therapy as a result. Is his behavior addictive? Is it compulsive? Or does it reflect the influence of conservative sexual beliefs about what constitutes typical sexual behavior? Depending on the perspective, the young man's behavior is all these things. Similarly, when Rowland (1986) asked Quadland what "being out of control sexually" meant, Quadland replied that it depended on the clinician's "value judgment about what is normal sexual behavior" (p. 45).

Regardless of how the concepts of sexual addiction or sexual compulsion are defined, they contain implicit comparisons to hegemonic erotic standards (Coleman, 1986; Wedin, 1984b, 1985). As applied presently, these concepts merely pathologize behaviors that diverge from the erotic standards held by the wider society (Levine, 1985).

Second, Quadland not only uses the term in a value laden fashion, but distorts the intended meaning of the compulsion concept. Barth and Kinder (1987, p. 21) argue that the use of the compulsion concept in the context of sexuality is "inconsistent with either of the *DSM-III's* (1980) two usages of the term 'compulsive'." The characteristics assigned to "sexual compulsives," for example, are not familiar to those of people labeled as having a "compulsive personality disorder" (e.g., perfectionism). According to the second use of the term, people classified as having an "obsessive-compulsive disorder" derive little or no pleasure from the compulsive pattern; it functions

> to produce or prevent some future event or situation. Since the [sexual] behavior is intended to be an escape from presently existing anxiety rather than from some future event, and since the behavior is intrinsically enjoyable, it should not be considered or labeled as a compulsion. (Barth & Kinder, 1987, p. 21)

Thus, strictly speaking, there is no such thing as sexual compulsivity.

Third, Quadland (1985a, 1985b; Quadland & Shattls, 1987) and others (Carnes, 1983; Coleman, 1986) regard anxiety as the primary cause of sexual compulsion: "Sexual activity functions to reduce anxiety often related to issues of loneliness, low self-esteem, poor interpersonal relationships and fears of intimacy" (Quadland, 1985a, p. 122). Yet when Quadland tested this hypothesis by asking self-defined sexual compulsives to indicate the nature of their feelings just before having sex, the results did not support the hypothesis. The sexual compulsives in his study did not experience significantly higher levels of frustration, anxiety, or loneliness before having sex than did the matched controls with whom they were compared. Nevertheless, Quadland continues to regard anxiety as the basis for sexual compulsion.

Incidentally, it is not surprising that Quadland's research failed to obtain significant differences between the affective states of so-called sexual compulsives and those of noncompulsives. There are a variety of ways to minimize negative feeling states by, for example, working, praying, parenting, or having sex. To label these learned responses as compulsions, however, is to render a moral judgment rather than a scientific description. The criteria used to distinguish occupational commitment from "workaholism," religious devoutness from religious fanaticism, and involvement with sex from sexual dependency are arbitrary and biased, perhaps announcing the investigator's subjective values rather than reflecting scientific objectivity.

Conclusion

Taking an interactionist approach to mental illness, we suggested that sexual compulsion and sexual addiction are therapeutic constructions (i.e., stigmatizing labels attached to behaviors that diverge from prevailing erotic standards). There is nothing intrinsically pathological in the conduct that is presently labeled as sexually compulsive or addictive; these behaviors have assumed pathological status only because powerful groups are beginning to define them as such. Rather than referring to actual clinical entities, the terms "sexual compulsion" or "sexual addiction" refer to learned patterns of behavior that are stigmatized, thereby suggesting that the concepts of sexual compulsion and sexual addiction are value judgments parading as therapeutic diagnoses (i.e., pseudoscientific euphemisms used to describe people who engage in nonnormative sex).

The twin concepts of sexual addiction and sexual compulsion emerged in response to shifts in the wider sociosexual landscape. The health threats associated with genital herpes, hepatitis B, and AIDS, national concern about drug use, addiction, and teenage pregnancy, a renewed interest in committed relationships, and the rise of politically powerful right-wing religious groups altered the societal values surrounding nonrelational sex. In response, some mental health professionals and members of sexual "self-help" groups came to regard people who engage in frequent sex, nonrelational sex, or sex in "inappropriate" settings as sex addicts or sexual compulsives.

On the other hand, we do not deny the existence of people who find it difficult to manage their sexuality within the normative boundaries mandated by the wider culture. We also acknowledge that some people learn to depend on sex as a means of coping with problematic issues. Finally, we do not deny the existence of ego-dystonic sexuality, the idea that people may be highly dissatisfied with the fashion in which they manage their sexuality. However, despite these acknowledgements, we maintain that "sexual addicts" and "sexual compulsives" do not possess clinical conditions that set them apart from nonaddicts and noncompulsives. They differ in external behavior rather than in internal make-up.

Sexual conduct is a learned behavior; it expresses a person's overall lifestyle. Thus the so-called sexual compulsives and addicts express and manage their sexuality in ways that violate prevailing societal expectations. Because these learned patterns of sexual conduct are an integral part of many people's lives, abandoning them and substituting new patterns is difficult. Yet all people experience problems of daily living—loneliness, guilt, shame, anxiety, and low self-esteem—at various times and places. In their discomfort they seek means of reducing these unpleasant feelings. They may learn to alleviate them through work, prayer, parenting, intimate friendships, or sex, behaviors that are valued to different degrees by the wider culture. People who have learned to depend on sexual release as a means of dealing with anxiety or loneliness might be described more accurately as "sex dependents."

The invention of sexual addiction and sexual compulsion as "diseases" threatens the civil liberties of sexually variant peoples. As we have seen, the definitions of sexual addiction and compulsion are highly subjective and value laden. Not surprisingly, such concepts can be (and have been) used to pathologize unconventional erotic activities. Consequently, mental health professionals must remain cautious about endorsing concepts which may serve as "billy clubs" for driving the erotically unconventional into the traditional sexual fold.

NOTE

This is a revised version of a paper presented at the annual meetings of the American Psychological Association, Washington, D.C., August 22–26, 1986.

REFERENCES

American Psychiatric Association. (1952). *The diagnostic and statistical manual of mental disorders.* Washington, DC: American Psychiatric Association.

American Psychiatric Association. (1980). *The diagnostic and statistical manual of mental disorders* (3rd ed.). Washington, DC: American Psychiatric Association.

Augustine Fellowship. (1986). *Sex and love addicts anonymous.* Boston: The Augustine Fellowship.

Barth, R. J., & Kinder, B. R. (1987). The mislabeling of sexual compulsion. *Journal of Sex and Marital Therapy, 13,* 15–23.

Becker, H. S. (1963). *Outsiders: Studies in the sociology of deviance.* New York: Free Press.

Bell, D. (1976). *The cultural contradictions of capitalism.* New York: Basic Books.

Carnes, P. (1983). *Out of the shadows: Understanding sexual addiction.* Minneapolis, MN: CompCare Publications.

Coleman, E. (1986). Sexual compulsion vs. sexual addiction: The debate continues. *SIECUS Report, 14,* 7–10.

Conrad, P., & Schneider, J. W. (1980). *Deviance and medicalization: From badness to sickness*. St. Louis, MO: C. V. Mosby.

Davis, N. J., & Anderson, B. (1983). *Social control: The production of deviance in the modern state*. New York: Irvington.

DeLamater, J. (1981). The social control of sexuality. *Annual Review of Sociology, 7,* 261–290.

Edwards, S. (1986). A sex addict speaks. *SIECUS Reports, 14,* 1–3.

Fletcher, C. R., Manning, P. K., & Smith, J. O. (1974). The labeling theory and mental illness. In P. M. Roman & H. M. Trice (Eds.), *Explorations in psychiatric sociology*. Philadelphia, PA: F. A. Davis.

Gagnon, J. H. (1977). *Human sexualities*. Glenview, IL: Scott, Foresman.

Gagnon, J. H., & Simon, W. (1973). *Sexual conduct: The social sources of human sexuality*. Chicago: Aldine.

Gallagher, B. J. (1987). *The sociology of mental illness*. Englewood Cliffs, NJ: Prentice-Hall.

Gershoni, Y. (1985, February 11–24). Overcoming sexual compulsion. *New York Native*, pp. 24, 28–29.

Goleman, D. (1984, October 16). Some sexual behavior viewed as an addiction. *New York Times*, pp. C1, C9.

Gove, W. (1970). Societal reaction as an explanation of mental illness. *American Sociological Review, 35,* 873–884.

Gregersen, E. (1983). *Sexual practices: The story of human sexuality*. New York: Franklin Watts.

Greenwald, H. (1958). *The call girl: A social and psychoanalytic study*. New York: Ballantine.

Harris, M. (1981). *America now: The anthropology of a changing culture*. New York: Simon & Schuster.

Laing, R. D. (1967). *The politics of experience*. New York: Ballantine.

Laws, J. L., & Schwartz, P. (1977). *Sexual scripts; The social construction of female sexuality*. Hinsdale, IL: Dryden Press.

Levine, J. L., & Schwartz, P. (1977). *Sexual scripts: The social construction of female sexuality*. Hinsdale, IL: Dryden Press.

Levine, M. P. (1985). Sexual compulsion: A critical appraisal. Paper presented at the Annual Meetings of the Eastern Region of the Society for the Scientific Study of Sex, Philadelphia, PA.

Levine, M. P. (1986, April 14). *An interview with Patrick Carnes*. Golden Valley, MN: Unpublished manuscript.

Lofland, J. (1969). *Deviance and identity*. Englewood Cliffs, NJ: Prentice-Hall.

Luker, K. (1984). *Abortion and the politics of motherhood*. Berkeley, CA: University of California Press.

Mattison, A. M. (1985). *Group treatment of sexually compulsive gay and bisexual men*. Paper presented at the Annual Meetings of the Eastern Region of the Society for the Scientific Study of Sex, Philadelphia, PA.

Mechanic, D. (1969). *Mental health and social policy.* Englewood Cliffs, NJ: Prentice-Hall.

Mott, P. (1986, June 20). Giving hope to sufferers of sexual addiction. *Los Angeles Times*, pp. 1, 23–24.

Mumford, E. (1983). *Medical sociology.* New York: Random House.

Quadland, M. C. (1983, November 7–20). Overcoming sexual compulsion. *New York Native*, pp. 25–26.

Quadland, M. C. (1985a). Compulsive sexual behavior: Definition of a problem and an approach to treatment *Journal of Sex and Marital Therapy, 11*, 121–132.

Quadland, M. C. (1985b, February 11–24). Compulsive sexuality and sexual freedom. *New York Native*, p. 26.

Quadland, M. C., & Shattls, W. D. (1987). AIDS, sexuality, and sexual control. *Journal of Homosexuality, 14*, 277–298.

Reich, C. A. (1970). *The greening of America.* New York: Random House.

Rowland, C. (1986c, January 21). Reinventing the sex maniac. *The Advocate*, pp. 43–49.

Saline, C. (1985, February). Indecent obsession. *Philadelphia, Gay News*, pp. 100–110.

Scheff, T. J. (1984). *Being mentally ill: A sociological theory* (2nd ed.). New York: Aldine.

Schur, E. (1976). *The American awareness trap: Self-absorption instead of social change.* New York: McGraw-Hill.

Schur, E. (1979). *Interpreting deviance: A sociological introduction.* New York: Harper & Row.

Schwartz, M. F., & Brasted, W. S. (1985). Sexual addiction. *Medical Aspects of Human Sexuality, 19*, 103–107.

Simon, W., & Gagnon, J. H. (1977). Sexual scripts. *Society, 22*, 53–60.

Szasz, T. (1970). *Ideology and insanity: Essays on the psychiatric dehumanization of man.* Garden City, NY: Anchor Books.

Szasz, T. (1980). *Sex by prescription.* New York: Penguin Books.

Wedin, R. W. (1984a). The sexual compulsion movement. *Christopher Street, 8*, 48–53.

Wedin, R. W. (1984b, April 9–22). The need for anonymous sex: A critique of the AA Approach. *New York Native*, pp. 3–6.

Wedin, R. W. (1985, April 22–May 5). Another way around. *New York Native*, pp. 22–23, 48.

Yankelovich, D. (1974). *The new morality: A profile of American youth.* New York: McGraw-Hill.

Yankelovich, D. (1981). *New rules: Searching for self-fulfillment in a world turned upside down.* New York: Random House.

Yankelovich, D. (1984). American values: Change and stability. *Public Opinion, 6,* 2–9.

Chapter Ten

The Motives of Gay Men for Taking or Not Taking the HIV Antibody Test

Karolynn Siegel, Martin Levine, Charles Brooks, and Rochelle Kern [1989]

The present paper explores the motives given by gay men for taking or not taking the HIV (Human Immunodeficiency Virus) antibody test. Following Mills (1940), we conceptualize these motives as reasons, explanations, or justifications for taking or not taking the test. Moreover, we also conceptualize HIV antibody testing as problematic behavior, mainly because of the momentous psychological and social risks and benefits associated with testing. As one noted chronicler of the AIDS (Acquired Immune Deficiency Syndrome) epidemic put it,

> To test or not to test clearly would become the most important personal decision most gay men would make in their adult lives. To be tested meant learning that you might at any time fall victim to a deadly disease; it was a psychological burden few . . . could imagine. However, not to be tested meant you might be carrying a lethal virus, which you could give to others (Shilts 1987, 540).

Other risks include stigmatization, discrimination, and disrupted social relationships (Miller 1987). Among the benefits connected with testing are the opportunity to learn of one's seropositive status and obtain available treatments, a reduction in the anxiety of individuals who test seronegative, the opportunity to plan more effectively for the future, and support for a differential diagnosis when HIV infection is suspected (Goldblum and Seymour 1987).

To date, not much is known about gay men's motives for taking or not taking the test (Coates et al. 1988). The little data available indicate that gay men's motives frequently refer to perceived consequences of learning test results or taking the test. For example, Lyter et al. (1987) used fixed choice mail questionnaires to investigate the reasons why participants in the Pitt Men's Study (the Pittsburgh component of the Multicenter AIDS Cohort Study) did or did not ask to be informed about their antibody test results. These men had their blood tested as part of the research protocol. Out of a total of 2,047 gay and bisexual men, 61 percent chose to learn their results. The chief reasons offered for learning test results were curiosity about possible infection with HIV and the belief that knowledge about antibody status would help them cope with fears of AIDS and reduce high-risk sexual practices. Conversely, the primary reasons for not learning test results were concerns that positive results would be psychologically harmful (in the sense that it would increase anxiety, depression, and worry), and the belief that the test does not predict the development of AIDS.

Another study directly tapped motives for not being tested among a community sample (N = 213) of gay and bisexual men living in the San Francisco area (Research and Decisions Corporation 1986). About three-quarters (73%) of the respondents were untested. The major reasons reported for not taking the test included concerns about emotional reactions to the test, uncertainties regarding the utility and meaning of the test, and fears about the confidentiality of the test.

This paper expands our understanding of the motives of gay men for taking or not taking the antibody test. In what follows, we discuss the research methods used to collect our data on gay men's motives, report the motives cited by our respondents, and close with a discussion of how the major cultural definitions of the HIV test are reflected in the respondents' reports.

Method

The data presented below come from an ongoing qualitative study of sexual decision making among gay men in the context of the AIDS epidemic. The study was undertaken in response to a recognition that, although self-identified gay men have participated in a number of survey studies concerning the extent to which the AIDS epidemic caused changes in their sexual lives and emotional well-being, there

was a notable lack of research on the meaning of AIDS as it is phenom-
enologically and pragmatically experienced by the men themselves.
The research was designed to address this gap in understanding by
using a primarily qualitative methodology that includes participant
observation, the use of a brief self-administered questionnaire, and
relatively unstructured but focused group and in-depth individual
interviews.

Respondents for the study were recruited through fliers distributed
and posted at a variety of gay service, political, and social organizations (including the large Gay and Lesbian Community Center which
serves the organized gay community in New York). In addition, recruiting announcements were run as advertisements in gay newspapers, as public service announcements on gay cable television, announced at various gay organizational meetings, published in a range
of gay newsletters, and distributed through a constantly growing
recruitment network.

To participate, respondents had to be between 18 and 65 years of
age, live in the greater New York metropolitan area, have not used
intravenous drugs in the past six months, and have not been diagnosed with AIDS. Seventeen men participated in initial group interviews. A total of 150 gay men eventually participated in two, two-hour
individual interviews. All interviews were conducted as relatively
unstructured open-ended discussions led by the project's interviewer.
Interview sessions began with a nine-minute videotape produced
by the study team as a projective stimulus for discussion. The video
contained five vignettes in which actors portray gay men articulating
their diverse views about safer sex and AIDS. The vignettes included
men who have adopted safer sex practices and express differing feelings about their choice as well as men who justify continuing to
engage in risky sex. By presenting varying views about safer sex,
the video was designed to give respondents permission to express
themselves candidly (e.g., to acknowledge disagreement with safer
sex recommendations or involvement in unsafe sexual practices). Interviews were audiotaped and transcribed verbatim.

The material presented here was derived from individual unstructured focused interviews (Merton et al. 1956) with a total of 120 men.
Of these, 41 percent were untested, 22 percent were seropositive,
and 37 percent were seronegative. One hundred and eleven of the
respondents were white, four were Hispanic, three were black, and

one was Asian. The mean age of the sample was 34.6 years and the median age was 33 years (range = 18 to 63 years of age). Eighty percent of the sample was between ages of 18 and 40 years. Respondents were well educated: 69 percent had at least a college education; about 26 percent had completed some college; and the remaining 5 percent were high school graduates. Approximately 22 percent of the respondents earned less than $20,000; 29 percent earned between $20,000 and $29,000; 19 percent earned between $30,000 and $39,999; and 30 percent earned more than $40,000. All interviews were conducted between May 1988 and May 1989.

The data reported below were either spontaneously volunteered by respondents or offered in reply to a general query by the interviewer asking them to discuss what led to their decision to be tested or not. Because the interviews were unstructured there were no standardized probes as a follow-up to their responses. That is, the interviewer did not systematically probe about the possible importance of factors other than those reported by the respondent. In this way, we believe that we captured the respondent's subjective perceptions and definition of the situation and insight into what factors were personally most salient to him in arriving at his decision. For the purposes of exposition the reasons offered by men for their decisions are segregated. In reality, however, men frequently expressed more than one reason for their decision, and one reason would seem to potentiate another. All of the motives reported below for undergoing testing were cited by men who were actually tested. Similarly, all of the motives presented for not being tested were offered by untested respondents.

In presenting the findings we have pooled tested men regardless of their test results. Because the decision to be tested obviously temporally precedes knowledge of one's antibody status, the latter should not be causally implicated in explaining decisions about whether or not to be tested. Still, it must be recognized that, as reports regarding why one was tested are in fact retrospective accounts, it is possible that a respondent's test result influenced his reconstruction of his earlier decision to take the test. In describing the experiences of respondents who have been tested, their antibody status will be noted.

Motives for Taking the Test

The men who said they had taken the test told us they did so primarily because of the medical and health consequences they believed might follow from knowing their serostatus (whether positive, meaning that the HIV is present, or negative). In addition, they sought to know their test status in order to make more informed decisions about their sexual and social lifestyles. We have grouped their comments into five categories of motives: (1) to enable medical treatments for HIV infection, (2) to become motivated to make needed health and lifestyle changes, (3) to clarify an ambiguous medical condition, (4) to inform sexual decision making, and (5) to relieve the psychological distress associated with not knowing HIV status.

To Enable Medical Treatments for HIV Infection

Most men who underwent testing reported being previously opposed to taking the test. At first, they believed that nothing could be done to help HIV infected individuals or prevent the disease from running its inexorable course. In addition, they believed that learning that one was seropositive carried grave psychological dangers. In this sense, "ignorance was bliss" under conditions of helplessness. Some further rationalized not being tested on the grounds that they practiced only safer sex, and therefore did not place any partners at risk. They viewed their decision not to be tested as socially acceptable rather than as selfish, self-protective, or irresponsible because they did not engage in practices that could potentially infect partners.

However, the perceptions of these men changed over time. Many came to believe that there were effective medical therapies for HIV diseases. These included prophylactic treatments (e.g., aerosol pentamidine) for some of the more common opportunistic infections and antiviral drugs (e.g., Azidothymidineor AZT) that slow the replication of HIV. Accordingly, they recognized that these treatments provided a means of exerting some control or influence over their future health and said or implied that this recognition motivated them to take the test. One 32-year-old seropositive man said,

> Up until a few weeks before I took the test, which is in December, I had
> a couple of the opinions that I heard on your videotape. And that was,

"No one really knows what they're talking about", and "There's nothing that can be done anyway." And I didn't hear this on the tape, but you know it's in line with that—ah, my feeling that the HIV test is just a blood marker and not an indication of whether or not one will get AIDS. I was thoroughly ignorant until December. And then I came upon information that was not consistent with what I had thought up until then. Someone told me that the HIV test is not just a marker any more. That is old information. Now there are prophylaxis measures that one can take if one tests positive, and you can keep, you can possibly keep your T-4 cells from dropping. So I ... got as much information as I could. And I found out that untreated HIV, the current wisdom is that untreated HIV will progress to AIDS in like 76 percent of the cases over six and a half to seven years time. And there's no other information ... right now. That is the current wisdom, and things can be done. Things can be done to possibly halt the degeneration of one's immune system.

Another, 26-year-old, who was tested but had not yet received the results, said,

Until recently, for myself, I thought that ... testing positive would just scare me. And that I was behaving, or trying to behave, you know, in my sex life, just as if I was positive and not putting other people at risk. And that I didn't see, I didn't see what I would gain from learning I was positive. Just seemed like there wasn't much I could do. You know unless I wanted to, you know, like go on a macrobiotic diet; or, you know, start swimming every day; or, you know, just do general things which make me healthier—which, you know, if I had the will to do, I would do anyway. Ah, but just recently, it just seems like there's a lot more people can do. I mean whether it's, you know, taking low dose AZT when it's in a symptomatic stage, or whether it's getting your T-cells monitored and doing aerosol pentamidine. Ah, you know, as well as nutritional and general health maintenance things. It just seems like there's enough, enough that people can do that it seemed like a rational decision.

A seropositive man, 41 years old, told us that:

Up until recently, I didn't feel that there was any prophylactic treatment. And now I'm encouraging people to go get their diagnosis because I think now with aerosol pentamidine, and we're doing experiments with AZT being given to people with ARC. And there are a couple of new drugs on the market that are AZT analogues with less side effects that I think more and more is gonna become, it's becoming advantageous to be diagnosed earlier. But until recently, I don't think this was true.

Some men also recognized that early implementation of these treatments could prolong health and life. They felt that those who did not take prophylactic actions were likely to be diagnosed when it was "too late," at an advanced stage of the disease, with a poorer treatment outlook and consequently shorter survival time. One man, 40 and seropositive, said,

> I feel that I'm better taken care of by my doctor. And the old saw, the old line used to be, "What difference does it matter if the doctor knows because there's nothing they can do." Well, now there are things they can do. Granted, not in terms of giving you ten years, but there are things they can do in giving you one and half years versus two years and a certain amount of quality time. Ah, someone who doesn't know whether he's HIV positive or not might very well go right up to getting a full-blown case of AIDS, without any prophylactic medication whatsoever. And I think that's regrettable because then it is indeed much harder to treat the person.

And a 34-year-old seropositive respondent said,

> I think gay men need to hear in a clear, concise, and convincing way that if their HIV status is known it could benefit them. It could in fact make the difference in years, added to or taken off of their life. 'Cause I believe that's the case. Ah, not knowing your HIV status, I think is very dangerous—psychologically as well as physically. I think it's a bad medical decision to have, if you're a homosexual and you've been sexually active over the past ten years, or maybe fifteen, you should have your status determined. . . . It's gonna, there are gonna be two situations. There will be those who, like myself, have sought help before they needed it. 'Cause I think in this it, when it's too late, it's too late. You wait too long and that's it. Ah, whereas those like myself who seek out the help, have their bloodwork done, and work with their health care professionals, and also work with their, work on their head too, you know, psychologically keep themselves healthy in every way, that they can influence—I think we can do quite well. Maybe I'll live to be 60 years old. You never can tell. But I think those on the other scenario, the other extreme, they're gonna die very quickly.

The diagnosis and subsequent rapid death of friends and acquaintances reinforced some men's perceptions of the medical benefits of early intervention. A few men previously felt they could adopt a "wait and see" stance, delaying the decision to take the test and/or the decision to take recommended medical treatments until the appearance of HIV-related symptoms. The experience of seeing untested and seemingly healthy gay men suddenly become very sick and diagnosed with AIDS altered this stance and motivated them to be tested. Knowledge of their serostatus would allow them to take appropriate medical treatments. For example, a 51-year-old seropositive man told us:

> I feel it's better to take it. If you know the results you can explore ways you can deal and cope with it. And there are support groups and so there someone can go for help. And then rather than not know about it, because there have been cases of friends of mine who did not take the test and suddenly were diagnosed and died instantly in about a few months. Whereas those who have taken the test a long time ago and have been practicing safe sex and using preventive measures, as well as vitamins, and a non—, ah, antitoxic drugs have been able to survive and are doing very well.

A man, 26, recently tested but who had not gotten the results, said,

> So I've been thinking for the past few months that I wanted to do it [get tested] and I was just a little nervous about actually doing it. Ah, but then, someone who I knew a little bit, a friend of a friend, just about three or four weeks ago, after I mean having no indication that he was HIV positive or had any health problem, you know. He had a cold which became a cough and it persisted. And it turned out he had pneumocystis pneumonia. And so, you know, he was diagnosed as having AIDS, just like that. And he is certainly someone with, you know, access to medical information and medical care. And, you know, like he could have been doing pentamidine, you know, if there was any reason for him to. Ah, and that sort of like jolted me into realizing that, you know, I really ought to do it.

Nearly all the men citing the possibility of medical treatments as the motive for undergoing testing, described their decision as one they made for themselves. Nevertheless, several reported that their personal physicians played an important role in influencing them. These men were obviously impressed that their doctors, who had previously shared their opposition to testing, had altered their stance in light of recent scientific data and clinical experience indicating the potential efficacy of available treatment options. One 29-year-old seronegative man commented:

> When I saw him [my doctor] a year and a half ago he did not recommend taking the test. He recommended *not* taking the test. And then,

then six months ago, it's really more like more like eight months ago. . . . I knew my former lover had ARC, so was positive—HIV positive. And I went to the doctor just for a general check up and told him this. He said at this point he was very insistent that his patients, people who think that there might be the possibility or just for—you know, he recommends the test because he now feels with AZT if you're symptomatic, but not diagnosed, there may be time to start treatment if necessary. . . . And he explained, he took out charts and he took, you know, he had articles about it and we talked about it. He was just, you know, he was very levelheaded about what he was saying to me.

Another seronegative man, 34, said,

Yeah, it was actually a hard decision. And I, I thought about it for probably two or three years before I did it. Ah, I have a doctor who is gay, who treats a lot of people with AIDS. And he, a lot of my decision was based on his recommendations. Ah, there was obviously a natural curiosity all through the years. Ah, I think that only after I was convinced primarily through his telling me so, that there would be good, there could be good to come from having taken the test and finding out that you were positive, in terms of there being certain medical things that could be done. . . . Previous to that he was a strong proponent of *not* taking the test because medically there was nothing that could be done.

To Become Motivated to Make Needed Health and Lifestyle Changes

Some men said they took the test to become motivated to make desired health and lifestyle changes. Although aware of the desirability of safer sex, sound nutrition, reduced alcohol and drug consumption, they said they were insufficiently motivated to initiate and maintain these behaviors in the absence of knowing they were positive. They felt that a positive result would represent a concrete and certain threat to their health and to their partners, which would motivate them to make appropriate behavioral changes. For example, a 31-year-old seropositive man said, "I also knew that I was really not taking proper care of myself—physically, safe sex speaking, and just everything [like] nutrition . . . and somehow I thought that it might give me just the jolt I needed." And a 28-year-old seronegative respondent said,

I defended my own reluctance to take the test by saying, much like one of the guys in here [on the videotape], "If I have it, I don't want to know. And if I don't have it it's not gonna change anything about me anyway because I can't, ah, there's no cure. There's nothing to do." You know, I'm a sitting duck. And then some friends of mine . . . had taken the test and their doctors began to—they tested positive—and then the next step was to be, to have the T-4 cells counted and all this other stuff. And it became clear to me that, if in fact I was positive, there were things I could do to protect myself. I could give up the alcohol I was drinking. I could give up the marijuana I was smoking. I could worry more about my diet. I could, ah, be more honest with myself and my future. Ah, whatever future I would have. Ah, it became . . . really a question of honesty and courage. And, and protecting myself to the extent that I could."

Another man, 51 and seropositive, believed a positive result would stimulate him to adopt holistic health practices:

I'd given it thought and I wanted to know whether I had the virus and that if I did, what I was going to do to help myself. And what preventative measures that it's gonna take to protect my life. And this is exactly what I did. I'm exercising. I wake up at five to do some meditation for half an hour. I do the Hatha Yoga exercises. I eat macrobiotic food cause I feel that's helped people in the past. [I take] minerals that inhibit the virus from manifesting itself, and I do megadoses of vitamin C like 10,000 grams per day.

To Clarify an Ambiguous Medical Condition

In some cases, the appearance of possible HIV-related symptoms motivated respondents to be tested. Where the prevalence of HIV infection is assumed to be high, as in New York City, physicians caring for gay men often consider this as a possible cause of an ambiguous medical condition, since the symptoms of HIV infection are often similar to those of other illnesses. Therefore, to arrive at a definitive diagnosis of a patient's condition, physicians treating gay men may recommend antibody testing. This was commonly reported by our respondents. Nevertheless, in a few instances respondents took the initiative and proposed to their physicians that they be tested. A 26-year-old seropositive respondent said he took the test "because I got really sick with a kidney infection. And it did not clear up with the antibiotics right way. And I knew I was gay. I knew that my sexual activity would definitely put me in that risk group." Another man, 27, and also seropositive, said,

> I had been seeing a physician for an unrelated problem [anal warts] that he was treating. And as he treated it, the recurrence he said was possibly indicative that I was HIV positive. . . . He said the recurrence of the warts possibly had to do with being HIV positive. I didn't believe him. I wanted to [take the test], I wanted to find out and prove to him and myself that I was negative.

A man, seronegative and 44, said, in response to the question of why he decided to take the test,

> Oh 'cause I think when I had I had this little basal cell carcinoma . . . I got very paranoid about it 'cause when it first showed up, it's this little red rash. Right on my clavicle. I was in St. Thomas when it happened. And I thought, "Oh well" and I ah—"Who knows what it is?" And then two weeks later it opened, you know, it bled, it ulcerated, it didn't close. And I thought, "Well, cancer." I knew enough about KS [Kaposi's sarcoma] to know that these lesions don't ulcerate that way. But it still, you know, the unconscious grip is much stronger than the rational one.

And a 36-year-old man who said he was seropositive commented:

> I found out I had a form of muscular dystrophy, so I went to the doctor; went to the hospital for ten days to find out exactly what it was, 'cause I, at the same time, I had bruises and everything. I thought it might have been AIDS. Ah, I found out I was just anemic. I had low platelets, and muscular dystrophy and everything. About six months later he [my doctor] decided to, "Let's try it [the HIV antibody test], if you want. Let's try to take the test 'cause I want to know if this is gonna, if this is related or not."

To Inform Sexual Decision Making

Some men explained that they had taken the test so that they could make more informed and responsible decisions about their sexual behavior. There were two subgroups among these respondents. The first consisted of those who felt a negative result would allow them to expand their sexual activities, such as one 27-year-old seronegative man:

Well I did it [took the test] because I was in a relationship. The one that I'm in now. It's been going on for eleven months. And I just, I tested negative twice. And he tested negative twice. But he had just recently been tested negative. And I just, we were having, we were pretty much having safe sex. I mean we blew it a couple of times. And so we were trying to decide if we wanted to have unsafe sex. And we knew we wanted to be mutually exclusive. And so I just wanted to do it one more time to make sure.

Another 34-year-old seropositive man, citing similar motives, commented:

I was sure I was negative. . . . In [the] autumn of 1986, I had a boyfriend and this guy was very hypochondriac. He had the test at least twice and he was negative. But he set very strict sex rules for us. And I thought that one of the reasons of our problems was that he couldn't have a relaxed sexual life because of that. Turned out that I was wrong. But, I couldn't know that. I thought, well, if I take the test, too, and I, of course, I'll be negative, then we'll be both negative. We'll make a pact of mutual total fidelity, sexual fidelity. And so we will be able not to have, not to follow safer sex guidelines anymore.

And a seronegative man, 26, said, "I think it [a negative test result] allowed me to perceive myself as being at less a risk, and to have fewer qualms about having unprotected oral sex."

The second subgroup was motivated to be tested because they wanted to know if their sexual activities presented any risk of infecting their partners. They believed that if they tested negative, they posed no risk to others, regardless of their behavior. One 27-year-old seronegative man said he took the test "for a variety of reasons. First off, I really thought I was going to be negative. But I also didn't want to pass it on to anybody else. I mean I was having—I, I didn't want to pass it on to anyone else."

Another man, 25 and who had tested negative, told us:

Well, what basically led up to it [getting tested] was in September I met my lover. And I felt something I had never really felt for anybody else before. And he told me I guess about a month into our relationship that he has been tested negative three times, because there was someone he had been with that told him afterwards that he had it. So he was quite upset from that. So he went and told me, you know, he took it three times. And he was negative all three times. And I just felt that this was something that was very important to me. And this was something that I really cared a great deal about. And I didn't want to be in the dark about it and risk something happening at some point. Ah, so I decided, you know for myself, but also for him that I wanted to try it out [be tested].

Another respondent, also negative and 24, spoke of the "responsibility" he felt to others:

But anyway, the reason I got tested was mainly because I wanted to know. It's a big responsibility. Ah, this is my counter to the argument of "I don't want to get tested." Because you have a responsibility to the person you are going to sleep with. You have a responsibility to make sure they are healthy when they leave you. And that's something that I take very seriously. I mean in terms of whether or not you want to know for yourself, doesn't hold up if you are going to endanger the life of somebody else. And that's basically my argument. So I really wanted to know for that.

To Relieve Psychological Distress Associated with Not Knowing HIV Status

Virtually all respondents recognized that they may have been infected through past sexual behaviors. Even those who had consistently practiced safer sex during the last several years and expected they were negative realized that they could have acquired the virus through their earlier behavior. Furthermore, even those who had remained asymptomatic for several years after stopping unsafe behavior worried about infection because they knew that the disease had a long incubation.

The ambiguity of their status left them psychologically vulnerable to persistent fears and suspicions that any symptom might be HIV related. To relieve this psychological distress, some respondents were motivated to take the antibody test. A 30-year-old man who had taken the test, with negative results, about a year earlier said.

I knew about the test I guess since it's been out. What was happening up until that point, you know, every time I'd be sick, I would think "Is this AIDS?" . . . [And] for a long time I was able to live with that fear. What I realized was that, you know, the stress of every disease that was coming up, every common cold—anything—the stress that I would put myself through by not knowing if I was exposed to the virus was just outweighing me getting a positive result back. You know it came to that point where I finally realized that if I got a positive result back it'd probably be less stressful than not knowing. So I went and took the test at that point."

For many men, learning that past partners or close friends tested positive or were diagnosed with AIDS heightened their own sense of vulnerability and finally raised their anxiety to an intolerable level. These men experienced a kind of "closing circle" effect as the illnesses of past partners and friends personalized the threat of the disease, making it harder to deny the immediacy of the peril to own health. A 63-year-old man who said he was seronegative described these feelings:

I was worried, I was very worried. . . . Ah, several partners, previous partners, got AIDS and died with AIDS which scared the hell out of me. . . . And each time I heard that someone got AIDS and subsequently died of AIDS, I used to say, "There but for the grace of God go I." Ah, then ah, anytime I'd see something on my skin or something unusual in my physical make-up, I'd get frightened. Uh oh, here's a symptom coming up. Ah, it was two years ago, I was on the beach in the, down in Florida in the wintertime. And I saw three spots on my calf I had never seen before. Holy shit! KS [Kaposi's sarcoma]. Ah, and I was living with those fears, and I just didn't like it. I felt if I was positive, I could cope with it, but I just wanted to know. Ah, I wanted to push paranoia aside or whatever.

A 28-year-old man with a seronegative test result said,

I had three good friends who died of AIDS. And it was all over the papers and all over everything. And I, in my mind I kept saying to myself, "Well, gee that it could be that chance that I have it." And it was just getting to me. And it was getting the best of me. And I don't usually let anything get the best of me, but it, it kind of was. And I said, "Well, fuck it. Let me go for my [test], just to see. And I did.

One 31-year-old respondent initially had chosen not to be tested, justifying his decision by saying that he felt that knowing he was positive would be like walking around with a "time bomb" inside of him. However, eventually he decided to be tested (obtaining a positive result) because he felt not knowing his status was equally psychologically distressing:

Then what happened was I, I think I started walking around with that anxiety and that time bomb feeling even without taking it [the test]. . . . AIDS was something I was always able to keep at a comfortable distance. You know even though I volunteered at GMHC [Gay Men's Health Crisis, a community-based AIDS service organization], I could still go home and forget about it. Ah, most of the people that I—all of the people that I knew that had become sick were acquaintances, not close friends. And over the past year and a half, it started to hit closer to home. Closer friends, just people in my social circle. And, ah, so I suppose I started feeling the time bomb syndrome anyway, and then really wanted, you know, the anxiety level was high and I wanted some affirmation either way.

Motives for Not Taking the Test

Respondents who had not taken the test spoke of the anticipated negative psychosocial consequences that a seropositive result might have. We organized these responses into four categories: (1) the desire to avoid the adverse psychological impact of a positive test result, (2) the desire to avoid social discrimination and repressive governmental actions, (3) the desire to avoid an ambiguous or unreliable test result, and, (4) the wish to avoid having to make undesired lifestyle changes.

To Avoid the Adverse Psychological Impact
of a Positive Test Result

Respondents most frequently cited the wish to avoid negative psychological consequences as their reason for not taking the test. The men feared a devastating emotional impact if they learned that they were infected and expected they would become severely depressed and even potentially suicidal if confronted with that knowledge. Some said they would feel that their lives would "be over," "destroyed" by such an awareness. These fears were usually based on the belief that most, if not all, infected individuals would eventually develop AIDS and die and that available medical treatments could not prevent that eventuality. A 39-year-old said,

As far as the test is concerned, I just feel for myself, I am not, I haven't taken it and I don't intend to. I sort of agree too, very much, that if you test positive, it seems now that just about everybody who tests positive is gonna get it, you know. And that if you know that, first of all your life, your life is destroyed; even if not physically, just as much destroyed."

And a man, 26, spoke of how knowing that he was positive would "destroy" him:

> I would never get tested. I mean it. It would take a lot for someone to convince me to be tested. Ah, if I found out that I was positive, it would destroy me. Whether you could tell me I was gonna live for seventy or five hundred years. I think I would start, I would really feel, start to think really negatively. As it is, I think I probably have the HIV virus. But I don't know. So it's almost like it's better for me living for me that way. I mean I go back and forth. It would be great to find out it was negative. But if I found out it was positive, it would be devastating. And that's too great a risk for me to take. Basically, it's—I feel that if I found out I was positive on a piece of paper, my life would be over. I would, I would think every day, "Well, I just wonder when it's gonna happen." Not *if* it's gonna happen. When. I'd wonder if it will happen, you know, like a year from now, or two years. I mean it would totally wreak havoc.

Another, about the same age, said,

> Ah, I know myself well enough to know that I'm not the sort of person who would respond well to that kind of information. So, ah I would rather not know. I don't take it because I conjecture that I would be really debilitated by it. I wouldn't be able to function well, knowing that I would worry. I would live a life of default. Ah, but at the same time, it's hard not to know. I mean if I were in the circumstance and at that point were faced with no option, but to cope with it or kill myself, I don't know. I don't know which I would do.

Other men saw the immediate psychological impact as less acute and devastating, but felt knowing they were positive would become a chronic stressor which would significantly compromise the quality of their lives. They felt they would become morbidly preoccupied with their health and possible death if they knew they were infected. They expected they would be continually anxious about the specter of the appearance of the first HIV-related symptoms and be alarmed by even innocuous symptoms and ailments. Most described themselves as already riddled with anxiety about their antibody status and future health. They believed that the certain knowledge that they were infected would only serve to heighten their worries and fears.

One 38-year-old respondent, who described himself as already in a panic because a former live-in lover had died of AIDS, said if he found out he was positive he would "be even more frightened. I'd think of when would it come. . . . What I would do. . . . It's a death sentence." Another man of the same age said he thought about being tested "every single day. . . . Will finding out I'm positive or not change what I do? No. Will it make me worry more? Yes. . . . And I don't need to worry more." And a 19-year-old respondent also said he preferred not to know:

> But I wouldn't take the test because if, God forbid, the results were positive, I, I couldn't take that. I'd feel like I'm a time bomb and I'm going to explode soon. I just wouldn't want to know. If I have it, I have it. Ah, and I don't—now I haven't been doing any sexual practices that would, you know, harm anyone that I'm in sexual contact with.

Several men recognized that their past sexual behavior placed them at high risk for exposure to the virus, and even presumed themselves to be seropositive. Still, they felt that not having definitive knowledge that they were positive permitted them to maintain a modicum of hope that they were uninfected and that was psychologically protective. One 33-year-old man described the importance of this hope as something that could "sustain" him:

> [If positive] I would worry, you know. I'm more, kind of a hypochondriac in a lot of ways. And I think that ah, I worry enough as it is. And that thing, that little point zero one percent hope that I might be negative, you know, may sustain you sometimes. . . . I don't want to deal with the fact that I'm probably positive.

When we asked him about the difference between assuming he is positive and knowing it, he responded, "Just that difference. That little bit of, you know, there's a little bit of hope there." Similarly, a 36-year-old man who said he assumed he was positive, spoke about how not knowing for sure gave him "that little five percent that says maybe I'm not. And so, ah, rather than be told, "Yes, you are", and having to deal with that." He preferred not to be tested.

A number of men felt that learning they were positive could have adverse physical consequences. These men believed that psychological stress damaged the immune system's functioning. A 39-year-old said,

"I feel good. If it's gonna happen, it's gonna happen. Ah, if I got the test and it was positive, I would probably worry about it and make matters worse. So if I don't know, then I'm gonna proceed on a healthy way of life." A man, 36, said knowing he was positive could result in "damaging stress" to his immune system, and he thus avoided the test. One 27-year-old, who had gone to be tested in the midst of what he described an "incredible anxiety attack" but decided not to return to learn the results, explained his decision this way:

> At that time it seemed so certain that you were going to die very soon if you had it, that I just didn't want to face that information. And I guess I believe in the holistic idea that a healthy mind can help a healthy body. I do believe that ah, if you are infected, if you worry about it constantly, it's much more likely to sort of undermine your immune system than if you don't have worry about that very real solid fact.

To Avoid Social Discrimination and Repressive Governmental Actions

Another motive mentioned for not being tested was to avoid social discrimination and repressive governmental actions. Many men doubted that their test results would remain confidential or be truly anonymous and thus feared that testing positive, or even just taking the test, could result in loss of jobs, insurance coverage, and civil liberties. While the dangers of repressive government actions against infected individuals were typically discussed as something that could happen in the future, fears about loss of insurance or employment were usually based on stories they had heard of the past experiences of others and were perceived as an immediate threat. These men seemed to put little credence in assertions by various institutions or officials that results would be kept confidential or that testing was anonymous. Our respondents expressed distrust of public officials, employers, insurers, and even the general public. One 46-year-old man spoke of his fear of "getting on somebody's list":

> You know, I think politically, I mean in pure politics, that we see our country frequently shifting into a real conservative bent. And when they are in power, there is nothing to stop them. And once you've been tested, I really think you're probably on somebody's list, whether it's the doctor's list or public health's list or something like that. . . . I'm also concerned about the insurance question, medical insurance. People

being refused it or dropped. Ah, I don't trust the American public. Especially when something selfish comes. I don't trust any public . . . I just, I feel that panic that we've seen at times. And it will probably get worse because there are all indications that it's going to go into—it's broadening its spectrum in terms of the number of people and kinds of people that it's hitting. But I would be fearful of getting on some list.

Another man, 35, also doubted the anonymity of the test results:

I think of a few of the horror stories about test results, about test results being released to insurance companies, to employment agencies, to these kinds of things. Unfortunately I don't believe we are at a point where these things are totally anonymous. I don't feel I'm being overly cautious. If I felt it was something, that being tested was going to save my life, I wouldn't care. But the idea that somehow my insurance would be dropped or something based on the fact that some worker in a health department somewhere was convinced by an insurance company employee that for X amount of money that certain records could be left open or copies could be made. I've heard many horror stories of men with AIDS who have been dropped from insurance programs, and it's pretty horrible. I don't think knowing whether I have the HIV virus or not is worth right now taking that risk.

A 26-year-old man who said he "worked in government relations" commented that he didn't

trust public authorities with any kind of information regardless of what they say about confidentiality, including this. Public policy advocates will use information in any way that they can to advance their cause. And those advocates are not always going to be people who are sympathetic to those people who have taken the test. And even though right now the balance of power may be such that you have nothing to worry about now, that doesn't mean it will be so in the future.

To Avoid an Ambiguous or Unreliable Test Result

The perceived ambiguity of and/or unreliability of the antibody test results, the significance of HIV as a "cause" of AIDS, and the meaningfulness of a positive or negative test for anticipating future health were also offered as reasons not be tested. These respondents seemed to feel that tolerating the uncertainty of not knowing their status was possibly no worse than submitting to the ambiguity of a potentially unreliable or inaccurate test result. A few men remained unconvinced that HIV was the etiologic agent in AIDS or that seropositivity was a useful predictor of future health. One man, 37, said he thought taking the test was "like flipping a coin":

> I have friends who tested negative up until the day they died. . . . I have heard it's as high as 40 percent false positive, false negative, for example, 40 percent on the ELISA [an initial test to screen blood for HIV antibodies]. The Western Bloc [a more precise confirmatory text for the antibodies] is 70 percent, fairly accurate. . . . [My roommate's second lover] hung himself in his hospital room. . . . One day his test was positive and the next day negative, right up until the end. And it was like, "Oh no, it's just lymphatic cancer you lucky dog," you know. Really, every couple of days it was "you've got it, you don't have it, you've got it, you don't have it," you know.

Another man, 24, spoke of his understanding that the test was not "100 percent accurate":

> It doesn't mean that you don't have it [HIV infection] if it comes out negative. So I guess that would be the main thing. So what would be the sense of you taking it and then it coming out negative, and then having sex and end up catch, you know, contracting AIDS anyway.

The men recognized both the dangers inherent in a false sense of security that a "false negative" can provide and the psychological devastation that a "false positive" can bring. A respondent, 26, said,

> So I get a negative? Great. Well, maybe it's a false negative. You know, who knows? Or then I have to go get tested again. If they come up with a sure-fire test that says, "you are definitely, 100 percent." Until then I don't really think it would do that much for me. And I think getting a positive, which again could be false, is actually worse than not being sure and sort of assuming you have it. I think that would be, that would be worse.

To Avoid Having to Make Undesired Lifestyle Changes

Other men had decided not to undergo testing because they felt a positive result would require changes in their lifestyle that they did not want to make. Ignorance of their status seemed to make it at least personally acceptable to maintain current practices. A man, 29, said,

> I kind of like, well I do like the way I live now. And I know my personality. And if someone were to tell me that I tested positive for

this, I wouldn't live my—I know I'm pretty sure I wouldn't live my life the same way. I would worry. I'd be in fear. At the same time, if I tested positive it would probably be the end of my sexual activities.

Like this man, others said that learning they were positive would obligate them to modify their sexual behavior or lifestyle, something they did not feel compelled to do in the absence of certain knowledge they were positive. A man, 27, spoke of the "moral issue" involved:

If I found out I tested positive, it's not real for me to say that I would stop having sex. It's not real for me to say I would find a lover who has AIDS and only have sex with him. Ah, so I would continue to not practice safe sex, but I would continue to have sex—a great deal of anonymous sex. And that's wrong.

We asked him why he thought that was "wrong":

Because you know that you are in effect poisoning people. . . . I agree with the first person [on the videotape] who said every person that has sex with you without asking you first [if you're infected] is taking a risk, and that's his responsibility, not yours. And it's an implied risk and so you're off the hook. Well yes, if you don't *know* you're going to contaminate this person. If you know you're infected, you know that you will contaminate him if what you do is unsafe. And that's, morally that's wrong. Worse [to me] than actually having the disease and dying would be to live the rest of my life and not be able to have sex with anyone or knowing I was killing whoever I was having sex with.

And finally, a 38-year-old man speculated about how knowing he was positive might affect his relationships:

I don't think that would necessarily stop me from having a relationship with another person. But I know that it would really curtail the sexual activity because of what I may contribute to the person's development. Who knows, it may be multiple infections or whatever, so it would probably be better not to have any, you know, contact with his semen. You know it would probably be bad for both of us.

Discussion

The motives our respondents offered for taking or not taking the HIV antibody test both reflect and constitute prevailing social constructions of the test. In this final section of the paper, we characterize these cultural constructions more broadly and comment on changes in the motives offered over time.

Within the broader culture there are three competing definitions of the HIV test, which can be labeled the public health, psychosocial, and medical constructions. The men we interviewed discussed their motives for taking or not taking the test by drawing on these definitions, applying them to their own circumstances, and thus revitalizing them as cultural constructions. An analysis of public health and gay literature shows that the first two, what we call the psychosocial and the public health definitions, emerged shortly after the development in 1984 and subsequent licensing in 1985 of a test for serum antibodies to HIV. The third, the medical definition, appeared following the growing recognition in 1987 and 1988 that HIV causes a spectrum of diseases that culminate in AIDS. All three constructions differ in regard to the meaning and anticipated consequences of the test.

The psychosocial construction of the test depicts it as a grave threat to individuals' basic human rights and psychological well-being. A perception of pervasive homophobia in the United States prompted gay community leaders and civil libertarians to become the main proponents of this perspective (Shilts 1987; Bayer 1988). According to this construction, all but anonymous testing procedures presumably are associated with the creation of registries of infected people or provide the potential for such registries to be established. Although assurances of confidentiality may currently exist, it is recognized that future laws or court orders could overturn these protections. Subsequent breaches of confidentiality could be exploited by anti-gay interest groups, possibly leading to employment and housing discrimination against registered individuals as well as loss of their health and life insurance protection.

This construction also holds that test results may be emotionally and socially disruptive to individuals in a number of ways. First, positive results can have profound adverse psychological consequences, including depression, anxiety, suicide, and the disruption of social relationships. Second, the technical limitations of the test, including the existence of a period after infection during which antibodies cannot yet be detected, an lead to inaccurate or inconclusive results. False positive results can engender the same adverse emotional consequences as accurate findings, and, of course, false negatives can allow those infected to unknowingly transmit the virus.

The campaign against testing within the gay community in New York City conveyed the psychosocial construction. The leading gay newspaper and AIDS organizations published editorials, advertisements, and informational brochures discouraging gay men from being tested for technical, social, and psychological reasons (Shilts 1987; Bayer 1988). A widely distributed GMHC pamphlet was typical of these campaign materials. Written in alarmist tones, this brochure warned gay men that test results were unreliable and ambiguous and could cause them to "lose their jobs or health insurance."

The motives cited in the interviews for not taking the test drew heavily upon the psychosocial definition. Most of the men reported avoiding being tested because they feared social discrimination, repressive governmental actions, and the adverse psychological impact of positive results. Many men feared that hostile groups would gain access to test results and use them for discriminatory purposes. In addition, they believed that a positive result, even if it was inaccurate, would leave them emotionally traumatized and devastated.

The medical construction views the test as a valuable tool for planning the most efficacious and appropriate clinical management of at risk individuals. AIDS clinicians, researchers, and treatment activists have been the major supporters of this perspective (Redfield and Burke 1988; Institute of Medicine 1988; Helquist 1989; Delaney 1989). In this definition, HIV is presumed to cause a sequence of disease conditions, ranging from acute infection to seropositivity to chronic HIV infection and, finally, to AIDS. Furthermore, the antibody test is regarded as an acceptably reliable indicator of HIV status, with a positive result indicating the presence of the virus and infectivity. Therefore, a positive test result is considered to be grounds for initiating medical treatments. Moreover, it is presumed that if left untreated seropositivity will inexorably progress to AIDS, and hence early intervention is considered central to prolonging health and survival.

Prominent gay clinicians and treatment activists began to articulate this definition in New York City in early 1988. At public forums and in articles in the gay press and the newsletters of AIDS organizations, they encouraged gay men to get tested in order to take advantage of emerging medical treatments for HIV infection. They recommended that seropositive men practice sound health maintenance, participate in holistic therapies, and take either antiviral drugs or medicines that can either boost the immune system or prevent opportunistic infections.

The men's motives for undergoing testing largely embodied the medical definition. Many of the men stated that they took the test in order to more effectively monitor their health status and plan medical interventions. Knowledge of their test results would allow them to determine whether or not they should take drugs that could either slow the replication of HIV or forestall opportunistic infections. Others stated that they needed this knowledge in order either to become motivated to lead a healthier lifestyle or to arrive at a definitive diagnosis of a problematic medical condition.

The public health definition views the test as an effective mechanism for controlling the spread of the HIV epidemic. Public health officials and policy makers were the principal advocates of this construction, with most favoring widespread, voluntary, and confidential testing (Bayer 1988; Brandt 1987; Koop 1986; Centers for Disease Control 1986). According to this interpretation, the antibody test is an acceptably accurate and reliable indicator of HIV infection. Hence, individuals who test positive are regarded as being infected and presumably infectious.

Furthermore, testing, especially among high risk populations, is regarded as an effective strategy for reducing HIV transmission. First, testing is believed to locate infected individuals who are unaware of their status; these people can then be counseled to cease behaviors associated with the transmission of the virus and to adopt health maintenance practices. Second, some proportion of the asymptomatic infected population who are currently unaware of their status and unknowingly infecting others will learn of their seropositivity and be motivated to cease practices that spread the virus. Finally, widespread testing presumably provides more accurate surveillance data concerning the geographic and demographic spread of the virus, enabling more intensive educational efforts to be targeted to those regions and groups with high rates of infection.

The motives offered in the interviews for taking or not taking the test drew slightly from the public health construction. For the most part, the men saw little personal benefits in the public health rationale for testing. Some commented that the civil liberties and psychological risks associated with testing far outweighed the public health need for more accurate surveillance data. Others felt that education, not testing, was what was needed to motivate gay men to practice safer sex.

Only one of the motives cited for being tested reflected the public health construction. A few men reported that they took the test in order to alter current sexual practices. They felt that knowledge of their test results would allow them to either expand their range of sexual practices to include risky behavior or restrict their conduct to practices that posed no risk of infecting others.

The interviews indicate that over time there was a shift in men's definitions of the consequences of the test. When testing initially became available, most respondents subscribed to the psychosocial construction of the test. Accordingly, they perceived it as having potentially far-reaching adverse social and psychological consequences while offering no meaningful benefits. With the emergence of the medical construction in 1987 and 1988 some men redefined their perception of the anticipated consequences of being tested. Testing came to be viewed as providing a means of learning one's HIV status, and if infected, initiating medical treatments that could prolong health and life. Conversely most of the respondents who have remained untested continue to adhere to the psychosocial construction of the test.

The respondents' accounts suggest that the medical construction is likely to take on increasing importance in gay men's motives for testing. For example, if evidence continues to accrue demonstrating the efficacy of treatments for HIV infection and the benefits of beginning treatments early, more men will be strongly motivated to be tested. Furthermore, as the data indicating that HIV infection is the first stage of a progressive disease that will culminate in AIDS proliferate, the value of learning early that one is seropositive is likely to be viewed as greatly increased. Nevertheless, the psychosocial construction continues to present formidable barriers to testing. As our study and others cited above indicate, anticipated psychological distress and discrimination are among the most frequently reported motives for not taking the test. To overcome these barriers, gay organizations, public health agencies, and AIDS commissions and community-based organizations have repeatedly called for the availability of anonymous testing procedures and laws safeguarding the confidentiality of and prohibiting discrimination against tested individuals (Bayer 1988; Institute of Medicine 1988). Without these protections, it seems likely that many gay men will continue to regard the risks of testing as unacceptable.

NOTE

This research was supported in part by a grant from the National Institute of Mental Health (MH42275). The authors acknowledge the assistance of Shona Brogden, Douglas Oliver, and Lisa Rosen.

REFERENCES

Bayer, Ronald. 1988. *Private Acts, Social Consequences: AIDS and the Politics of Public Health.* New York: The Free Press.

Brandt, Allan. 1987. *No Magic Bullet: A Social History of Venereal Diseases in the United States from 1880.* New York: Oxford University Press.

Centers for Disease Control. 1986. Additional Recommendations to Reduce Sexual and Drug-Abuse Related Transmissions of Human T-Lymphotorophic Virus Type III Lymphadenopathy Associated Virus. *Morbidity and Mortality Weekly* 35:152–55.

Coates, Thomas, Ron D. Stall, Susan M. Kegeles, Bernard Lo, Stephen F. Morin, and Leon McKusick. 1988. "AIDS antibody testing: Will it stop the AIDS epidemic? Will it help people infected with HIV?" *American Psychologist* 43:859–64.

Delaney, Martin. 1989. "Staying alive. Making the ultimate political statement: new reasons to consider taking the antibody test." *Advocate* (February 28): 33–37.

Goldblum, Peter, and Neil Seymour. 1987. "Whether to take the test: counseling guidelines." *Focus: A Guide to AIDS Research* 2:1–3.

Helquist, Michael. 1989. "Update on getting tested" *Advocate* (June 6) 36.

Institute of Medicine. 1988. *Confronting AIDS: Update 1988.* Washington, DC: National Academy Press.

Koop, C. Everett. 1986. *Surgeon General's Report on Acquired Immune Deficiency Syndrome.* Washington, DC: U.S. Department of Health.

Lyter, David, Ronald O. Valdiserri, Lawrence A. Kingsley, William P. Amodoso, and Charles R. Rinaldo Jr. 1987. "The HIV antibody test: Why gay and bisexual men want to know their results." *Public Health Reports* 102:468–74.

Merton, Robert K., Marjorie Fiske, and Patricia L. Kendall. 1956. *The Focused Interview.* Glencoe, IL: The Free Press.

Miller, David. 1987. *Living with AIDS and HIV.* London: Macmillan.

Mills, C. Wright. 1940. Situated actions and vocabularies of motive. *American Sociological Review* 5:904–13.

Redfield, Robert, and Donald S. Burke. 1988. "HIV infection: the clinical picture." *Scientific American* 259:90–99.

Research and Decisions Corporation. 1986. *Designing an Effective AIDS Prevention Campaign Strategy for San Francisco: Results from the Third Probability Sample of an Urban Gay Male Community.* San Francisco, CA: The San Francisco AIDS Foundation.

Shilts, Randy. 1987. *And the Band Played On: Politics, People and the AIDS Epidemic.* New York: St. Martin's Press.

Chapter Eleven

Unprotected Sex
Understanding Gay Men's Participation

Martin Levine and Karolynn Siegel [1992]

In the absence of a curative treatment or vaccination, behavioral change remains the most effective means for curtailing the spread of the human immunodeficiency virus (HIV) epidemic (Coates 1990). Individuals must be persuaded to refrain from practices associated with the transmission of infection (Institute of Medicine 1988), which, in the case of gay men, primarily include unprotected anal and oral intercourse (Turner, Miller, and Moses 1989). Accordingly, HIV prevention efforts aimed at the gay community have encouraged the use of condoms during insertive and receptive anal and oral sex and have presented protected intercourse as a socially acceptable and responsible action (Siegel, Grodsky, and Herman 1986; Connell et al. 1989).

Prevention campaigns have succeeded in fostering some normative, attitudinal, and behavioral change with respect to protected sex among gay men living in epicenters of HIV infection (Turner, Miller, and Moses 1989). Prior to AIDS, cultural rules within these gay communities proscribed condom usage during homosexual relations (Williams 1979). Gay men perceived condoms as chiefly a contraceptive device and thus irrelevant to same-sex contacts. Moreover, the easy availability of curative treatments for most venereal diseases prompted gay men to eschew condoms as a prophylaxis against these illnesses (Judson 1977). In this sense, gay men considered the health risks of unprotected intercourse as acceptable when weighed against the perceived sexual and psychological benefits. Hence, prophylaxis was rarely considered or used during homosexual acts (Martin 1987; Ross 1988a).

However, the threat of HIV disease has transformed norms and attitudes toward protected anal sex within gay communities located in areas that are the foci of the epidemic (Stall, Coates, and Hoff 1988; Becker and Joseph 1988). Available evidence suggests that gay men dwelling in these communities now regard unprotected anal intercourse as an extremely efficient means of transmitting HIV and condom use as a normative, necessary, and effective means of preventing infection during anal sex (Turner, Miller, and Moses 1989). For example, in 1987 Communication Technologies researchers asked a random probability sample of self-identified gay and bisexual men living in San Francisco to rate the risk of HIV transmission during unprotected anal sex on a 10-point scale on which 10 indicated that this practice was very associated with the risk of transmission and 1 indicated it was not associated with transmission. The mean reported risk score was 9.8. In addition, the investigators questioned the sample about the extent to which they agreed with the following two statements: (a) "The only way I will have anal sex is with a condom." (b) "Most of my friends believe that I should only have anal intercourse with a condom." Again, a 10-point scale was used on which 10 represented complete agreement. The mean acceptance score for the first statement was 8.2; for the second it was 8.8.

Significant behavioral modifications of anal sexual practices have paralleled these normative and attitudinal shifts (Stall, Coates, and Hoff 1988; Becker and Joseph 1988). Survey data from gay men residing in cities with high rates of HIV infection indicate striking increases in the frequency of protected anal intercourse (Martin 1987; McKusick, Wiley et al. 1985; McKusick, Hortsman, and Coates 1985; Siegel, Bauman, Christ, and Krown 1988a; Stall, McKusick, Wiley, Coates, and Ostrow 1986; Communication Technologies 1987). For example, using longitudinal data from a community-based convenience sample of self-identified gay men living in New York City, Martin, Dean, Garcia, and Hall (1989) found that the percentage of men reporting always using condoms during receptive anal sex increased from 2% in 1981 to 62% in 1987. Similarly, the percentage indicating always using condoms during insertive anal intercourse rose from 2% in 1981 to 58% in 1987.

Despite these substantial changes, these same surveys also record the persistence of participation in unprotected anal sex among a significant percentage of men in epicenter gay communities (Stall, Coates, and Hoff 1988; Becker and Joseph 1988). For example, Communication Technologies (1987) researchers found that almost one third (31%) of their sample had practiced unprotected anal intercourse with a primary partner during the past 6 months and that 5% of the sample behaved similarly with a secondary partner during the same time period. Other studies indicate occasional relapses into unprotected anal sex among a substantial proportion of men studied (Siegel, Mesagno, Chen, and Christ 1988b; Stall et al. 1986).

Additional data from these surveys suggest minimal changes in norms or attitudes toward protected oral sex (Turner et al. 1989). Typically, gay male residents of areas that are at the center of the epidemic perceive oral sex without ejaculation as an unlikely means of HIV transmission and, hence, reject protection during this act (Martin et al. 1989). For example, Communication Technologies (1987) researchers also asked their sample to rank the risk of HIV transmission during oral sex without semen exchange (again using a 10-point scale on which 10 indicated the practice was very associated with transmission and 1 indicated the practice was not related to transmission). The scores signified that the men regarded this act as about as risky as protected anal intercourse. The mean reported risk score for oral sex without ejaculation was 3.7; it was 3.5 for protected anal intercourse. It is not surprising that unprotected oral sex, albeit usually without ejaculation or semen ingestion, remains prevalent in epicenter communities. In fact, Martin et al. (1989) found that, as of 1987, approximately 85% of their sample had engaged in either unprotected insertive or receptive oral sex at least once during the past year.

The reasons for the persistence of unprotected intercourse among gay men living in epicenter communities remain poorly understood. Unfortunately, studies of behavioral change within these locales commonly only ask questions about the magnitude and correlates of protected intercourse and rarely directly examine motives for unprotected sex (Coates, Stall, Catania, and Kegeles 1988; Siegel, Bauman et al. 1988a; Siegel, Mesagno et al. 1988b; Martin 1987; Martin et al. 1989; McKusick, Wiley et al. 1985; McKusick, Hortsman et al. 1985; Stall et al. 1986; Ross 1988a, 1988b, 1988c; Valdiserri et al. 1987; Valdiserri et al. 1988). Only one survey tapped gay men's reasons for engaging in unprotected anal intercourse. In this study (Communication Technologies 1987), researchers found that partner status, condom unavailability, coitus interruptus, condom acceptability, and partner seronegativity were the most frequently offered reasons for unprotected anal sex. More than half (54%) of the sample reported that they eschewed protection because they only had anal sex with primary partners; one quarter (25%) indicated that they did not use protection because condoms were not available; about one fifth (18%) stated that they avoided protection because they withdrew before ejaculation; a similar proportion (18%) reported that they shunned protection because they did not like condoms; and approximately one tenth (13%) indicated that they eschewed protection because both they and their partners were seronegative. To date, then, not much is known about why most gay men perceive oral sex as an inefficient means of transmitting HIV or about why some gay men continue to practice a behavior (unprotected anal sex) that they define as risky.

This chapter expands our understanding of the motives of gay male residents of HIV epicenters for engaging in unprotected intercourse. In what follows, we discuss the research methods used to collect our data on gay men's explanations for this behavior, report the reasons for unprotected intercourse cited by our respondents, and comment upon how the major social constructions of the risk of HIV infection during intercourse and culturally available motives for improper sexual conduct are reflected in our respondents' comments.

Following Scott and Lyman (1968), we conceptualized the men's reports as "accounts" and typologized them as either "justifications" or "excuses." Accounts are culturally determined narrative statements offered to explain untoward or problematic behavior. Justifications assume responsibility for committing the act but deny that it was unseemly or questionable behavior. Excuses admit that the act is improper or inappropriate but dispute culpability for committing it through either scapegoating or appealing to reasons such as accidents, defeasibility, or biological drives.

Method

The data presented below are from a qualitative study of sexual decision making among gay men in the context of the AIDS epidemic. The study was undertaken in response to a recognition that, although self-identified gay men have participated in several survey studies concerning the extent to which the AIDS epidemic fostered changes in their sexual lives, there has been a notable lack of research on the meaning of AIDS as it is pragmatically experienced and cognitively structured by the men themselves. The study was designed to address this problem using a primarily qualitative methodology that included participant observation, the use of a brief self-administered questionnaire, and primary reliance on unstructured but focused individual interviews (Merton, Fiske, and Kendall 1956).

Respondents for the study were recruited through flyers distributed and posted at a variety of gay service, political, and social organizations (including the large Lesbian and Gay Community Center, which serves the organized gay community in New York). In addition, recruiting announcements were run as advertisements in gay newspapers and as public service announcements on gay cable television, announced at various gay organizational meetings, published in a range of gay newsletters, and distributed through a constantly growing recruitment network.

To participate, respondents had to be between 18 and 65 years of age, live in the greater New York metropolitan area, not have used intravenous drugs in the past 6 months, and not have been diagnosed with AIDS. We excluded intravenous drug users because the study aimed at understanding behavioral change among individuals for whom sexual practices constituted the principal risk behavior. Men with AIDS were not included because we felt that their physical and mental symptomatology might be more significant explanatory factors for their sexual behavior than the kinds of interpersonal, social, and cultural factors we were trying to elucidate.

All interviews were conducted as relatively unstructured open-ended discussions led by the project interviewer. Interview sessions began with a 9-minute videotape produced by the study team as a projective stimulus for discussion. The video contained five vignettes in which actors portrayed gay men articulating their diverse views about safer sex and AIDS. The vignettes included men who had adopted safer sex practices and expressed differing feelings about their choice as well as men who justified continuing to engage in risky sex. By presenting varying views about safer sex, the video was designed to give respondents permission to express themselves candidly (e.g., to acknowledge disagreement with safer sex recommendations or involvement in unsafe sexual practices). Interviews were audiotaped and transcribed verbatim for analysis.

The findings presented here were derived from the focused interviews with a subset of 124 men, out of a total of 150 respondents, who reported having engaged in unprotected anal or oral intercourse (with and without ejaculation) during the preceding 6 months. Of these, 40% were untested, 32% were seropositive, and 29% were seronegative for HIV antibodies. Of the respondents, 110 were white, 6 were Hispanic, 3 were black, and the remaining 5 were from diverse racial and ethnic groups. The mean age of this subsample of respondents was 34, and 78% of the subsample was under 40 years of age. The men were well educated: 94% had completed some undergraduate education, and 71% had completed some undergraduate education, and 71% had completed college or attended graduate school. All interviews were conducted between May 1988 and January 1990.

The data reported below were usually offered in reply to a general query by the interviewer asking respondents to discuss what led to their participation in reported incidents of unprotected sex. The interviewer also directly questioned the men about the context in which these encounters occurred. Because the interviews were unstructured, there were no standardized probes as a follow-up to their responses. That is, the interviewer did not systematically probe to explore the possible importance of factors other than those reported by the men. In this way, we believe that we captured the respondents' subjective perceptions and definition of the situation and gained insight into what factors were personally most salient to them in arriving at their decision to participate in unprotected sex. For the purpose of exposition, we segregated the reasons offered by the men in their accounts of this decision. In reality, their accounts typically contained several interrelated reasons.

Accounts

The men participating in our study typically regarded unprotected intercourse as improper or problematic behavior and, therefore, readily offered accounts for their actions, which took the form of either justifications or excuses. The men citing justifications intentionally and routinely engaged in unprotected sex. Although these men accepted responsibility for their conduct, they disputed the notion that the behavior risked transmitting HIV. They either openly doubted the

validity of a practice's classification as risky (this was limited primarily to unprotected oral sex) or believed they could eliminate, or at
least minimize, the risk of HIV transmission during unprotected intercourse through strategies that prevented the transmission of infected
body fluids into the bloodstream.

Conversely, the men offering excuses inadvertently and irregularly
engaged in unprotected sex. Typically these men perceived participation in unprotected intercourse as risky and, therefore, usually used
protection during anal or oral sex. They regarded instances of unprotected sex as an unintended relapse from their normal pattern of
protection, which emerged from either "extenuating circumstances"
or "external forces" beyond their control.

Justifications

The justifications cited by our respondents generally reflected their
perceptions of how HIV was transmitted during intercourse. Typically
the men believed that the transmission of HIV required the passage of
infected body fluids (blood, semen, or preseminal fluids) directly into
the bloodstream through lacerations on the penis or the interior lining
of mouth or anus. Our respondents specified that three conditions
were required for HIV transmission. First, they believed that either
one or both of the partners had to be infected with HIV. Second, they
felt that the infected partner had to deposit sufficient quantities of an
infected body fluid into the mouth or anus of the uninfected partner.
Third, they believed that the infected body fluid had to directly enter
the uninfected partner's bloodstream through tears on the skin or
lining of the penis, anus, or mouth.

The men offering justifications typically felt that their sexual behavior was not risky because one or more of the conditions required for
the transmission of HIV was not present. We have grouped their
comments into four categories of reasons: (a) no signs of infectivity,
(b) no transmission of either semen and/or preseminal fluids, (c) no
lacerations, and (d) the belief that saliva, gastric juices, and urethral
acids either inhibit or kill the virus.

No Signs of Infectivity. Many respondents defended acts of unprotected
intercourse on the grounds that both they and/or their partners were
known or assumed to be uninfected. Typically these men saw no risk of

HIV transmission during unprotected sex between uninfected partners. They regarded unprotected intercourse between an infected and uninfected partner similarly, as long as the uninfected partner took the insertive role or precautions were taken to ensure that infected body fluids did not enter the bloodstream of the uninfected partner.

The men offering this explanation based their presumption of their own or their partners' uninfected status on a variety of medical and social criteria. These men reasoned that either they or their partners were uninfected because there was either medical proof of seronegativity or social indicators of a low-risk status.

Medical Evidence of Seronegativity. Some men perceived normal T-cell counts and negative HIV antibody test results as medical evidence of their virus-free status. Several, for example, stated that they had unprotected sex with current lovers because they had both tested seronegative for HIV antibodies. One 33-year-old technical writer reported having unprotected oral-genital contact with his lover because "he [the lover] knew he was negative and I knew I was negative, and ah so it seemed that we, neither of us, . . . was at risk." Others mentioned seronegativity as a reason for ceasing protected sex with lovers. For example, a 24-year-old customer service representative who had tested negative told us that he and his lover "stopped using condoms" after they both tested negative. A few men justified having unprotected receptive oral intercourse on the grounds that their partners were seronegative. One man, who was 30 and had tested positive, stated that he fellated his last two lovers without condoms because his lovers were both "negative, and my doctor said that [he did not] see what the risk is." The men typically believed that the insertive partner in oral intercourse was not at risk if there were no tears or cuts on the penis.

Nearly all the men citing seronegativity as a reason for engaging in unprotected sex accepted the validity of their test result. The possibility of a false negative result was almost never mentioned, even by men who were surprised at testing negative or who had had risky sex shortly before taking the test and thus might have not yet seroconverted.

Social Evidence of a Low-Risk Status. Other men construed sexual history and geographic locale as social markers of a low-risk status. Some of these men assumed that either they or their partners were not infected because prior to or throughout the epidemic they had been monogamous, relatively sexually inactive, or rarely took the receptive role during anal intercourse, which minimized their chance of exposure to HIV. For example, a 30-year-old waiter who had tested negative told us that he repeatedly had unprotected sex with his former lover because "I thought he was only seeing me . . . and I'm into one man relationships . . . and therefore the possibility of either of us having the virus was slight." An unemployed 24-year-old, who was untested, felt that "fucking" his steady partner was safe because the partner had "been with only one person for five years [and] there's no way [he] could have it." One seronegative 32-year-old Hispanic respondent had a number of episodes of unprotected anal sex with a priest. He explained his behavior by saying that, although he knew he couldn't be "100 percent certain" that the priest was uninfected, he was confident that the priest's life-style had greatly restricted his opportunity for encounters with many different partners and thus limited the probability of his having become infected.

Typical of those who believed that men who either avoided or rarely engaged in receptive anal sex were most likely to be uninfected was an untested college student in his early twenties. He justified regularly fellating his lover without condoms on the grounds that his lover had never been the receptive partner during anal sex, which he presumed meant that his lover was uninfected. He commented:

I mean I would say that he's at zero risk. He's at virtually none. He ah, he's ten years older than me. He'll be 32 at the end of the month. But he was a virgin until six months before I met him. . . . And he had only had very safe sex with a couple of people before I met him. All of whom I know. Save one, one whom I haven't met. But I know who he is. And ah, he'd only been very very safe. So I don't worry about him at all.

Other respondents assumed that their partners were uninfected because they came from locales with a low prevalence of AIDS cases, and, therefore, probably a low incidence of HIV infection, which greatly diminished their chance of becoming exposed to the virus. These men believed that unprotected intercourse with partners from low-prevalence areas (e.g., Michigan, Canada) who had either recently moved to New York or were just visiting the city was not risky. For example, a 38-year-old Hispanic counselor who was untested explained that he did not use condoms with men who were "imports," that is, partners from countries that he thought had few AIDS cases, because their chances of being infected were minimal. Similarly, men traveling to low-incidence areas either abroad or within the United States felt that they could have unprotected intercourse during these excursions with little fear of becoming infected.

No Transmission of Either Semen and/or Preseminal Fluids. Some men justified engaging in unprotected receptive intercourse on the grounds that there was no transmission of either ejaculate and/or preejaculatory fluids. There were two subgroups among these respondents. The first consisted of those who defended this practice on the basis of not receiving semen. Almost all of these men regarded ejaculate as transmitting HIV. Accordingly, they felt that they could minimize the danger of infection during receptive sex by avoiding semen. For example, the college student cited above commented on the risk associated with unprotected receptive oral intercourse with his lover:

> We'll give each other blow jobs but won't cum in each other's mouths. Ah, we never ejaculate in each other's mouths. And I consider that pretty safe as well.

Most of these men also regarded preejaculatory fluids as an ineffective transmitter of HIV. Typically they felt that preseminal fluids did not harbor or contain sufficient amounts of the virus to cause infection. Consequently, they believed the fluids posed little risk of transmission of infection to the receptive partner. For example, a 41-year-old accountant who had not been tested justified unprotected receptive anal sex with his lover on the grounds that his lover "didn't cum in me [and] precum isn't a risk factor." Another man, a 35-year-old actor who had not taken the HIV antibody test, doubted that there was enough preejaculatory fluid to transmit the virus during receptive oral intercourse. He based his belief on a conversation with a registered nurse at a community-based health clinic for gay men, who showed him a takeout Chinese food carton and said, "That's how much preejaculation would have to be in your mouth for you to swallow to get AIDS."

The second group defended unprotected receptive oral sex on the basis of not ingesting semen or preseminal fluids. Unlike the first group, these men believed that both ejaculate and preejaculatory fluids carried the virus. Hence, they felt they could minimize the risk of transmission during receptive fellatio by not allowing these body fluids to enter the mouth.

These men described two procedures for avoiding the ingestion of these fluids during oral intercourse. In the first, the receptive partner stimulated the scrotum and the shaft of the penis with his tongue and mouth but did not take the glans (head) of the penis into the mouth and, therefore, avoided ingesting any fluids. A 29-year-old seronegative college student said that he practiced this technique by stimulating "around—but not the head; but sort of around, you know, balls and everything."

In the second procedure, the receptive partner inserted the penile glans and shaft into his mouth only when semen and preseminal fluids were not present. The accountant referred to above, who had sexual relations with a male prostitute while his lover of 19 years was dying from AIDS, believed that the absence of these fluids reduced the risk of unprotected receptive fellatio:

> He [the prostitute] knows by now what I want. Ah, the second time I was with him, I put his cock into my mouth, and I have ever since. He has no precum. . . . You know I've tried putting a condom on him. But he has no precum and I say, "Well, it's basically safe" and he doesn't cum. He doesn't have an orgasm with me. Which again is fine. You know what I'm saying? All I want is to get off, and have some enjoyment that's safe and "bye."

Similarly, a 33-year-old journalist who did not yet know the results of his HIV antibody test told us that he regarded receptive fellatio as safe when his partners were "dry." He said:

> If I see that the person tends to be ah, to have precum, I don't go down on him. If I see that the person tends to be dry and the person is attractive and I feel like it, then I would maybe go as far as taking it in my mouth.

No Lacerations. Many men justified engaging in unprotected sex on the grounds that there were no tears, sores, or cuts on the skin or lining of the penis, anus, or mouth. Almost all these men believed that HIV-infected body fluids entered the bloodstream during intercourse through either anal, oral, or genital lacerations. Moreover, they felt that these tears commonly occurred during receptive anal sex, largely because of the friction associated with the thrusting of the penis and the fragility of the interior walls of the anus. Hence, they believed that receptive anal intercourse was quite risky.

Nevertheless, most of these respondents openly doubted the risk classification of insertive anal and receptive oral intercourse. Usually these men felt that lacerations were generally absent during these practices, which prevented infected body fluids from entering the bloodstream. They believed that tears rarely occurred during insertive anal sex because the sphincter muscles of the receptive partner were usually relaxed and thus penetration did not lacerate either the interior of the anus or the skin of the penis. The journalist, quoted above, who did not know the results of his HIV antibody test, told us:

> I must say that I feel there is virtually no danger in penetrating unless there is a great deal of pain and laceration and whatever else. Otherwise I feel that if everything is relaxed then there is no great danger.

Later in the interview he continued:

> Penetrating another guy without a condom? I tend to believe that it's not risky. Again, unless you are putting a great deal of effort in penetration, then there's lesions and all that. When it just comes real easy and natural, when it's smooth, then I feel that it's OK.

These men also discounted the likelihood of wounds during receptive oral sex on the grounds that most men rarely had bleeding gums or sores in their mouths. A 44-year-old hair stylist who tested positive said that "oral sex is not, unless you have sores or lesions in your mouth, as difficult or as dangerous as everybody thinks." The actor, referred to above, who was counseled by the nurse at the community-based health clinic, felt similarly and said:

> I think that oral sex is safer [than anal sex]. I do think that if you have bleeding gums or sores in your mouth or herpes sores on your mouth, you run a great risk.

He again based his belief on what the nurse told him, which was this:

> Having someone perform oral sex on you is low risk. The only way that it could be risky to you is if someone was performing on you if they have severe cuts all the way in the back of their mouth, periodontal problems.

A handful of respondents felt that the absence of lacerations precluded risk even during receptive oral sex with ejaculation. Typical of those who believed this was a 32-year-old, HIV-antibody positive, writer, who commented:

> I will have oral sex. The subject of ejaculation has not come up lately but I honestly think that, theoretically, to me, that it is OK. I'm assuming that one did not floss twenty minutes ago [causing bleeding gums].

Saliva, gastric juices, and urethral acids either inhibit or kill the virus. Many men justified engaging in unprotected intercourse on the grounds that saliva, gastric juices, and urethral acids either destroyed or inhibited the infectivity of HIV. There were two subgroups among these respondents. The first consisted of those who defended the ingestion of either ejaculate or preejaculatory fluids during receptive oral sex. Generally these men believed that the chemical agency of saliva and gastric juices neutralized the infectivity of HIV in semen and preseminal fluids. A seropositive man, who was 43-years-old and the head of a nonprofit organization, commented:

> As well versed as I am on this [the safer sex guidelines], I really don't believe that. I mean I just, I can see how contact would occur—bleeding gums or whatever. But the intestinal tract and the salivary, the saliva and everything else that works to break [it] down; it just seems the virus couldn't take that.

The unemployed 24-year-old respondent cited above told us that

> there's nothing wrong with oral sex without a condom. I know that they say you can swallow someone's cum and that kills it automatically in your stomach.

Similarly, a 39-year-old talent agent, who did not know the results of his antibody test, said:

> There's just too many stories about saliva being able to kill the virus, and certainly the digestive juices I believe, would kill the virus.

Several men also believed that the agency of these fluids neutralized HIV during fellatio because ejaculate and preejaculatory fluids contained negligible amounts of the virus. Typical of these was a 23-year-old seronegative executive who thought that preseminal fluids were not a risk factor because

> it's such a negligible amount [the amount of HIV in preejaculatory fluids]. And what's in your mouth is probably gonna kill it first. And

well depending upon how you're having the oral sex, there's probably gonna be some air around to kill any little bit that's there.

A few men further defended this belief on the basis of the prevalence of receptive oral sex with ingestion of semen and preseminal fluids among gay men before AIDS. These men felt that the agency of saliva and/or gastric juices must neutralize HIV because most gay men received ejaculate and preejaculatory fluids into their mouths, especially during anonymous encounters, both before and, to a lesser extent, since the epidemic. They reasoned that more gay men would be ill or dead if these fluids did not inhibit HIV, given the ubiquity of this practice. A 33-year-old financial researcher who did not know his test results commented:

> And I've read or heard that the whole process of ingesting semen is different than when you're getting fucked. Because of the saliva, the digestive juices and everything, by the time it gets into the bloodstream it's neutralized.

Later in the interview he added:

> I think you could cum in somebody's mouth or they could cum in my mouth and I don't think that's one of the main modes of transmission because, from what I've viewed throughout my life, in places like the balcony of The Saint or in movie theaters or tea rooms or whatever, sucking was the main sex because it's the easiest and quickest. Then I figure if it were one of the main means, a hell of a lot more people would have it.

The second group felt that the inhibitory agency of either saliva or urethral acid prevented HIV from being transmitted through the urethral opening to the insertive partner during unprotected anal and oral intercourse. Typical of these was a 30-year-old seropositive caterer who told us that the insertor in anal sex was not at risk because the "urethra is too acidic" for HIV to survive. A 36-year-old attorney, who decided not to learn the results of his HIV antibody test, doubted that the amount of saliva present during oral sex was sufficient to transmit the virus through the urethral opening:

> Now it's been my understanding that you can't get it from kissing. Or at least it's not known anyone ever has. And since it appears to me that the amount of saliva that you're exposed to, if someone gives you a

blow job, is very very small compared to the amount you get when you're kissing, it seems to me that there's nominal risk.

Excuses

The men offering excuses for unprotected intercourse generally felt that their sexual conduct was risky but attributed their behavior to forces they were unable to control. We organized their responses into four categories of reasons: (a) the influence of drugs and alcohol, (b) sexual passion, (c) emotional needs, and (d) partner coercion.

The Influence of Drugs or Alcohol. The most commonly cited excuse for unprotected sex was the use of drugs or alcohol. Almost all of the respondents offering this excuse insisted that unprotected intercourse was atypical behavior that occurred only when they were "high" or "stoned." These men contended that drugs or alcohol impaired their judgment, lowered their inhibitions, or reduced their ability to resist a partner's urging or pressure to engage in unprotected oral or anal sex.

Characteristic of respondents claiming that insobriety was responsible for unprotected intercourse was a 27-year-old seronegative lawyer. During the interview, this man told us about an episode of unprotected anal sex with a physician. Although the respondent began to put a condom on his penis, the doctor said to the respondent, "No, you don't need that. You're OK." The respondent assumed that the doctor was positive and that, therefore, "it didn't matter to him" if the respondent took the insertive role in anal sex and did not use protection. The respondent said that he then proceeded "to fuck" the physician without a condom because "I was really drunk and not thinking about it." He then added that he "felt sorry about it later."

Similarly, two other men attributed unprotected intercourse to the effects of drugs and alcohol. Both respondents felt that insobriety impaired either their judgment or their will. The first, an untested, 27-year-old graduate student, commented:

I met this guy and we went home. And ah, I was very drunk. And I don't know whether he was drunk or not. But I did, and I'm not real proud of this, fuck him without a condom. I didn't cum in him, but ah, that was because I was drunk. I shouldn't say that was because I was drunk because I, that sort of abrogates responsibility, but I was.

The second, who was a 30-year-old coordinator of an AIDS information service and seropositive, remarked:

> Ah there was, I was introducing condoms to people and being safe with
> people I had sex with. Ah, but there was one time I was doing, ah I was
> doing a lot of cocaine. And I let this guy fuck me, and he wouldn't use
> a condom. And I asked him to just make sure that he pulled out. And I
> think he did, or I thought he did, but he might not have because I was
> high.

Sexual Passion. A second frequently offered reason for unprotected
intercourse was sexual desire or lust. Nearly all the men offering
this excuse felt their behavior was uncharacteristic of them and attributable to uncontrollable urges, which overwhelmed their intent to use
protection. These men typically described these urges as powerful
biological needs and drives, which they dubbed passion or "horniness." For example, a 29-year-old seropositive consultant told us that
he occasionally anally penetrated without a condom two of his regular
partners because of "sexual passion." Another, a 24-year-old word
processor who was seronegative, sometimes allowed men to ejaculate in his mouth because he didn't "have the willpower to pull away"
because he "really wanted it." This same respondent also let
"a stranger" anally penetrate him without a condom because he was
"so horny" that he lost his "sense of reality" and didn't "think ratio-
nally."

Several other men attributed unprotected sexual conduct to overwhelming erotic desires. One respondent, a 26-year-old computer op-
erator who was infected, said:

> The first time we met there was unprotected oral sex. And he is HIV
> positive. . . . There was unprotected oral sex and unprotected anal sex
> where he did not cum. . . . And the second time—we've only had sex
> twice—we had brought condoms, the whole bit. You know what I
> mean, like we were all ready to go. And you know, somewhere along
> the course of action we forgot to put, you know, to bring out the
> condoms. . . . And he did cum inside of me. And you know, we both felt
> bad, so stupid about it. There hadn't even been drinking. . . . It just
> happened. It was passion.

Another, who was a 41-year-old seronegative pharmacy supervisor,
told us:

I mean it's you know, sometimes you go with all good intentions. And you say to yourself, "You're not gonna let yourself do this. You're not gonna suck the head. Right!" But you know, you see him with a, you know, big cock in your face, and it's not always easy to say, you know, "No, I'm not gonna do it." It's, you know, there are certain basic instincts I guess that take over. And ah, you can't always be as controlled as you want to be.

And a third, who was a 57-year-old cab driver and seropositive, stated:

Ah, I know there's one particularly hot guy. Well he, he works in the movies, I guess. Just a stud, you know. Ah, just completely rejecting the idea [of using a condom during anal sex.]. Ah, and so once, we did have a session and he fucked the hell out of me. And I'm happy to say, he just, he couldn't cum at all. And even though I was so overwhelmed by the passion of the moment that I would have permitted him that pleasure, things sort of lucked out, as it were.

Emotional Needs. Some men explained incidents of unprotected sex as an expression of love, affection, or acceptance. Typically these men participated in unprotected intercourse to demonstrate their emotional feelings for their partners who were usually their lovers or boyfriends. Many described their behavior as a sacrifice made for their partners, which was attributable to understandable and even altruistic motives.

For example, a 28-year-old waiter who had not been tested engaged in unprotected oral sex with a regular partner because he really cared for this partner and viewed the act as "an expression of [his] love for him." Another man, a 39-year-old model who was seropositive, had unprotected receptive anal sex with his lover whom he knew was infected because he wanted to show the lover "that he was going to be loved and nurtured and all." He stated that he wanted to be sure he did not make the lover "feel like a pariah." Similarly, a 34-year-old seronegative journalist participated in unprotected insertive anal intercourse, albeit without ejaculation, with his lover who had AIDS. He told us that he did it because "it was psychologically for our relationship at that point important."

Partner Coercion. Other men claimed that their partners coerced them into engaging in unprotected intercourse. Generally these men perceived themselves as victims of either other men's pressure or their deceptive conduct. They insisted that they intended to use protection but that their partners undermined their resolve.

There were two subgroups among these respondents. The first included respondents who were pressured into participating in unprotected sex. Typically their partners either refused or urged them not to use protection. The cab driver quoted above told us that, on the increasingly rare occasions when he did not use a condom, the "problem was with the other partner," who just "absolutely refused to use condoms." Another, a 27-year-old man who was untested, insisted that he "went into a situation saying, 'I'm not . . . there's not going to be any oral-genital contact here.' " However, he admitted that he often got "weak in [his] strength" and could not maintain his intent to practice safer sex in the face of his partner's desire for unprotected fellatio. Finally, a 30-year-old seropositive graduate student said he stopped seeing his HIV-positive boyfriend because "he forced me to do things sexually that I didn't want to do" such as "sucking him off" and ingesting the semen. The respondent felt that he had been "raped" by the lover and "forced to have sex against [his] will."

The second group consisted of a handful of men who were deceived into having unprotected receptive anal sex. These men usually thought the insertive partner used protection but later discovered that this was not the case. For example, a 23-year-old untested artist's assistant reported he noticed after one instance of receptive anal intercourse that the insertive partner did not use protection. This respondent assumed that the insertor was going to put on a condom before entering his anus because "there was a condom right next to him," that is, on the bedside table.

Discussion

The men's accounts of unprotected sex both embody and constitute social constructions of the risk of HIV transmission during intercourse and culturally available explanations for untoward sexual behavior. In this final section of the chapter, we describe these risk definitions and explanations more broadly, further differentiate men using justifications from those citing excuses, and comment upon the implications of our findings for HIV prevention.

Within the cultural milieu surrounding our respondents, there exist two competing constructions of the risk of HIV transmission associated with unprotected intercourse; they can be labeled the *public health* and the *folk* constructions. The men we interviewed justified or excused their unprotected sexual behavior by drawing upon these risk definitions, applying them to their own situation, and thus revitalizing them as cultural constructions. Our review of public health, HIV prevention, and gay literature indicates that the public health definition emerged shortly after the early (1981–84) epidemiological studies of the risk factors for AIDS and the discovery of HIV in 1984. The folk construction appeared later, following the appearance of epidemiological and laboratory evidence concerning the effect of saliva and gastric juices on HIV and the presence of HIV within preseminal fluids. Both definitions differ in regard to the relative risk of HIV transmission during unprotected anal and oral intercourse.

The public health construction of risk depicts all forms of unprotected oral and anal intercourse as risky unless both partners either had been monogamous from the mid-1970s or had tested seronegative 6 months after their last unsafe encounter (Wofsky 1988). These practices are regarded as risky because they have the potential for transmitting HIV-infected body fluids (blood, saliva, semen, preseminal fluids) directly into the bloodstream through either the urethral opening or tiny lacerations in the skin or linings of the anus, mouth, or genitals (Jaffe and Lifson 1988). The transmission of this virus during intercourse may occur in three distinct ways: First, the thrusting of the penis during anal sex may cause small tears on its surface or in the lining of the anus, which may provide infected body fluids a portal of entry into the bloodstream. Second, periodontal and sexually transmitted diseases, dental flossing and brushing, and deep kissing can create similar cuts or sores on the penis or mouth. During oral intercourse, these lacerations may permit infected body fluids to enter the bloodstream. Third, HIV also can enter the bloodstream during intercourse through the mucous lining of the urethral opening (Koop 1986; Mass 1985).

This construction also holds that there are relative differences in the level of risk associated with anal and oral sex (Jennings 1988). Available epidemiological data indicate that unprotected receptive anal intercourse with ejaculation of semen is the most consistently identified risk behavior for the transmission of HIV throughout the epidemic (Institute of Medicine 1986, 1988; Turner et al. 1989), probably due to the strong likelihood of anal lacerations from penile thrusting (Jennings 1988). However, the risk of infection from unprotected oral-genital relations and unprotected insertive anal intercourse appears to be less. Although several epidemiological studies found no statistical association between oral-genital contact and HIV infection (Lyman et al. 1986; Moss et al. 1987; Detels et al. 1989), a handful of isolated and often unsubstantiated case reports have described infection through receptive oral sex (Wofsky 1988; Jaffe and Lifson 1988). In addition, only a few epidemiological studies have reported statistical relationships between unprotected insertive anal intercourse and HIV infection (Detels et al. 1989). Thus available data seem to indicate that unprotected receptive anal intercourse is a highly efficient means of transmitting HIV, and there is probably less risk of infection through unprotected fellatio and insertive anal intercourse (Institute of Medicine 1986, 1988; Turner et al. 1989; Detels et al. 1989).

Within metropolitan New York, local public health agencies and AIDS organizations have been the principal advocates of the public health definition of risk (Siegel et al. 1986). These groups, which have mounted continuous HIV prevention campaigns aimed at gay and bisexual men, have in their guidelines for safer sex sought to eliminate all HIV transmission risk during intercourse.

Accordingly, although their guidelines often acknowledged different levels of risk for anal and oral sex, they, nevertheless, have recommended the use of condoms during both these practices. In addition, the guidelines promulgated by such gay organizations such as Gay Men's Health Crisis (GMHC) have recommended not taking ejaculate, preejaculatory fluids, or the glans of the penis into the mouth during unprotected receptive fellatio (Gay Men's Health Crisis 1986).

The men we interviewed were quite familiar with the public health construction of risk. As was the case in previous research (Becker and Joseph 1988; Stall et al. 1988), our respondents spoke knowingly about the public health model of HIV transmission and prevention. Many reported learning about this model from reading articles in the gay and mainstream press, attending GMHC or the Body Positive's (an organization serving seropositive individuals) workshops and forums, and talking to friends and community health activists and practitioners.

The accounts cited in the interviews partly drew upon the public health construction of risk. Many of our respondents justified engaging in unprotected intercourse on the grounds that they avoided the conditions the public health model of transmission specified as necessary for the transmission of HIV. Some defended their behavior on the basis of medical evidence that they or their partners were not infected, usually based on a negative result on the HIV-antibody test. Others rationalized their behavior on the grounds that they followed the guidelines for safe unprotected receptive fellatio. Typically these men claimed that they did not take the glans of the penis into their mouths and thus avoided ingesting semen or preseminal fluids during receptive oral sex.

The folk construction asserts a different model of HIV infection and prevention during intercourse. According to this definition, the transmission of HIV requires the passage of infected blood or semen directly into the bloodstream through lacerations either on the penis or on the interior lining of the mouth or anus. Unlike the public health construction, the folk model regards preejaculatory fluids and the urethral opening as ineffective transmitters of HIV. The model maintains that laboratory findings provide no conclusive evidence that preseminal fluids contain HIV and also indicate that the chemical agency of saliva and gastric juices neutralize the infectivity of the virus (Jennings 1988, pp. 53–59; Fox et al. 1988). Hence, the chances of viral infection through the urethral opening during oral sex are minimal.

This construction also perceives wide differences in the relative risk of anal and oral intercourse. In this definition, unprotected receptive anal sex with ejaculation constitutes the only form of intercourse proven to be risky. The failure of epidemiological studies to demonstrate a consistent relationship between HIV infection and insertive anal sex and/or oral-genital contact indicates, according to this construction, that it is highly unlikely that these acts effectively transmit the virus. In addition, the documented inhibitory effect of saliva on the infectivity of HIV almost completely diminishes the risk of transmission during fellatio.

The folk construction also uses medical and social indicators to discern the HIV status of potential sexual partners. The determination of this status is based on medical tests for the presence of antibodies to HIV and for immune functioning as well as social evidence of illness, promiscuity, or a high-risk past (Communication Technologies 1987; Valdiserri et al. 1987). Men are presumed to be infected if they test seropositive, have low T-cell counts, look unhealthy, engage in anonymous sex, have sexual histories of high-risk behavior, or come from areas with a high prevalence of the disease.

Many of our respondents' accounts of unprotected intercourse embodied the folk construction. Most of the men justified participating in unprotected intercourse on the grounds that they avoided the conditions specified in the folk model of transmission as necessary for the transmission of HIV. Many defended their behavior on the basis of social evidence of seronegativity—either a sexual background or a geographic locale that could be characterized as low risk. Other men rationalized engaging in unprotected oral sex on the basis of avoiding the exchange of either semen and/or preseminal fluids. Typically these men felt that their behavior was safe because they did not ingest fluids that could potentially contain HIV. Others justified acts of unprotected insertive anal intercourse and fellatio on the grounds that there were no lacerations, which they believed precluded transmission of the virus. Finally, some men defended participating in unprotected insertive anal sex and oral-genital relations on the basis of the chemical agency of saliva, gastric juices, and urethral acid, which they felt killed or inhibited the infectivity of HIV.

The accounts cited in the interviews also reflected culturally available explanations for problematic erotic conduct. Within the broader culture, there are a set of socially legitimate reasons for engaging in improper sexual behavior (Luker 1975). Typically these explanations affirm the validity of normative expectations but attempt to neutralize reputational damage by denying the risk of discovery, pregnancy, or disease as well as individual responsibility for participating in the act. That is, they assert that the act was wrong but maintain that there was almost no chance of either being found out or becoming pregnant or sick and attribute responsibility for this behavior to situations and forces that were usually out of the individual's control, such as insobriety, lust, affection, pleasure, or duress (Masters, Johnson, & Kolodny 1982).

The justifications and excuses reported by our respondents incorporated these explanations. Generally, the men offering justifications defended their behavior on the grounds that there was no risk of becoming infected. In addition, respondents citing excuses blamed their behavior on insobriety, sexual passion, emotional needs, and coercion.

These constructions also account for some of the attitudinal, emotional, and behavioral differences observed among respondents offering excuses and justifications. The men citing justifications usually accepted either the public health or the folk definition of risk. Consequently, these men believed that unprotected intercourse was safe in the absence of infectivity, ejaculation, lacerations, or insertion of the penile glans into the mouth. Hence, the men rarely expressed regret or guilt about their own episodes of unprotected sex that occurred in the absence of these conditions. They felt their behavior was safe and conformed to normative expectations within the gay community, calling for the avoidance of risk during intercourse. It is not surprising that the men knowingly and frequently engaged in unprotected intercourse with multiple partners when they perceived that the conditions existed to make such practices safe.

Alternately, respondents offering excuses usually accepted the public health construction of risk. Consequently, these men believed that unprotected intercourse was always risky unless it occurred between two men who both tested seronegative for HIV antibodies. Hence, the men frequently expressed regret, guilt, or remorse for participating in unprotected sex, which they often regarded as "irresponsible," "stupid," or "wrong" behavior. (By acknowledging these feelings, they appeared to be trying to soften the reactions of others—in this case, the interviewer and/or research team—to their disclosure of normative violation.) Moreover, these men generally described their episodes of unprotected intercourse as isolated and unintended relapses from their normal pattern of safer sex, usually resulting from insobriety, sexual passion, emotional need, or coercion.

The accounts cited in the interviews have implications for HIV prevention. Most prevention campaigns have sought to induce compliance with safer sex guidelines among gay and bisexual men by both raising individuals' levels of knowledge about practices implicated in HIV transmission and creating a normative expectation within the gay community that men will practice only safer sex. Although these strategies have been somewhat effective, the explanations offered by the men in our study for participation in unprotected intercourse suggest that there are several additional factors to be considered. First, in the absence of compelling epidemiological/scientific data about the risk of transmission associated with insertive anal sex and oral-genital relations, men draw conclusions about the relative risk inherent in those behaviors from experimentally acquired folk constructions. Efforts must be made either to clarify the level of risk associated with these practices or, in the meantime, to emphasize their uncertain safety rather than their uncertain risk.

Second, gay men are making various assumptions in evaluating the risk inherent in a given sexual encounter that are likely to be highly unreliable. For example, men are appraising the likelihood that a potential partner is infected based on the partner's unsubstantiated reports of prior behavior, past level of sexual activity, and past locales of that activity. Prevention efforts must stress the poor and unreliable predictive value of these folk definitions of risk status.

Finally, sexual activity is a highly charged, interpersonal mix of physical pleasure and complex psychological states. Accordingly, persuasion or coercion, physical attraction or desire, and emotional bonds or needs exert a powerful influence over erotic conduct. For example, the influence of a sexual partner can undermine an individual's intent to practice safer sex and prompt him to engage in risky conduct. Similarly, the powerful drives associated with love, affection, and desire can foster further episodes of risk behavior. These intense interpersonal dynamics will be difficult to influence solely through education and normative change and may instead require interventions that focus on enhancing skills in interpersonal dynamics.

NOTE

This research was supported in part by a grant from the National Institute of Mental Health (MH42275). The authors acknowledge the assistance of Shona Brogden, Douglas Oliver, and Lisa Rosen.

REFERENCES

Becker, Marshall H. and Jill G. Joseph. 1988. "AIDS and Behavioral Change to Reduce Risk: A Review." *American Journal of Public Health* 78:394–410.

Coates, Thomas J. 1990. "Strategies for Modifying Sexual Behavior for Primary and Secondary Prevention of HIV Disease." *Journal of Consulting and Clinical Psychology* 58:57–69.

Coates, Thomas J., Ron D. Stall, Joseph A. Catania, and Susan M. Kegeles. 1988. "Behavioral Factors in the Spread of HIV Infection." *AIDS* 2 (Suppl.):S239–45.

Communication Technologies. 1987. *Designing an Effective AIDS Prevention Campaign Strategy for San Francisco: Results from the Fourth Probability Sample of an Urban Gay Male Community.* San Francisco: San Francisco AIDS Foundation

Connell, R. W., June Crawford, Susan Kippay, G. W. Dowsett, Don Baxter, and Lex Watson. 1989. "Facing the Epidemic: Changes in the Sexual Lives of Gay and Bisexual Men in Australia and Their Implications for AIDS Prevention Strategies." *Social Problems* 36:384–402.

Detels, Roger, Patricia English, Barbara R. Visscher, Lisa Jacobson, Lawrence A. Kingsley, Joan S. Chmiel, Janice P. Dudley, Lois J. Eldred, and Harold M. Ginzburg. 1989. "Serocoversion, Sexual Activity, and Condom Use Among 2915 HIV Seronegative Men Followed for up to 2 Years." *Journal of Acquired Immune Deficiency Syndromes* 2:77–83.

Fox, P.C., A. Wolff, C. K. Yeh, et al. 1988. "Salvia Inhibits HIV-1 Infectivity." *Journal of the American Dental Association* 116:635–37.

Gay Men's Health Crisis. 1986. *An Ounce of Prevention Is Worth a Pound of Cure: Safer Sex Guidelines for Gay and Bisexual Men.* New York: Gay Men's Health Crisis.

Institute of Medicine. 1986. *Confronting AIDS: Update 1988.* Washington, DC: National Academy Press.

———. 1988. *Confronting AIDS: Directions for Public Health, Health Care, and Research.* Washington, DC: National Academy Press.

Jaffe, Harold W., and Alan R. Lifson. 1988. "Acquisition and Transmission of HIV." Pp. 19–27 in *The Medical Management of AIDS.* Edited by M. A. Sande and P. A. Volberding. Philadelphia: W. B. Saunders.

Jennings, Chris. 1988. *Understanding and Preventing Aids: A Book for Everyone.* Cambridge, MA: Health Alert Press.

Judson, Franklin N. 1977. "Sexually Transmitted Disease in Gay Men." *Sexually Transmitted Diseases* 4:76–78.

Koop, C. Everett. 1986 *Surgeon General's Report on Acquired Immune Deficiency Syndrome.* Washington, DC: U.S. Department of Health.

Luker, Kristine. 1975. *Taking Chances.* Berkeley: University of California Press.

Lyman, David, Warren Winkelstein, Michael Ascher, and Jay A. Levy. 1986. "Minimal Risk of AIDS-Associated Retrovirus Infection by Oral Genital Contact." *Journal of the American Medical Association.* 255:1703.

Martin, John L. 1987. "The Impact of AIDS on Gay Male Sexual Behavior Patterns in New York City." *American Journal of Public Health* 77:578–81.

Martin, John L., Laura Dean, Mark Garcia, and William Hall. 1989. "The Impact of AIDS on a Gay Community: Changes in Sexual Behavior, Substance Abuse, and Mental Health." *American Journal of Community Psychology.* 17:269–93.

Mass, Lawrence. 1985. *Medical Answers about AIDS.* New York: Gay Men's Health Crisis.

Masters, William H., Virginia E. Johnson, and Robert C. Kolodny. 1982. *Human Sexuality.* Boston: Little, Brown.

McKusick, Leon, William Hortsman, and Thomas J. Coates. 1985. "AIDS and Sexual Behavior Reported by Gay Men in San Francisco." *American Journal of Public Health* 75:493–96.

McKusick, Leon, James A. Wiley, Thomas J. Coates, Ronald Stall, Glen Saika, Stephen Morin, Kenneth Charles, William Hortsman, and Marrus A. Conant. 1985. "Reported Changes in the Sexual Behavior of Men at Risk for AIDS, San Francisco, 1982–84: The AIDS Behavioral Research Project." *U.S. Public Health Reports* 100:622–29.

Merton, Robert K., Marjorie Fiske, and Patricia L. Kendall. 1956. *The Focused Interview.* New York: Free Press.

Moss, Andrew R., Dennis Osmond, Peter Bacchetti, Jean Claude Chermann, Francoise Barre-Sinoussi, and James Carlson. 1987. "Risk Factors for AIDS and HIV Seropositivity in Homosexual Men." *American Journal of Epidemiology* 125:1035–47.

Ross, Michael W. 1988a. "Attitudes towards Condoms as AIDS Prophylaxis in Homosexual Men: Dimensions and Measurement." *Psychology and Health* 2:291–99.

———. 1988b. "Personality Factors That Differentiate Homosexual Men with Positive and Negative Attitudes toward Condom Use." *New York State Journal of Medicine* 88: 626–28.

———. 1988c. "Relationship of Combinations of AIDS Counseling and Testing to Safer Sex and Condom Use in Homosexual Men." *Community Health Studies* 12:322–27.

Scott, Marvin, and Stanford Lyman. 1968. "Accounts." *American Sociological Review* 33:46–62.

Siegel, Karolynn, Laurie J. Bauman, Grace H. Christ, and Susan Krown. 1988a. "Patterns of Change in Sexual Behavior among Gay Men in New York City." *Archives of Sexual Behavior* 17:481–97.

Siegel, Karolynn, Phyllis B. Grodsky, and A. Herman. 1986. "AIDS Risk Reduction Guidelines: A Review and Analysis." *Journal of Community Health* 11:235–43.

Siegel, Karolynn, Frances Mesagno, Jin-Yi Chen, and Grace Christ. 1988b. "Factors Distinguishing Homosexual Males Practicing Risky and Safer Sex." *Social Science and Medicine* 28:561–69.

Stall, Ron, Thomas Coates, and Charles Hoff. 1988. "Behavioral Risk Reduction for HIV Infection among Gay and Bisexual Men: A Review of Results from the United States." *American Psychologist* 43:878–85.

Stall, Ron, Leon McKusick, James Wiley, Thomas J. Coates, and David G. Ostrow. 1986. "Alcohol and Drug Use During Sexual Activity and Compliance with Safe Sex Guidelines for AIDS: The AIDS Behavioral Research Project" *Health Education Quarterly* 13:359–71.

Turner, Charles F., Heather G. Miller, and Lincoln Moses, 1989. *AIDS: Sexual Behavior and Intravenous Drug Use.* Washington, DC: National Academy Press.

Valdiserri, Ronald O., David W. Lyter, Lawrence A. Kingsley, Laura C. Leviton, Janet W. Schofield, James Huggins, Monto Ho, and Charles R. Rinaldo. 1987. "The Effect of Group Education on Improvising Attitudes about AIDS Risk Reduction." *New York State Journal of Medicine* 87:272–78.

Valdiserri, Ronald O., David Lyter, Laura Leviton, Catherine M. Callahan, Lawrence A. Kingsley, and Charles R. Rinaldo. 1988. "Variables Influencing Condom Use in a Cohort of Gay and Bisexual Men." *American Journal of Public Health* 78:801–5.

Williams, Daniel C. 1979. "Sexually Transmitted Diseases in Gay Men: An Insider's View." *Sexually Transmitted Diseases* 6:278–80.

Wofsky, Constance B. 1988. "Prevention of HIV Transmission." Pp. 29–43 in *The Medical Management of AIDS.* Edited by M. A. Sande and P. A. Volberding. Philadelphia: W. B. Saunders.

Chapter Twelve

The Implications of Constructionist Theory for Social Research on the AIDS Epidemic among Gay Men [1992]

> The aims, then, of a sociological approach to homo-
> sexuality are to begin to define the factors—both indi-
> vidual and situational—that predispose a homosex-
> ual to follow one path as against others; to spell out
> the contingencies that will shape the career that has
> been embarked upon; and to trace out the patterns of
> living in both their pedestrian and their seemingly
> exotic aspects. Only then will we begin to understand
> the homosexual. This pursuit must inevitably bring
> us—though from a particular angle—to those com-
> plex matrices wherein most human behavior is fash-
> ioned.
>
> —Simon & Gagnon (1967, 185)

In this chapter, I examine the implications of constructionist theory for social research on the HIV (human immunodeficiency virus) epidemic within the gay community. My aim is to review the status of the existing social inquiry on the HIV epidemic among gay men; identify the cultural definitions of sexuality, homosexuality, and HIV disease embedded in this research; and conclude by proposing a construction-ist approach to AIDS research.

Constructionism (symbolic interactionism) constitutes a major theo-retical paradigm within the social sciences (Coser 1977). Drawing upon basic axioms within 20th-century European philosophy and the history of science (Kuhn 1962; Law & Lodge 1984), constructionism includes three basic assumptions (Denzin, 1989). First, social reality is socially constructed: The objects that constitute social life lack intrinsic meaning. Instead, these objects take on meaning through human actions. The cultural definitions, symbols, and identities attached to these objects are thus acquired through the process of social interaction. Second, human interaction entails mental processes in which individuals fashion a point of view that accords with the behavior of other actors. These mental processes involve the manipulation of symbols, words, meanings, and languages. Consequently, social interaction is symbolic, emergent, negotiated—and frequently unpredictable. Third, self-reflexive conduct distinguishes human beings from other forms of life. Individuals are capable of shaping and directing both their own actions and those of other people.

The constructionist perspective transformed social science thinking about human sexuality (Gagnon & Simon 1973). It challenged us to see the conceptual categories through which individuals interpret eroticism are not, as previously thought, as biologically or psychologically determined but are socially constituted (Simon & Gagnon 1987). Culture, that is, provided the conceptual meanings through which people distinguished sexual feelings, identities, and practices. It thus effectively claimed that these definitions were culturally relative (Plummer 1975).

Constructionism directly challenged the essentialist approach to homosexuality, which prevailed within the social sciences (Troiden 1988). Essentialism regarded homosexuality as a form of gender inversion that arose from such presocial forces as genes, hormones, instincts, or specific kinds of developmental psychodynamics (Richardson 1981). In other words, it viewed same-sex desire and its perceived behavioral pattern of gender nonconformity as "a manifestation of some" biological or psychological "inner essence" (Greenberg 1988, 485). It regarded homosexuality as a distinct and separate form of being, with modes of expression that transcended time and place (Troiden 1988).

Conversely, constructionism interpreted homosexuality as a conceptual category that varied between cultural and historical settings (Troiden 1988). Definitions of same-sex eroticism were viewed as cultural inventions that were specific to particular societies at particular times. It also held that conceptualizations of homosexuality determined the forms same-sex eroticism took within a given a society (Greenberg 1988). In other words, the social meaning of homosexuality shaped the domain of emotion, identity, and conduct associated with sex between men.

The anthropological and historical record supports constructionist propositions concerning the behavioral patterns associated with human sexuality (Ford & Beach 1951; Gregerson 1983). The enormous variation in the social meaning and organization of heterosexual and homosexual eroticism shown in this record discounts the possibility of a presocial origin for these behavioral patterns (Gagnon & Simon 1973; Troiden 1988). Instead, the historical and cross-cultural variability demonstrates how cultural definitions organize the forms of sexual expression both between and within the sexes (Adam 1985).

Social Research on the HIV Epidemic among Gay Men

Epidemiological and public health concerns have largely framed the theoretical perspectives, research questions, and methodologies used in social inquiry on the HIV epidemic within the gay community. Epidemiological interest lay primarily in uncovering both the determinants and the distribution of HIV disease among gay men. Hence epidemiologists initiated studies of the social attributes and risk behaviors associated with the disease. At first, mainly heterosexual researchers, typically physicians with public health or epidemiological backgrounds, conducted descriptive studies that used case reports and survey questionnaires to provide data regarding the geographic, sociodemographic, and life-style attributes of the original HIV cases (Oppenheimer 1988). The survey instruments reflected to a great extent assumptions about a causal relationship between the illness and behavioral features of the urban gay life-style (Murray & Payne 1988). The raging epidemic of sexually transmitted diseases during the 1970s within urban gay communities made many investigators suspect that the new disease was attributable to the prevailing life-style of drugs, discos, and anonymous sex (Oppenheimer 1988). Hence the survey schedules usually asked numerous questions about erotic conduct and substance abuse.

Subsequent epidemiological inquiry became more analytic in orientation and designed case control and prospective studies to identify the specific risk factors associated with HIV infection and the rate of progression through the sequential stages of the disease. Although more social scientists participated in the research, the investigators remained chiefly heterosexual physicians. Only a handful of gay men worked on these studies, but many were deeply or partially closeted. The case control studies attempted to identify the nutritional, residential, and life-style attributes that distinguished the gay AIDS (acquired immune deficiency syndrome) cases from the healthy gay or heterosexual controls (Oppenheimer 1988). Generally, the gay cases were recruited from the practices of gay physicians. The prospective studies attempted to examine processes of disease progression over time among large cohorts of individuals thought to be at high risk for infection; survey questionnaires, physical examinations, and specimen collections (for laboratory and serological purposes) were used. Typically, the prospective studies enrolled large community-based convenience samples of gay and bisexual men who were recruited primarily from gay organizations, health facilities, or gathering places that were located in areas with elevated rates of HIV disease. Only one study used a population-based (probability) sample that also included a heterosexual cohort (Winkelstein et al. 1987).

Public health interest lay primarily in prevention, that is, halting the spread of the disease among gay and bisexual men. Consequently, prevention-oriented investigators implemented prospective (longitudinal) or cross-sectional (at one point in time) studies of the magnitude and correlates of changes in those sexual practices or life-style features known or suspected to be associated with the transmission of HIV (Turner, Miller, & Moses 1989). Again, most of the researchers were heterosexual physicians and social scientists. However, some were closeted or openly gay men, including a few of the principal investigators. Furthermore, most of the prospective studies were piggybacked onto broader investigations of the natural history of the disease. These studies commonly used self-administered questionnaires and community-based convenience samples of gay and bisexual men living mainly in epicenter areas (Turner et al. 1989). Only two prospective studies in San Francisco used probability-based samples (Communication Technologies 1987; Winkelstein et al. 1987), and one prospective study in New York used face-to-face interviews (Bauman & Siegel 1986; Siegel, Bauman, Christ, & Krown 1988; Siegel, Mesagno, Jin-Yi Chen, & Christ 1989).

Public health or psychological models of behavioral change shaped most of the attempts within these studies to identify the correlates of changes in risk practices. These models were drawn from either preexisting theories of health conduct or the attitudinal basis of social behavior. The models derived from theories of health conduct assumed that already identified predictors of health conduct were also correlates of changes in risk behavior for HIV (Siegel et al. 1988). The recognized predictors of health behavior included (a) knowledge about the disease, (b) perception of vulnerability to the disease, (c) beliefs about the efficacy of health care, (d) accessibility to health or preventive care, (c) dispositional barriers to health or preventive care, (f) degree of affiliation within a social network, (g) normative structure of the social network, and (h) demographic characteristics such as age, class, race, residence, and relationship status (Cummings, Becker, & Maile 1980). The assumed correlates of risk behavior for HIV were (a) knowledge of HIV etiology, transmission, and prevention; (b) perceived risk of HIV disease: (c) perceived efficacy of HIV risk reduction behavior; (d) perceived difficulty in sexual impulse control; (e) belief in biomedical technological cures or prevention for HIV disease; (f) degree of integration into gay social networks; (g) perceived peer support for HIV risk reduction; and (h) perceived level of emotional support from peer group (Emmons et al. 1986; Siegel et al. 1988).

The studies found that the predictors derived from models of health behavior poorly explained alterations in risk behavior for HIV (Becker & Joseph 1988; Siegel et al. 1989; Stall, Coates, & Hoff 1988). For example, Joseph et al. (1987) reported that the predictors taken from this model accounted for only 30 to 50 percent of the variability in longitudinal risk reduction behavior observed in their cohort of gay and bisexual men. The predictors used in their study included (a) knowledge of AIDS, (b) perceived risk of AIDS, (c) perceived efficacy of behavioral change, (d) perceived difficulty with sexual impulse control, (f) belief in biomedical cure or prevention for AIDS, (g) perceived social norms supportive of behavioral change, and (h) gay social network affiliation. Moreover, they believed that the inclusion of initial risk reduction behavior in their linear regression model explained most of the observed effect:

> Closer inspection of these results suggests, however, that this is primarily due to the inclusion of S1 behavior in the model; as has frequently been reported in analyses of longitudinal or panel data, many behaviors are relatively stable across time, and initial behavior is one of the strongest predictors of subsequent behavior. (Joseph et al. 1987, 86–87)

Joseph and her associates (1987) also found that the effects of these predictors diminished over time. The cross-sectional analysis indicated a relationship between knowledge of AIDS, perceived risk of AIDS, perceived efficacy of behavioral change, perceived difficulty with sexual impulse control, belief in biomedical cure or prevention for AIDS, and perceived social norms supportive of behavioral change—with reductions in HIV-related risk practices. Nevertheless, the number and magnitude of these relationships either diminished or disappeared in the longitudinal analysis. To clarify, all of these factors except that of perceived efficacy had no effect on risk reduction from the first to the last assessment interval. In addition, the effect of perceived efficacy was greatly reduced.

Notwithstanding, several studies reported a strong association between two predictors derived from health behavior models and longitudinal risk reduction. These predictors included perceived peer support for HIV risk reduction and perceived level of emotional support from peer group. For example, Joseph and her co-researchers (1987) found that perceived social norms supportive of behavioral change were highly related to risk reduction over time. In addition, Siegel et al. (1989) reported an equally strong relationship between perceived adequacy of peer emotional support and longitudinal risk reduction.

Attitudinal models of behavioral change also shaped efforts within one of these studies to determine the correlates of risk behavior. Communication Technologies (1987) researchers assumed that the factors specified in Fishbein's (Ajzen & Fishbein 1980) theory of the attitudinal basis of social behavior affected risk practices. Fishbein maintained that an individual's intention to behave in a certain manner reflected that person's beliefs about the attitudinal and normative status of this behavior. Indeed, an individual's beliefs informed that person's attitude toward the behavior, which may be either positive or negative. An individual's beliefs about the normative standing of a behavior in the eyes of other people and groups similarly influences that person's perception of the normative prescriptions and proscriptions affecting the behavior.

Following Fishbein, Communication Technologies (1987) investigators examined the extent to which beliefs about the risk, enjoyability, and normative status of HIV risk behavior influenced anal and oral risk practices with secondary partners during the 30-day period before the interview among a probability-based sample of gay and bisexual men in San Francisco. They found that enjoyability and perceived social norms significantly influenced participation in unprotected intercourse. For example, the correlation coefficient between enjoyment of anal intercourse with the exchange of semen and engagement in this practice was +.26. Similarly, the enjoyment of other unsafe practices was linked to participation in this act. The correlations between oral-anal relations, anal fisting, and oral intercourse with ejaculation— and anal sex with ejaculation—were, respectively, +.18+15, and +.13.

It is surprising that the researchers reported that the effect of enjoyability weakened for unprotected oral sex. The correlation between enjoyment of oral intercourse with the exchange of semen and the practice of this behavior was +.16. This effect reversed for enjoyment of safer erotic practices. The correlations between enjoyability of mutual masturbation, anal intercourse without ejaculation, oral sex without ejaculation, protected anal intercourse, and deep kissing—and oral sex with ejaculation—were, respectively, −.23,−.19,−.15,−s.13, and −.13.

Furthermore, these investigators found significant associations between perceived social norms and engagement in unprotected sex. They reported, for example, that the correlation coefficient between the belief that friends disapproved of anal sex without a condom and anal intercourse with the exchange of semen was −.21; again, the relationship declined for unprotected oral sex. The correlation between the belief that friends disapproved of oral sex without a condom and oral intercourse with ejaculation was −.13.

Moreover, the researchers found little relationship between perceived risk of intercourse with semen exchange and participation in this behavior. The correlation between perceived risk of oral sex with ejaculation and the practice of this act was −.08. However, this association weakened for unprotected anal sex. The correlation between perceived risk of anal sex with ejaculation and engagement in this practice dropped to −.0.3.

Public health concerns about prevention also elicited efforts to evaluate the effect of HIV antibody testing and prevention campaigns upon risk behavior within the gay community (Office of Technology Assessment 1988). Typically, these studies examined the impact of antibody testing or particular educational interventions on risk reduction among a community-based convenience sample of gay and bisexual men through self-administered questionnaires (Valdiserri 1989).

Finally, public health interest in care for individuals with HIV disease fostered attempts to investigate HIV-related volunteering, coping behavior, emotional reactions, and social support (Mori 1988). Again, through self-administered questionnaires or in-depth interviews, the studies explored these issues among either clinical or community-based samples of HIV-infected gay or bisexual men who frequently resided in areas that were the foci of the epidemic.

Cultural Definitions Embedded in Social Research on the HIV Epidemic among Gay Men

Epidemiological and public health-oriented social inquiry on the HIV epidemic within the gay community reflected prevailing cultural conceptualizations of homosexuality, sexuality, and HIV disease. An essentialist construction of same-sex eroticism informed much of the early epidemiological research on this epidemic. According to this definition, presocial forces engendered both homosexual desire and behavioral patterns: "Homosexuality" was a monolithic entity characterized by a common origin and life-style.

The background and training of the original band of epidemiological investigators predisposed them to hold an essentialist point of view. The initial researchers were chiefly heterosexual physicians (Astor 1983) and, therefore, "outsiders" (Merton 1972) to the gay world, who were recruited largely from the Centers for Disease Control's Division of Venereal Disease Control (Oppenheimer 1988). Their medical schooling led them to hold essentialist constructions of homosexuality. Typically, they discounted social science findings concerning cross-cultural and historical variability in the social meaning and organization of homosexuality and the diversity of the sexual habits of U.S. gay men (Greenberg 1988). Same-sex eroticism was regarded instead as either a psychological or a physiologically induced pathology characterized by hyperpromiscuity.

The investigators' professional experiences corroborated essentialist assumptions about the erotic patterns of gay men. Prior to the epidemic, most of these researchers studied sexually transmitted diseases among gay men (Oppenheimer, 1988). It is not surprising that this research brought them into contact with gay men who were quite sexually adventurous and active. Hence they viewed multiple partners and esoteric acts such as anal fisting as characteristic of gay men's sexuality (Batchelor 1984).

Most of the original epidemiological theories about the etiology of AIDS reflected essentialist constructions of homosexuality. Many investigators reasoned that the agent causing the disease was related to either a presocial determinant of same-sex desire or the urban gay life-style (Oppenheimer 1988). For example, some felt that the genetic or hormonal determinants of homosexuality caused AIDS. Typically, they linked the disease to hypothesized genetic abnormalities in the immune system of gay men. Others thought that the urban gay life-style of promiscuity and recreational drug use was responsible for AIDS (Murray & Payne 1988). The disease in this view was associated with either an unknown sexually transmitted agent or the ingestion of drugs or semen thought to cause immunosuppression.

Essentialist constructions also appeared in the initial epidemiological definitions of risk groups. At the onset of the epidemic, epidemiologists defined gay men as a group that was at high risk for AIDS. They based this classification on the early epidemiological findings that showed that the initial AIDS cases were overwhelmingly sexually active gay men who consumed recreational drugs. However, this categorization reflected essentialist perceptions about the behavioral patterns of gay men. It assumed that most gay men were at risk for the disease because they were commonly hyperpromiscuous drug users.

Essentialism blinded these researchers to the diversity of behavioral patterns within the gay community. Gay men vary widely in their sexual and drug habits (Bell & Weinberg 1978; Jay & Young 1977; Saghir & Robins 1973). Only a small minority of gay men were promiscuous and took drugs. Furthermore, only those men within this minority who lived in areas with elevated rates of AIDS were at risk for the disease. In sum, the assumption that all gay men were at risk reflected a distorted view of the erotic and drug use patterns of gay men and the spatial distribution of the virus.

Moralistic and medical constructions of HIV disease to a large extent also informed much of the public health-oriented research on the epidemic among gay men. The available literature reveals four major definitions of HIV disease both among and within the societies affected by the epidemic: the moralistic, contagion, conspiratorial, and medical constructions. All four definitions differ in regard to the etiology, transmission, and prevention of the illness.

The moralistic definition maintains that HIV disease is a moral problem. In this view, the illness emerges not from a virus but from immoral actions. Disease results not from HIV as such but from promiscuity, homosexuality, and drug use. Obviously, this construction confuses etiology with transmission. It associates the cause of the disease with some of its behavioral routes of transmission. Predictably, of course, this definition sees traditional morality as the chief means of prevention. It considers abstinence from drugs, sodomy, adultery, and premarital sex as the only way to avoid infection.

The contagion definition views HIV disease as a public health problem. According to this construction, HIV is a highly contagious virus that can be casually transmitted in a manner similar to the common cold. Consequently, effective prevention requires the segregation or quarantine of individuals infected with HIV.

The conspiratorial construction regards HIV disease as a political problem. In this view, the epidemic constitutes politically planned genocide for socially stigmatized peoples. In other words, homophobic, racist, and classist elites either launched or inadequately responded to the epidemic to kill morally, racially, or economically devalued populations. The genocidal crusades supposedly took two forms: In the first, the U.S. elite instructed the Central Intelligence Agency to invent and disseminate HIV as part of a germ warfare campaign against gay men, drug addicts, promiscuous heterosexuals, racial minorities, welfare recipients, and the populations of Africa and Latin America. In the second, national elites prevented North American and European governments from providing adequate funding for HIV-related care, research, and prevention in order to decimate gay and Third World communities. It is not surprising that this definition sees political protest and pressure as the mechanism for forcing North American and European governments to provide the needed resources for care, research, and prevention.

The medical construction views HIV disease as a medical problem. According to this definition, medical science has established both the etiology and the transmission of the illness. A multitude of medical studies indicate that the disease results from a newly discovered virus, called HIV, which is transmitted by the exchange of infected body fluids such as blood, semen, and vaginal secretions during such behavioral practices as needle sharing and unprotected (without a condom) intercourse. In addition, this construction views behavioral change as the most effective means of prevention. In the absence of an immediate cure or treatment, halting the behavior implicated in the transmission of the virus through explicit and culturally specific educational interventions constitutes the most effective procedure for preventing infection.

The moralistic and medical constructions of HIV disease influenced the risk classifications for sexual behavior used in public health-oriented research on the epidemic. The moralistic definition considered promiscuity to be a high-risk behavior. The medical model defined this practice as primarily unprotected intercourse. These classifications were uncritically incorporated into most studies of the changes in erotic conduct among gay men. These studies usually measured the frequency and correlates of promiscuity (partner numbers) and unprotected intercourse.

The classification of promiscuity as a risk behavior was scientifically indefensible (Murray & Payne 1988). As the medical evidence makes abundantly clear, promiscuity was not implicated in the transmission of HIV. The virus was not spread through numbers of sexual partners but through the erotic acts performed with these partners. Risk was not associated with how many partners an individual had but with the erotic acts that person engaged in with these partners.

The medical construction also affected the way in which intercourse was conceptualized. The medical definition regarded intercourse as a health behavior because it could potentially transmit HIV. Moreover, it categorized intercourse as either healthy or unhealthy on the basis of this potential. Protected intercourse was healthy because there was a low risk of transmission. Conversely, unprotected intercourse was unhealthy because it carried a high risk of transmission.

Most of the studies of the correlates of changes in erotic behavior used the medical construction of intercourse. They construed intercourse as a "health behavior" similar to smoking, drinking, eating, and wearing a seat belt. This medicalization of intercourse accounts for the use of models of health behavior within these studies. These studies assumed that the already identified predictors of health conduct were also correlates of changes in risk behavior among gay men because they conceptualized intercourse as a health behavior.

The use of theories of health behavior can be faulted on three grounds: First, these theories denuded intercourse of its social, cultural, and psychological meanings and motivations. Typically, people participated in intercourse for reasons that have more to do with these meanings than with health concerns. Second, these theories stripped intercourse of its interpersonal context. Models of health behavior were predicated upon individual actors making solitary decisions about health-related practices. However, decisions around intercourse were fundamentally dyadic. Choices around intercourse always involved negotiations with another person. Third, these theories denuded intercourse of its noncognitive motivations. Models of health behavior assumed that individuals take health-related actions on the basis of cognitive assessment of such factors as the possible costs and benefits of this practice. Nevertheless, decisions around intercourse are often influenced by deep-seated psychological needs that may lie outside the individual's immediate awareness.

Conclusion

The constructions embedded in social inquiry on the HIV epidemic among gay men led to the crucial questions about the disease being inadequately formulated. Essentialist constructions of homosexuality led epidemiologists to distort the social reality of HIV infection within the gay community. The belief that AIDS was linked to a presocial determinant of same-sex desire wastefully misdirected initial research efforts into the etiology of the illness. In addition, the classification of homosexuals as a risk group for AIDS foolishly ignored the diversity of erotic, residential, and drug use patterns among gay men.

These essentialist definitions also impeded attempts at HIV prevention. As several studies indicated, the perception that AIDS was a gay white disease seriously hindered prevention efforts within the black and Hispanic communities and among sexually active heterosexuals, especially adolescents and college students (Valdiserri 1989). Moreover, the perception that AIDS was an illness associated with the urban gay life-style impeded prevention crusades within the gay community. Many gay men justified engaging in unprotected intercourse on the grounds that neither they nor their partner was promiscuous, took drugs, or lived in cities that were the foci of the epidemic (Stall et al. 1988).

The medical construction of HIV disease also distorted efforts at prevention. The medicalization of sexual intercourse as health conduct prompted the use in prevention of models of health behavior change and decision making. However, these models were inapplicable because they stripped intercourse of its social, cultural, and psychological meanings and motivations. It is not surprising, then, that these models could not adequately explain risk behavior among gay men. Indeed, the most commonly identified correlates of behavioral change within this population were social in nature. As many studies demonstrated, age, ethnicity, peer norms, relationship status, and geographic location were associated with risk reduction (Stall et al. 1988).

The constructionist approach to this research must recontextualize the behavior involved with HIV disease in several ways: First, this approach directs our attention to the psychic and sociocultural meanings and motivations attached to intercourse among gay men. Second, this approach presupposes the use of methodologies better suited for capturing the domain of meaning and motivations associated with HIV illness. To date, most research has used survey instruments constructed from a priori assumptions about the nature of the problem typically held by outsiders to the gay community. Constructionism demands the use of qualitative techniques that can tap into the definitions of the situation prevailing among gay men. Third, this approach broadens the research questions asked about the effect of HIV within the gay community. Until now, these questions have reflected epidemiological and public health interests, either the distribution and determinants of the disease or the magnitude and correlates of behavioral change among gay men. A focus on the subjective experience raises entirely new questions such as those concerning the loss of a way of life or cultural community. Ultimately, our understanding of these meanings and motivations will take us to the matrix from which all sexual behaviors are derived—the sociocultural order.

REFERENCES

Adam, B. D. 1985. Age, structure, and sexuality: Reflections on the anthropological evidence on homosexual relations. *Journal of Homosexuality, 11,* 19–33.

Ajzen, L. & Fishbein, M. 1980. *Understanding attitudes and predicting social behavior.* Englewood Cliffs, NJ: Prentice-Hall.

Astor, G. 1983. *The disease detectives.* New York: New American Library.

Batchelor, W. F. 1984. AIDS: A public health and psychological emergency. *American Psychologist, 39,* 1279–84.

Bauman, L. J., & Siegel, K. 1986. Misperception among gay men of the risk for AIDS associated with their sexual behavior. *Journal of Applied Social Psychology, 78,* 329–50.

Becker, M. H., & Joseph, J. G. 1988. AIDS and behavioral change to reduce risk: A review. *American Journal of Public Health, 78,* 394–410.

Bell, A. P., & Weinberg, M. S. 1978. *Homosexualities: A study of diversity among men and women.* New York: Simon & Schuster.

Communication Technologies. 1987. *A report on designing an effective AIDS prevention campaign strategy for San Francisco. Results from the fourth probability sample of an urban gay community.* San Francisco: San Francisco AIDS Foundation.

Coser, L. A. 1977. *Masters of sociological thought: Ideas in historical and social context* (2nd ed.). New York: Harcourt Brace Jovanovich.

Cummings, K. M., Becker, M. H., & Maile, M. C. 1980. Bringing the models together: An empirical approach to combining variables used to explain health action. *Journal of Behavioral Medicine, 3,* 123–45.

Denzin, N. K. 1989. *The research act: A theoretical introduction to sociological methods.* Englewood Cliffs, NJ: Prentice-Hall.

Emmons, C., Joseph, J. G., Kessler, R. C., Wortman, C. B., Montgomery, S. B., & Ostrow, D. G. 1986. Psychosocial predictors of reported behavior change in homosexual men at risk for AIDS: *Health Education Quarterly, 13,* 331–45.

Ford, C. S., & Beach, F. A. 1951. *Patterns of sexual behavior.* New York: Harper & Row.

Gagnon, J., & Simon, W. 1973. *Sexual conduct: The social sources of human sexuality.* Chicago: Aldine.

Greenberg, D. F. 1988. *The construction of homosexuality.* Chicago: University of Chicago Press.

Gregerson, E. 1983. *Sexual practices: The story of human sexuality.* New York: Franklin Watts.

Jay K., & Young, A. 1977. *The gay report: Lesbians and gay men speak out about sexual experiences and lifestyles.* New York: Summit.

Joseph, J. G., Montgomery, S. B., Emmons, C., Kessler, R. C., Ostrow, D. G., Wortman, C. B., O'Brien, K., Ellen M., & Eshleman, S. 1987. Magnitude and determinants of behavioral risk reduction: Longitudinal analysis of a cohort at risk for AIDS. *Psychology and Health, 1,* 73–96.

Kuhn, T. S. 1962. *The structure of scientific revolutions.* Chicago: University of Chicago Press.

Law, J., & Lodge, P. 1984. *Science for social scientists.* London: Macmillan.

Merton, R. K. 1972. Insiders and outsiders: A chapter in the sociology of knowledge. *American Journal of Sociology, 78,* 9–47.

Morin, S. F. 1988. AIDS: The challenge to psychology. *American Psychologist 43,* 838–42.

Murray, S. O., & Payne, K. W. 1988. Medical policy without scientific evidence: The promiscuity paradigm and AIDS. *California Sociologist, 11,* 13–54.

Office of Technology Assessment. 1988. *OTA Staff Paper: How effective is AIDS education?* Washington, DC: U.S. Congress.

Oppenheimer, G. M. 1988. In the eye of the storm: The epidemiological construction of AIDS. In E. Fee & D. M. Fox (eds.), *AIDS: The burdens of history* (pp. 267–301). Berkeley: University of California Press.

Plummer, K. 1975. *Sexual stigma: An interactionist account.* Boston: Routledge & Kegan Paul.

Richardson, D. 1981. Theoretical perspectives on homosexuality. In J. Hart & D. Richardson (eds.), *The theory and practice of homosexuality* (pp. 5–37). Boston: Routledge & Kegan Paul.

Saghir, M. T., & Robins, E. 1973. *Male and female homosexuality: A comprehensive investigation.* Baltimore: Williams & Wilkins.

Siegel, K., Bauman, L. J., Christ, G. H., & Krown, S. 1988. Patterns of change in sexual behavior among gay men in New York City. *Archives of Sexual Behavior, 17,* 481–97.

Siegel, K., Mesagno, F. P., Jin-Yi Chen, & Christ, G. 1989. Factors distinguishing homosexual males practicing risky and safer sex. *Social Science and Medicine,* pp. 561–69.

Simon, W., & Gagnon, J. H. 1967. Homosexuality: The formulation of a sociological perspective. *Journal of Health and Social Behavior, 8,* 177–85.

Simon, W., & Gagnon, J. H. 1987. A sexual scripts approach. In J. H. Geer & W. T. O'Donohue (Eds.), *Theories of human sexuality* (pp. 363–84). New York: Plenum.

Stall, R. D., Coates, T. J., & Hoff, C. 1988. Behavioral risk reduction for HIV infection among gay and bisexual men: A review of the results from the United States. *American Psychologist, 43,* 878–85.

Troiden, R. R. 1988. *Gay and lesbian identity: A sociological analysis.* Dix Hills, NY: General Hall.

Turner, C. F., Miller, H. G., & Moses, L. E. (eds.). 1989. *AIDS: Sexual behavior and drug use.* Washington, DC: National Academy Press.

Valdiserri, R. O. 1989. *Preventing AIDS: The design of effective programs.* New Brunswick, NJ: Rutgers University Press.

Winkelstein, W., Jr., Samuel, M., Padian, N. S., Wiley, J. A., Long, W., Anderson, R. E., & Levy, J. A. 1987. The San Francisco Men's Health Study: III. Reduction in human immunodeficiency virus transmission among homosexual/bisexual men, 1982–86. *American Journal of Public Health, 76,* 685–89.

Epilogue
Martin P. Levine, 1950–1993

Martin Levine was one of the pioneers in the sociological study of homosexuality. He was also one of the most vital, visible, and vocal champions of gay men and lesbians within the profession of sociology.

Born and raised in a poor, working-class family in Brooklyn, New York, Levine was proud of his professional accomplishments that marked his upward mobility. The first member of his family to attend college, he graduated from the State University of New York at Binghamton in 1972 with a B.A. in Sociology. He received his M.A. (1977) and Ph.D. (1986) in sociology from New York University.

Levine's work adds a significant chapter in the sociological study of homosexuality. He was among the first sociologists produced *by* gay liberation who then turned around to study his own community. He was an "organic intellectual" in the Gramscian sense—produced by his community, he then used the theoretical tools of organized disciplines to make sense of it, but in a way that would ultimately be of service and of use to his community. Levine was a gay sociologist, who thought sociology provided the tools for understanding homosexuality and who believed that sociology had a responsibility to serve the gay community.

Levine's major work was his Ph.D. dissertation, which has become the core of this book. *Gay Macho: An Ethnography of the Homosexual Clone* placed gay male sexuality squarely within a social constructionist perspective of masculinity and male sexuality. Based on extensive field work at various sites of gay male sexual expression (bars, bathhouses, sex clubs), Levine chronicled the changing masculinities of the gay community that emerged from gay liberation. He saw a transition from a self-hatred as "failed men" to the self-awareness of "real men" as evidence of the socially constructed nature of both sexuality and gender.

Levine's teaching and research revolved around making gender and homosexuality visible within the academy, within his professional organization, the American Sociological Association, and in the world at large. He was one of the first sociologists to define homosexuality as a legitimate field of study. His edited collection, *Gay Men: The Sociology of Male Homosexuality* (Harper and Row, 1979), was a pioneering anthology that used sociological concepts to understand the emergence of a gay male community.

Levine completed the work on *Gay Men* while a graduate student at NYU, where he also developed an innovative course on "Society and Sexual Variations." Using the university's Greenwich Village location as a natural laboratory, Levine began to bring social science perspectives to the study of homosexuality in new and important ways.

In 1980, while researching his dissertation, Levine was hired by the sociology department at Bloomfield College, where he taught as Assistant and Associate Professor until 1991. There, his extraordinary teaching abilities blossomed. He was an especially gifted teacher, utterly devoted to his students. He twice won the "best teacher" award at Bloomfield, and prided himself on the fact that as a gay white man, he was the faculty advisor to the black student organization, the gay student organization, and one of the college's fraternities. Rarely has anyone been able to bridge those communities on any campus.

In 1991, Levine accepted a position as Associate Professor at Florida Atlantic University. He was excited at the prospect of training graduate students, and looked forward to living in Miami Beach's famous Art Deco district in South Beach. Unfortunately, his illness prevented him from fully integrating himself into that community, and in 1992 he returned to New York, to be among his friends.

While his work with undergraduate students at Bloomfield was enormously satisfying, Levine was also devoted to the mentoring of graduate students who were undertaking research on homosexuality, gender, and human sexuality, and, later, on the AIDS epidemic. He was among the organizers of the American Sociological Association's Gay and Lesbian caucus, and founded the Sociologists AIDS Network. Through his professional activities, he worked informally with graduate students from all over the country, providing a level of nurturing and support that went far beyond any expectations. Many younger gay and lesbian scholars got their first break on a conference panel he organized, or through his careful and considerate commentary and critique of their work. It is consistent with his life that even at his death, he remained committed to serving as a mentor and supporter of those younger scholars who are undertaking research on homosexuality, AIDS, or human sexuality, using the largest share of his estate to establish a fellowship to support a graduate student during the final year of his or her thesis writing.

At the annual conventions of the American Sociological Association, Levine was a constant and visible presence, arguing pointedly for the inclusion of gays and lesbians from the floor of the ASA council or at open business meetings, organizing sessions and presenting current research. He also organized some of the most enjoyable and memorable caucus parties, and bar-hopping expeditions in the cities where the conventions were held.

As the gay and lesbian community became increasingly preoccupied with the AIDS epidemic, so too did Levine's work. Even before he was diagnosed as HIV-positive in 1988, he had begun to look for ways to bring the concerns of social scientists and the AIDS community together to develop responsible and responsive research opportunities. He pioneered undergraduate courses about AIDS, developing one of the first courses in the country about AIDS and homosexuality.

Levine also co-directed a National Institute of Mental Health study of sexual decision making among gay men, advised Commissioner Frank Lilly of the Presidential Commission on the Human Immunodeficiency Virus Epidemic, and testified about AIDS antibody testing, violence against gay men and lesbians, and employment discrimination against lesbians and gay men before the United States Congress, the Colorado State legislature, and the New York City Council. At the time of his death, he was also a Research Associate at the Memorial Sloan-Kettering Cancer Institute in New York City, and served on the National Academy of Sciences panel that was monitoring the social impact of the AIDS epidemic. He was also a community liaison with the Burroughs Wellcome Corporation, assisting the company in channeling some of its AZT profits back into the communities affected by the epidemic.

In his teaching and his research, Levine did not simply celebrate clone culture, even as he participated in it and was among its primary explicators. He saw clone culture as having been formed by men who responded to both the political stigmatization of homosexuality and the self-fulfillment ethic of the 1960s by coming out as both gay and proud. It thus fused masculinity and consumerism in a particularly potent blend. Levine was critical of the excesses of clone culture, and refused to go along with the casual misogyny that often accompanied clone masculinity. Levine was a both a gay activist and pro-feminist. Although he focused on gay men, he was also critical of their unquestioning acceptance of a masculinity that had negative consequences for women. He was a colleague, mentor, and friend to many women, both heterosexual and lesbian. That one of his articles, "Discrimination against Lesbians in the Workforce" (with Robin Leonard) was published in the special "Lesbian Issue" of *Signs* (1984) especially tickled his pro-feminist political sensibilities.

This book presents Levine's major work, his Ph.D. dissertation, and a series of articles that followed up the concerns of the dissertation. In the dissertation, Levine explored the emergence of the gay clone, and located that emergence at the intersection of gender conformity, gay liberation, and the self-fulfillment ethic, and elaborated and articulated clone masculinity. In later work, he explored the consequences of this form of gay masculinity in the AIDS epidemic. Levine's work represents a pioneering effort to both normalize male homosexuality through the prism of gender conformity and critique that expression of masculinity from within, as one of its practitioners.

Martin Levine died of AIDS at his home in New York City on April 3, 1993. He was 42 years old.

EDITOR'S NOTE

This epilogue is based on an obituary, co-authored with John Gagnon, that appeared in ASA *Footnotes*.

Index

Abortion, 164–66
Abstinence (from sexual activity), 141; to avoid AIDS, 76, 146, 149–50, 153, 198, 241; as violation of masculine norms, 147, 150
Acquired Immune Deficiency Syndrome. See AIDS
Adventure or risk-taking (as masculine norm), 13, 92, 95–96, 145–48, 150, 152, 153, 155; among clones, 27
Advocate, The, 41
Aerosol pentamidine, 182, 183, 185
Africa, 144
African Americans, 10–11, 32, 82, 243; and Tuskegee syphilis experiment, 127–37
Aggression (as masculine norm), 13–14, 17, 145
AIDS (Acquired Immune Deficiency Syndrome): beginning of epidemic of, 2, 4, 125–26; conjectures about causes of, 196–97, 199, 240–43; contribution of masculine norms to, x, 126, 143–57; as disease afflicting men, 143–57; education about, 149–54, 202, 228, 242; emotional support for people with, 126, 142, 154–55; impact of, on "butch" presentation, 76; impact of, on clones, x–xi, 8, 138–42, 249; impact of, on gay male community, x–xii, 5, 6, 8, 138–42; Levine's experience with, x–xi, 248–49; Levine's writings on, 126, 127–57, 178–246, 250; medical treatment for, 182–88, 192, 200–202; prevention of, campaigns for, 150–52, 154, 224, 227, 235, 242; prevention of, and peer support, 237, 239, 244; prevention of, strategies for, 147–52, 205, 227–28, 237; sanctions for, 147, 195–96, 199–202; and transformation of sexual practices, 5, 8, 76, 138–42, 151–52, 165–67, 173, 197–98, 202, 205, 235–36;

241–42; transmission of, 146. *See also* AIDS testing; ARC; Drug use; HIV; Sexual practices
AIDS Activity Group, 126, 135–36
"AIDS Play Safe" campaign, 151
AIDS testing, 126, 249; benefits associated with, 178–79, 182–92; confidentiality concerns about, 136, 195–96, 199, 200, 202–3; effects of, on sexual practices, 188–90, 197–98; interpretations of results from, 212, 223, 225–26; medical constructions of, 199, 200–201; as method of AIDS prevention, 147–48, 238; opposition to, in gay community, 200; psychosocial constructions of, 199, 202; public health constructions of, 199, 201–2; reliability concerns about, 196–97, 199–200; risks associated with, 147–48, 178–79, 192–98
Alcoholics Anonymous (AA), 167, 168
Alcohol use: among clones, 30, 85–86, 96; among older homosexuals, 27, 71; and unprotected sexual activity, 219–20
Altman, Dennis, 7
American Red Cross, 127
American Sociological Association, 248, 249
Anal fisting, 52–53, 95, 238, 240
Analingus (rimming), 24, 94, 238
Anal intercourse, 24, 93; and AIDS transmission, 144, 146, 205, 242–43; "bottoms" in, 66, 97–98; condom use in, 206; ramming in, 92, 93; "tops" in, 66, 97–98; unprotected, 205–8, 210, 212–16, 218–27, 238, 243
Andrew Hospital (Tuskegee Institute), 131, 132
Anonymous sexual activity (tricking), 7, 8, 28, 48; and AIDS, 139, 140, 198, 226, 234; avoidance of, 24–25, 28; as clone

About the Editor

Michael S. Kimmel is Professor of Sociology at SUNY at Stony Brook. His books include *Changing Men* (1987), *Men Confront Pornography* (1990), *Men's Lives* (4th edition, 1997), *Against the Tide: Profeminist Men in the United States, 1776–1990* (1992), *The Politics of Manhood* (1996), and *Manhood: A Cultural History* (1996). He edits *masculinities*, an interdisciplinary scholarly journal, a book series on men and masculinity at the University of California Press, and the Sage Series on Men and Masculinities. He is the Spokesperson for the National Organization for Men Against Sexism (NOMAS) and lectures extensively on campuses in the United States and abroad.